CRUISING SOLO

The Single Traveler's Guide to Adventure on the High Seas

by Sally J. Maisel

MARIN PUBLICATIONS

*This book
is dedicated
with love
to my grandparents*

Table of Contents

Chapter 7: Getting To Know...Everyone! 79

Chapter 8: Are You Hungry Yet? 87

Chapter 9: Shipboard Activities 99

Chapter 10: It's Ashore Thing 111

Chapter 11: Spice Up Your Language 121

Chapter 12: Special Events 135

Chapter 13: Isn't It Romantic? 143

Chapter 14: Take A Tip From Me 157

Chapter 15: Turning Lemons Into Lemon Drops 165

Chapter 16: So Long! Farewell! Goodbye! 175

PART TWO: The Cruise Lines

Acknowledgements

In a lot of ways, this is like giving the Academy Award speech that we little folks dream about but will never deliver. We're grateful to so many people, but know we'll be hooted off the stage if we reel off names of folks who mean nothing to the rest of the audience yet are so integral to our personal project.

I'm so grateful, in fact, I could fill this book with people who deserve my thanks. Of course, nobody wants to read my personal Rolodex. Instead, I'll have to thank, with all my heart and gratitude, for all their support and enthusiasm:

My most immediate and my important family, and you know who you are;

My most immediate and my close friends, and you know who you are, too;

All the cruise lines people who, through their cooperation and assistance, represented their companies with pride and professionalism;

All the wonderful people I met on my cruises who supplied me with anecdotes and experiences, then consistently asked, "So, are you going to write a whole chapter about me?";

And my dog, Nemo, who sat at my feet while I wrote this book and waited for me to return from my adventures on the high seas.

PART ONE

The Adventure

Introduction

*There ain't no surer way to find out
whether you like people or hate them
than to travel with them.*

Mark Twain

Traveling with a companion can be a week of adventure or a week of hell.

One of my friends relates the story of a new traveling companion, and it's a tale that escalates in mirth each time she retells it. When the two women walked down the beach, the friend complained, "The sun is too hot." As they walked down the street, the woman carped, "The cobblestones hurt my feet." Every restaurant had terrible food, abominable service and horrible sanitation. After a week together, my friend needed a vacation to recover from her vacation. Even now, when I travel with a friend and someone starts to get crabby, all we have to do is say in a mocking voice, "The cobblestones hurt my FEEEEET!" and the moment is gone and we're back into perspective.

The wonderful thing about traveling alone is that there is no one to complain about sore feet and cobblestones. And if you travel on a cruise, you'll leave those cobblestoned streets and come back to a ship full of luxury and attention.

Traveling is a series of adventures, and not all of it is what we're used to in the comforts of our own space back home. But it doesn't have to faze you if you prepare yourself about what to expect and turn each situation into a positive. Remember, forewarned is forearmed, making the transition of a new, unknown situation that much easier.

When trying to decide where to go on my well-earned vacation, and with whom to travel, I discovered something very telling. First, I narrowed down the field of my friends to those I knew wouldn't complain about cobblestones hurting their feet. Next, I dissected personalities to assess which of those remaining had an independent spirit. While I might like to lie by the pool, I didn't want to be responsible for someone who needed to be constantly entertained. Conversely, if I wanted to hike into town, and she wanted to relax by the pool, I wanted to be sure that there would be no recriminations about abandonment.

Once I had weeded out those undesirable people, I was down to a select few. And then the old axiom came up: Those that had the time didn't have the money to spare on a vacation. And those that had the money didn't have the time.

That led me to this conclusion: I had worked all year for a vacation and wasn't going to waste it because I had no one with whom to travel. I would (gulp!) have to consider going somewhere alone.

At the time, the idea of traveling alone was disconcerting. Even going out to *dinner* alone was intimidating. I'd go to a restaurant, register with the hostess, and be told to wait. I felt very conspicuous sitting in the bar alone, and even more so when the hostess announced my name over the loudspeaker, telling everyone in the place that my TABLE FOR ONE was ready. The thought of a whole week of TABLE FOR ONE was pretty daunting, indeed.

I also was concerned about the cost. I knew that ONE can fly as cheaply as ONE on the airlines, but ONE cannot live as cheaply as ONE at a beach-front hotel. Then I thought of spending each day at the beach, reading a Danielle Steel novel, followed by showering and dressing, all to eat a lonely, expensive dinner in a lovely tropical setting, after which I would be grateful for a small smile from the waiter as he poured me my second cup of coffee. The scenario was not very appealing.

What to do? What to do?

Club Med! Here was a resort with no single supplement. I had talked to people who were Club Med fanatics, and listened to their stories about wild and carefree picnics, topless sunbathing in remote locales, unlimited water sports, free wine and beer at lunch and dinner, and a large percentage of single people looking to let go on their vacation.

Also, for one set price, the vacation included transportation, accommodations, all meals, and a lot of sports activities. Best of all, Club Med boasted it was "the antidote to civilization." Unfortunately, the reality of Club Med didn't correspond with my idea of the ideal vacation.

The Club Med experience turned out to be just fine, although I was less than pleased with a few facets. While I enjoyed my week, I longed for a bit more of a civilized approach. These were the things I hoped to improve on for my next vacation: the food, the accommodations, the people, the entertainment, and the locale.

In terms of food, I would hope on my next vacation that I could enjoy Eggs Benedict for breakfast, instead of scrambled eggs scooped out and plopped on my plate. A nice dinner, complete with asparagus vinaigrette, shrimp cocktail, or some other treat would be a welcome addition. A little service at meals would be nice, too. While I don't mind passing the plate at family gatherings, it seemed more like chowing down instead of dining at Club Med, although Club Med does offer a choice of different and very nice restaurants at many of their resorts.

I also started getting antsy to see something other than the thin strip of beach upon which the club is located. Many of the Club Meds are located a couple of hours from everything, specifically for the purpose of getting away from civilization. The distinguishing features of a favorite vacation spot are usually the local people, the culture, the artwork, the food. At a Club Med, the villages are self-contained and pretty much the same wherever you go.

Before it sounds like I'm complaining about the cobblestones hurting my feet, consider the fact that I really did have a nice vacation doing what I wanted to do when I wanted to do it. I did, however, want a little more variety, a little more service, and a little more adventure.

Then I thought of going on a cruise. I had been on a cruise before, but never alone. In fact, that first cruise seemed like a lifetime ago and all that remained were some very distinct impressions: excellent cabin service, including a fresh basket of fruit by our bed each night and clean towels twice a day; well-prepared meals, with filet mignon cooked exactly right and seconds on the escargot, just for the asking; friendly staff, including dozens of waiters bringing flaming Baked Alaska into the dining room; lovely days in port, featuring a beautiful afternoon touring Haiti, gambling in Puerto Rico; and shopping and sunbathing in St. Thomas.

I also was attracted to the idea that, as with Club Med, one price included the meals, transportation, transfers and activities. Unfortunately, I also knew that to go alone on all the ships I looked at would require paying about 50 percent more than I had paid before.

Finally, through a great deal of research, I discovered there were many different options available to the solo traveler. After reading this book, you'll be able to take advantage of those options, too.

Nothing can match the wonder of your first cruise—it's like falling in love for the first time. Everything is new and exciting. The sense of wonder and discovery seems unequalled. But like most things in life, cruising gets better the more you know and the more you go.

I have never had a bad cruise and neither will you if you follow the advice in this book.

May the cobblestones never hurt your feet and may you always have a Bon Voyage.

Why A Cruise?

I must down to the seas again,
to the lonely sea and the sky,
And all I ask is a tall ship
and a star to steer her by.

John Masefield

Remember when you were a kid and you got to go away to camp? Everything held a sense of discovery and your whole summer was devoted to having fun! You'd wake up each morning with the expectation of spending the entire day doing all the things you *wanted* to do: playing sports, eating lunch and snacks with the other campers, horsing around in the swimming pool, making things in arts and crafts and maybe even finishing the night around the campfire, singing songs and feeling a sense of kinship with the other campers.

As you got a little older at camp, you might have even felt your blood race as you snuck out of your cabin for a secret rendezvous across the lake with those forbidden members of the opposite sex, with whom you might try to share a borrowed cigarette, a clandestine taste of beer and a stolen kiss.

I always thought camp was wasted on the young and should be reserved for those who needed it most: hard-working, beleaguered adults.

Obviously, somebody had the idea before me, because cruising today is not so much designed for transportation from Point A to Point B as it is a glorious camp for adults, catering to adult whims. Today's cruise ship is a fabulous international playground for every age and sophistication of adult, ingeniously satisfying needs each person didn't even know he or she had.

Just like the camp of yore, when your parents plunked down a lump of money and sent you off for the summer, you'll plunk down a wad of cash and go off for the week. But instead of a rickety bus taking you to a bug-infested cabin in the

Courtesy Crystal Cruises

Passengers don't even have to get out of the pool to enjoy a refreshing cocktail break aboard the *Crystal Harmony*.

woods, you'll fly on a super-fast jet to a luxurious floating resort on the sea. Instead of burnt wienies and mystery meat, you'll dine on Oysters Rockefeller, Beef Wellington and Crepes Suzette. Instead of sneaking a sip of beer, an attentive bartender will pour it for you, and light your cigarette, too, if that's your vice. And instead of a hard-as-a-rock cot, you'll find your nice, soft bed turned down each night, and perhaps a mint on your fluffy pillow.

Cruises appeal to so many people not only for the luxury but also for the simplicity. For the person traveling alone, the sheer logistics of a vacation can be a nightmare. Go to a travel agent, tell him or her you want to go on vacation alone, and the fun/agony begins. Unless you go to an all-inclusive resort, you've got a lot of decisions to make and a lot of plans to arrange.

Let's say you want to spend a week in Mexico. First you book your air fare and hotel. Once you've arrived, you've got to figure out how to get to the hotel. Is there a bus? Perhaps, but it's mostly for locals and probably doesn't go to the resort area. Does the hotel have a shuttle? Probably not, unless it's a major hotel charging megabucks. Could you take a cab? That's the most likely possibility, and even then you'll have to find a cab, negotiate the rate, and then pay for it.

You'll have none of these problems when you take a cruise. You can be as adventurous or as timid as you like. You can strike out on your own, walking among the natives, speaking the language, using local currency and eating dubious foods from a street vendor, or you can sit back and be taken care of, opting for the ship's shore excursion in an air-conditioned bus with an English-speaking guide.

Experience Personal Growth

There's a very good reason for cruising alone: Not only do you discover new people and new places, you also uncover a part of you that has been sheltered and harbored.

When you get on the ship and realize that you don't know a soul in the world, you can either hide out in your room and go only to scheduled activities, or you can take a chance and literally discover a whole new world, both of geography and friendship.

Although you might not have known you had it in you, you'll be forced to conquer your fear of loneliness; you'll come out of yourself while learning to meet and greet new people of all age groups and all nationalities. The new social skills you'll acquire will stay with you, even off the ship, and will be a valuable asset in the future.

People who cruise with a friend, lover or spouse rarely take advantage of these new opportunities that await them on a cruise—they simply are not forced to expand their horizons. Watch a couple of people around the pool or in the showroom, be they married or two friends traveling together. They might speak to the people next to them, but the majority of their conversation is to each other. They discuss what they're going to have for dinner and what they had for lunch. They talk about what might be happening back at home and what they're going to do tomorrow on shore. They ponder how tired they are, and when one decides to leave the pool for a nap, they both go. At the end of the cruise, they might be relaxed but they haven't had the exhilarating experience of facing new challenges.

Do What You Want To Do, Go Where You Want To Go

For many people, traveling together is composed of a lot of compromises. *He* wants to play golf; *she* wants to go shopping. What do they do instead? They take a pre-packaged tour of historic mansions on a bus filled with other squabbling couples.

It never occurred to them that *he* could play golf and *she* could take a cab into town. People who travel together stay together, even when they don't want to. Most couples are used to spending their evenings together, while enjoying their freedom during the day at their jobs or their chores. Put two people together on a cruise—24 hours a day, three or more meals a day, day in and day out in a smaller-than-used-to cabin—and even the best of friends or lovers get on each others' nerves.

You, on the other hand, can speak with whomever you want to speak (without anyone getting jealous), eat what you want to eat (without anyone pointing out the calories or cholesterol), do what you want to do (without someone complaining about how boring it is) and go where you want to go (without another person whining about it being too hot, dusty, expensive or exhausting).

Aren't you glad you're cruising solo?

Enjoy An All-Inclusive Package

The great thing about cruising for the solo traveler is that just about every-thing is included in one price, and all the arrangements are made for you. Select a cruise to, say, the Caribbean and in one phone call everything is taken care of. When you get your documents, you'll find an airplane ticket getting you to the port of embarkation. If you're traveling from a distant time zone, the cruise company might even fly you in the night before and put you up in a hotel at no extra charge. They'll meet you at the airport and take you to your accommodations or directly to the ship.

Once on the ship, all the food you could possibly want, from room service to buffets, is included. Entertainment—piano bar music, Broadway- and Las Vegas-style shows, classical concerts—is there for the taking and a cover charge is unthinkable.

Write one check, or put one charge on your credit card, and the majority of your vacation is taken care of in one decisive action.

For your information, here's what's not included in the flat rate:

⚓ **Port Charges**
While port charges are not included in the price of the cruise, they are listed in the brochure and are paid for at the time the cruise is finalized. Port charges vary, not surprisingly, on the number of ports visited and what they individually charge. Typical port charges for a seven-day Caribbean cruise are $70 to $80.

⚓ **Tips**
Some cruise lines include the price of the tips in the tariff, and some simply do not allow the distribution of gratuities. On most, how-ever, tipping is the rule rather than the exception. You should allo-cate about $60 for tipping on a 7-day cruise.

⚓ **Drinks**
Some ultra-deluxe lines include a fully stocked mini-bar, cocktails in the public rooms, and wine with meals. On most cruise lines, however, drinks are extra, although there is no obligation to pur-chase beverages, even in the show lounges.

⚓ **Shore Excursions**
You're welcome to walk into town or rent a cab for transportation or a tour, but you're encouraged to purchase the shore excursions of-fered by the ship. Again, there is no obligation to do so.

⚓ **Gambling**
Think about it—if gambling were included, would it really be gam-bling? Gambling not only refers to the casino, but also to bingo, horse racing, and anything else in which you can win or lose money.

⚓ **Some sports and activities**
A very nominal charge is levied on some sports, such as trapshooting, and some activities, such as wine tasting or crafts, to cover the cost of materials.

⚓ **Photos**

The ship's photographers seem to be everywhere, capturing your every move. The photos are posted in a gallery and business is brisk. If you choose to purchase the photos, you'll shell out about $6 for a 5x7, slightly higher for portraits. Don't like the angle they use? Don't like the way your smile looks? Been using your own camera anyway? Don't want to shell out $6? You don't have to buy a thing.

Courtesy Royal Cruise Line

People who started off strangers end up friends after a week of dining on the *Crown Odyssey.*

Be Assured Of Dining Companions

When you sign up for a cruise, you'll also be signing up for a dining-room seating and table. Although some ships have continuous open seating for meals, the majority of ships have two seatings and assigned dining companions.

The people at your dining-room table are the people you'll be seeing every evening. While the conversation might be limited initially, you'll find that as the days go by you'll look forward to the growing friendship . It's a reassuring feeling knowing that not only will you never eat alone, but you'll be dining with people who are rapidly becoming close friends.

When you're not dining at your regular table, you'll have the opportunity to meet people at the open-seating meals while in port or at the numerous buffets served in special restaurants or on deck. Dining need never be a lonely experience.

Meet New People

Meeting people aboard a cruise ship is easy: It's what people do on ships, as opposed to their normal lives. Initiating conversation is expected and there's a commonality all cruise passengers share that enhances the vacation experience.

Because cruising is such an easy and positive experience for a solo traveler, you'll have the chance to meet a variety of other solo travelers from around the country. Because there are so many different types of shore excursions and activities aboard the ship, it's easy to meet people with similar interests. And because there is a cruise staff trained and excelling in facilitating fun and communication, interaction among passengers is high.

In addition, cruising is an excellent opportunity to meet people in age ranges or from foreign cultures that most of us rarely encounter. It is so easy to make friends, in fact, that many people end up booking their next cruise with people

Courtesy Renaissance Cruises

This is what awaits you if you choose one of the luxurious Renaissance Cruises ships.

they've met at sea. Others never meet again, because of the distance between their home towns, but do manage to stay in touch over the years, remembering birthdays, sending Christmas cards and chatting over the phone.

Luxuriate at a Floating Hotel

You can forget lugging around your suitcase from island to island. Unpack once and enjoy the luxury of your floating hotel. Once settled in, you only need to pick up the phone and your needs are taken care of.

Getting a little hungry? Call room service.

Need a massage? Pick up the phone and set up an appointment with the masseuse.

Ready to pour yourself a drink? Call for a bucket of ice.

Don't have anything to drink ? Call down, and a drink will be delivered.

Notice a chip in your nail polish? There's a manicurist ready to remedy the problem.

Today's cruise ships have all the amenities of the best luxury hotels, with individualized service to go along with it. Here's one place where the solo traveler is never a second-class citizen.

Visit a Variety of Locations Effortlessly

My friend Cindy was very excited about her three-island Hawaiian vacation. Her seven-day trip included stays in Honolulu, Maui and Kauai. What she didn't realize when she booked the trip was that three days would be spent on those islands but four days would be spent getting there and back.

Day One: Cindy flew to Honolulu and checked into her hotel. After getting from the airport and unpacking, she had just enough time to watch the sun set over the beautiful Waikiki beach. Day Two: Cindy took a tour of Diamond Head and Pearl Harbor. Day Three: Cindy packed, checked out of her hotel, got to the airport and flew to Maui. Once there, she traveled to her hotel, unpacked, and had just enough time to watch the sun set over the beautiful Kaanipali beach. Day Four: Cindy windsurfed and sunbathed. Day Five: Cindy packed, checked out of the hotel, headed out to the airport and flew to Kauai. Once there, she traveled to her hotel, unpacked and had just enough time to watch the sun set over the beautiful Poipu beach. Day Six: Cindy slept. Day Seven: Cindy packed and went home.

If Cindy had taken, say, an American Hawaii or a Princess cruise, she could have seen all of these islands and more during that same week. She'd have seen the sights during the day and the ship would have traveled at night, arriving in port with Cindy refreshed and ready for her next experience.

In addition, you'll be able to experience a variety of cultures, foods, experiences and geographic splendor, all on the same trip. Once day you might be eating fresh-caught shrimp in Cancun, the next jerk chicken in Jamaica and, a few days later, you could even be having bangers and mash in Britain.

There are many reasons to take a cruise, and even more reasons to take a cruise if you're traveling alone. All you have to do is make the decision to treat yourself to a new type of adventure.

Choose Your Cruise

The difficulty in life is the choice.

George Moore

You've decided to take the plunge and actually set off to sea. Or, you've already cruised and can hardly wait to once again feel the wind against your back and the luxury at your beck and call. Either way, you've got some pretty weighty decisions to make before you set foot on the ship.

The first thing to be decided is: What ship should you choose?

Before you plunk down your money and take your chances, you should decide what the primary objective of this vacation is. Many people say they just want to sit back, relax, be pampered and left alone after a harried year at a hectic job. Theoretically, you can accomplish this goal on any ship, because the decision about what to do while on board is left up to you. If all you want to do is eat and sleep, every ship has good food and comfortable staterooms.

For many other people, the type of vacation desired is quite varied. Some want to shop. Some want to frolic in the water. Some want to meet other single people. Some desire history and ruins. Some want to commune with nature.

Different cruise lines offer different cruise experiences. Interestingly enough, you can get a real feel for the ships through the cruise line's advertising slogans. See if you can tell which line projects which image by taking the quiz on the following page.

Choose Your Ship's Itinerary

For many first-time and neophyte cruisers, the most important aspect is the ship's itinerary. If you've never been to St. Thomas and want to buy, buy, buy at duty-free prices, you should check out the various ships' brochures and narrow it down to those lines that offer Caribbean routes which include this renowned duty-free port. For other people, snorkeling and water sports are of prime importance, so stops in Cozumel and Grand Cayman may be the deciding factor. Some people yearn for exotic ports in the Far East or South Pacific while others have been waiting half a lifetime to view penguins in their natural habitat. With today's cruise market, there are very few places left on the face of the earth that you can't visit by ship.

Cruise Motto Quiz

If knowledge truly is power, you might end up as ruler of the high seas after taking this quiz. Simply match up the cruise line with the motto with which it's associated, and find out how much power you really do have. Get a perfect score and you might have a future in the travel business.

1____ American Canadian Caribbean Line

2 ____ Carnival

3 ____ Celebrity

4 ____ Clipper

5 ____ Costa

6 ____ Cunard Line

7 ____ Dolphin

8 ____ Holland America

9 ____ Majesty

10 ___ Norwegian Cruise Line

11 ___ OdessAmerica

12 ___ Premier

13 ___ Princess

14 ___ Seabourn

15 ___ Seawind

16 ___ Star Clippers

17 ___ Windstar Cruises

A. The Fun Ships

B. A Tradition of Excellence

C. The Big Red Boat

D. In The Spirit Of Adventure

E. Tallest of the Tall Ships

F. 180 degrees from ordinary

G. It's more than a cruise, it's the Love Boat

H. The Way the Well-Traveled Make Sure They Travel Well

I. Cruise Line of the Czars

J. The Classic Cruise for Connoisseurs

K. The Small Ship Cruise Line

L. If you want to be yourself, be our guest

M. Italian-style cruising

N. Elegant, Yes. Stuffy, Never

O. Allow us to exceed your expectations

P. The official cruise line of Hanna-Barbera

Q. We're not the best because we're the oldest. We're the oldest because we're the best.

Answers: 1-K; 2-A; 3-O; 4-D; 5-M; 6-Q; 7-P; 8-B; 9-L; 10-N; 11-I; 12-C; 13-G; 14-H; 15-J; 16-E; 17-F

Choose Your Ship's Size

Nowadays, more and more cruise lines are putting into service "megaships," huge floating resorts exceeding 70,000 tons in weight and accommodating nearly 3,000 passengers when completely full. Other ships in the same line may serve only 750 passengers, providing a more personal setting. Some ships deliver the

Courtesy Seabourn Cruise Line

The intimate *Seabourn Pride* carries a maximum of 204 pampered guest on the 10,000-GRT (Gross Registered Tonnage) vessel.

same luxury of the bigger ships—in fact, they are often more luxurious—while maintaining a yacht-like feel with 200 or fewer passengers.

There are advantages and disadvantages to the various ship sizes, and only you can decide what is best at this stage of your life and travels. A smaller ship provides you more intimacy and the opportunity to get to know more people faster. If there is only one pool and three lounges, chances are you'll keep running into the same people again. There is a feeling of camaraderie among the passengers as you all walk around deck, spotting friendly faces from yesterday's skeet shooting or bingo game. On the other hand, you may feel your choices are limited in meeting traveling companions with the same interests as you, and you may feel the choices of entertainment are a bit lacking.

Darlene took her first vacation on an 18,000-ton ship, serving about 750 people. The night of the first formal occasion, she set out to the lounge for a drink, hoping to meet some congenial souls who wanted company while waiting in the reception line to meet the captain. There were three lounges on that ship, but one was being used for the captain's reception, one was the disco and not open until 11 p.m., and the third was closed because the waiters and bartenders were needed for the captain's cocktail party. Darlene ruefully crept back to her room to wait for the big event, feeling a bit foolish and lonely.

The next night, Darlene went to the main bar before dinner for a cocktail and conversation only to discover she was the lone passenger having pre-dinner drinks.

The *Rotterdam* is a mid-sized ship weighing in at 38,000 tons and accommodating 1,075 guests at double occupancy.

She did, however, enjoy a nice, friendly chat with the bartender. In the long run, Darlene valued that particular cruise experience more than many others she'd been on because she still felt she had a variety of options without getting bored on a small ship or feeling lost on a large ship.

On a larger ship, one accommodating 2,500 or more passengers, Darlene would never have been the only person sitting alone. Some ships have as many as 9 or 10 public rooms and, while some are closed at various times, there is always something going on until the wee hours of the morning. Often, the choices on a big ship are overwhelming: Do I go to the lounge on 8 Deck with the pre-dinner dance music, or the bar on 7 Deck with the piano player, or the open-air atrium on 5 Deck with the string quartet?

Another advantage of a larger ship is that the entertainment is reputedly of a higher quality. A larger ship with more passengers means a bigger main stage and a grander entertainment budget, both in the main showroom and the smaller lounges.

The larger ships are also the newer ships, so you'll find they're more likely to have certain amenities, such as refrigerators and safes in the cabin, as well as movies and satellite feeds on the television in your cabin. A real advantage to the television is that most ships rebroadcast informational lectures, such as shore lectures, shopping guides, and disembarkation procedures. If you were unable or unwilling to tear yourself away from an activity or a nap to attend one of these lectures, you'll probably be able to catch it on the TV while you're leisurely dressing for dinner.

Courtesy Royal Caribbean Cruise Line

The *Majesty of the Seas* is one of the most popular megaliners afloat, weighing in at 73,941 tons and holding 2,744 passengers when all berths are occupied.

If you're traveling alone and looking to meet someone of the opposite sex, larger is often better because, through sheer dint of numbers, there will be that many more people to meet.

There are, of course, disadvantages to a megaship. It's very frustrating to meet some fun people the first night at sea and never see them again. With 2,500 people aboard and so many places to visit and things to do, you could spend the week searching for someone. Plus, it's easy to feel lost on a large ship, both physically and emotionally.

If you've never taken a cruise before and are traveling alone, I would recommend starting with a smaller ship to get your feet wet. After you've spent a week cruising, you'll feel like a pro and will be ready to tackle the challenge of a megaship. But for your first experience, I would suggest starting small and working your way up instead of being overwhelmed the first time.

Choose Your Ship's Fare

For many people, the cost of a cruise is a major consideration. If money is no object to you, I offer my congratulations and want you to know that I am available for adoption. For the rest of us, the cost of a cruise often determines which ship we'll choose for sailing.

The cost of a cruise is explained right up front in the cruise brochure, so you can compare the various tariffs of the ships. Of course, prices will vary based on itinerary (yes, it does cost more to cruise to Europe than along the Mexican Riviera) and based on number of days (yes, an 11-day cruise will run more than a seven-day trip), but you will know in advance what the fare is and can compare the various lines based on your vacation goals and itinerary desires.

Another price consideration is the selection of the up-scale or luxury ships. While all ships feel luxurious when the service is up to par, some ships do promote themselves as ultra-luxury liners. You can spend a week in the Caribbean for as little as $125 per day on a very nice ship, or you can opt for a luxury craft and pay as much as $700 a day. The choice is up to you and your budget.

Choose The Number Of Days

There is a general rule of thumb that the longer the cruise (in number of days) the older the passengers (in number of years.) While the average age of passengers has steadily decreased over the years, I think it's safe to say that the general rule still holds true.

Here's why: The longer the cruise, the more time required and the more expensive the tariff. Young, single people, honeymooners just starting out, and younger, married couples simply do not have the time or money to take a long cruise around the world (or even a two- or three-week cruise.) Older retirees have worked hard all their lives and have put aside money for travel. Since they don't have jobs to return to or young kids to get back to care for, they can indulge themselves with exotic or longer vacations.

For a single person taking his or her first cruise, a three-day party-boat cruise is an excellent initiation into the joys of a vacation at sea. These weekend jaunts leave out of major ports, such as San Pedro, California or Miami, Florida and are accessible and affordable to the majority of the population. There are even a number of one-day excursions which, while not exactly classified as a cruise, will give you a sense of what being aboard ship is like. Many people find the seven-day cruise in the Caribbean or on the Mexico coast to be the ideal vacation.

Choose The Time Of Year

When to go on the cruise is up to you. There are cruises going to ports around the world every day of the year. You'll probably take your cruise when your boss tells you your vacation is due. But if you have some flexibility, there are some times of year that are better than others.

Cruise prices are usually divided into three sections, often called Economy, Value and Peak. These times are determined by demand and weather, so your cruise tariff will reflect this. There are certain times of year that are extremely popular, such as New Year's Eve, and you'll probably end up paying a surcharge. On the other hand, there are times that are flat for the cruise business. During these times, some cruise lines will alter their policies so that the solo traveler will have a real incentive to travel then.

Choose Your Cabin

Take a look at a cruise brochure and be prepared to be overwhelmed by the deck plan and the categories available to you as the potential cruiser. Sure, there's a difference between an outside and an inside cabin, and sure there's a difference between a cabin and a suite—but is there that much of a difference to the solo traveler that you'd be willing to pay twice the price?

As a solo traveler, you won't be spending much time in your cabin. In fact, if you're spending time in your cabin other than sleeping and changing clothes, you haven't got the hang of this cruise thing yet. Since you're on this cruise to meet new people, eat a lot of food, have a lot of fun, relax by the pool, take in new ports and enjoy the amenities the ship has to offer, why would you be spending time in your cabin?

As noted, there is a difference between an inside and outside cabin and the difference is very simple: Outside cabins have a porthole or a window. On most ships, these portholes are sealed shut, so you won't be able to open them to smell the sea breeze anyway. But it is nice to be able to sense the sun as you wake up and look outside at the azure sea and cloudless skies. In an inside cabin, the room is always dark until you turn on the lights, so when you wake up you have no sense of time. Your watch may say 7 o'clock, but sometimes it's hard to remember if you took a nap and it's time for dinner or if you slept peacefully all night and you're early for breakfast.

In general, the best location on the ship is in the middle because it's least affected by the motion of the ocean. That means, you should be happy with a cabin that's halfway between the stern and the bow, and halfway from the top deck to the bottom. With today's modern ships and advanced stabilizers, the location doesn't seem to make that much of a difference.

Most people who travel solo book the cheapest inside or outside cabin. Since there is often a single supplement charged, why pay an additional percentage on a luxury cabin when you're only using part of it anyway? And how much different is a standard outside cabin from a larger outside cabin from a deluxe outside cabin? You're still going to have great service. In addition, there is always the possibility of a free upgrade, so don't be intimidated by a travel agent talking you into a higher cabin category (so he or she can get a higher commission).

Your last decision in selecting a cabin is whether to choose one with two lower beds or one with an upper and a lower. The choice depends on whether you plan on booking the cabin alone or accepting a guaranteed share, which means the cruise line will match you up with another solo traveler. If you book a guaranteed share, the arrangement might be awkward when these accommodations are split with a stranger. Upper/lower cabins are smaller and, during the day, the upper berth is put back in place in the wall, leaving one small bed. If both you and your roommate return to the cabin for a 4 p.m. nap, some shuffling and calling of the steward must be arranged. In addition, there's always the question of who takes the upper and who sleeps in the lower.

Of course, if you have the cabin by yourself, there is no problem. You won't need the upper berth, you won't care that the cabin is small, and you'll save a bit of money in the bargain.

Deck Layout of The SeaBreeze

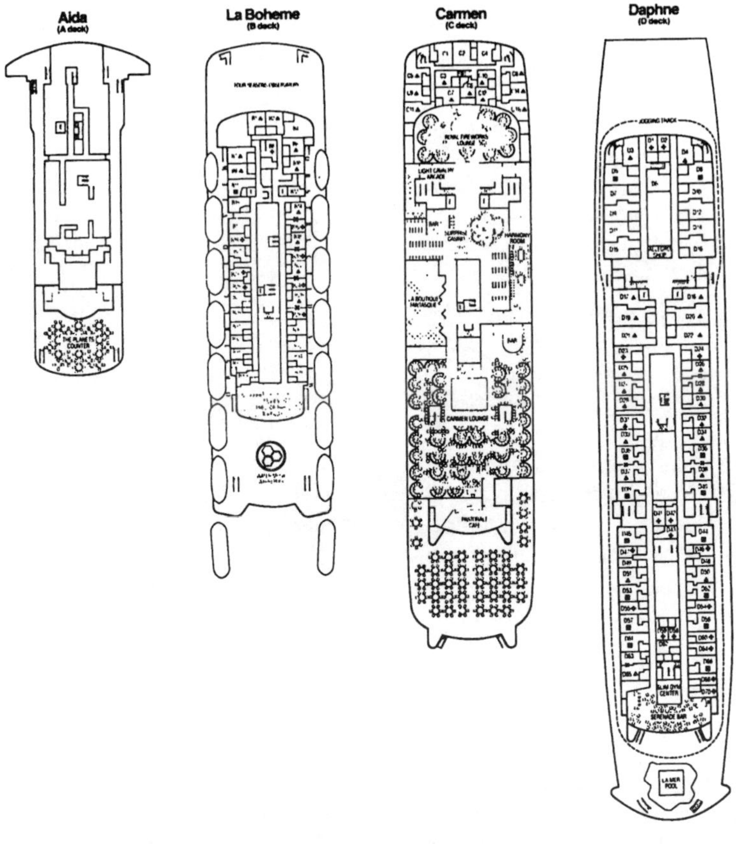

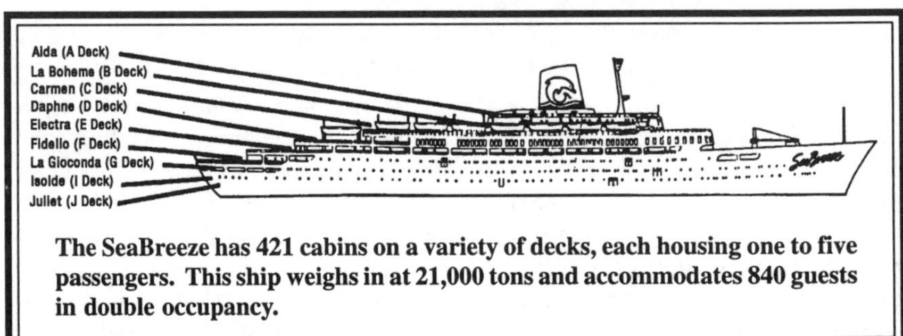

The SeaBreeze has 421 cabins on a variety of decks, each housing one to five passengers. This ship weighs in at 21,000 tons and accommodates 840 guests in double occupancy.

Choose When To Book

When you book—whether you commit yourself months in advance to get an early-booking discount or you book late, to get last-minute deals—depends on the cruise line, its popularity, its policies, and your own emotional makeup.

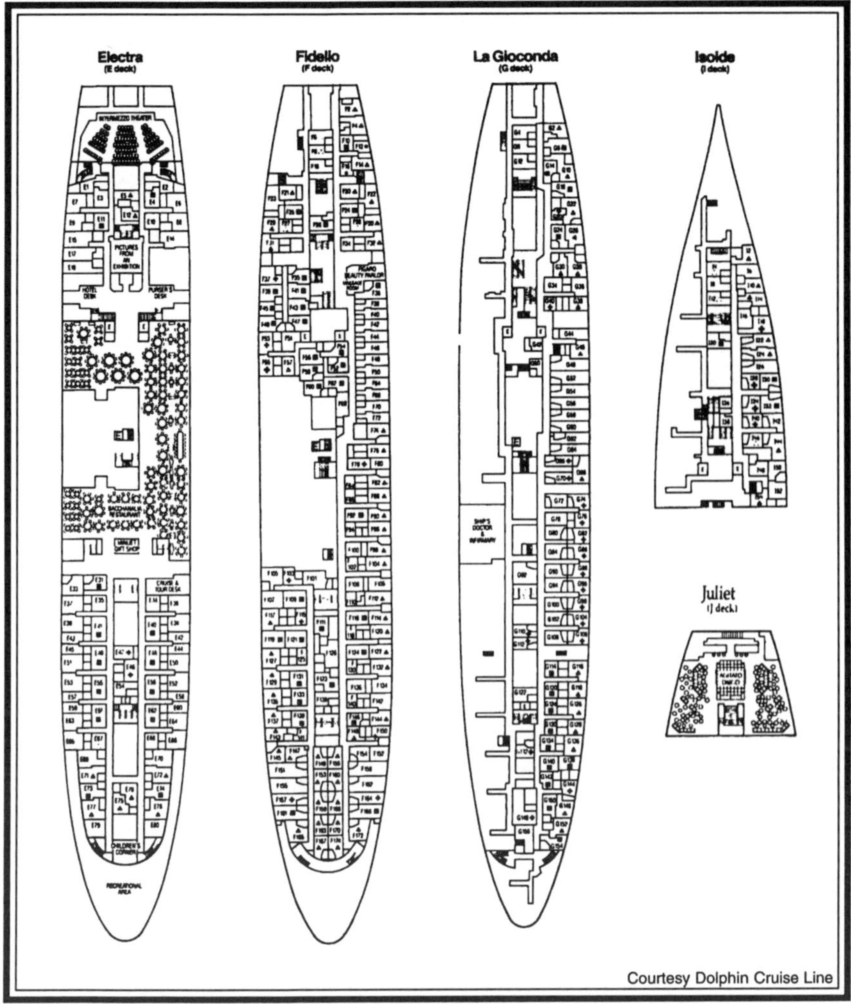

If you know way in advance that you will be getting one week's vacation in March and you know you want to go on a particular ship during that week, it makes sense to book early. You could receive a substantial discount for making this commitment, and you will have a good selection of cabins. On the other hand, you might be able to snag a bargain by waiting two or three week before you want to travel. Certain cruise lines are willing to allow solo occupancy of a cabin at no surcharge, or a reduced rate, if the occupancy for that week is particularly light.

It would also seem that booking late would give you a better shot at getting a cabin to yourself despite paying for a guaranteed share. Here's the logic: The very last person to book on a guaranteed share will either fill out the second berth in a two-berth cabin or will get a cabin to himself. Seems there's a 50-50 chance for the last person getting the cabin alone, unless the cruise line declines to sell the stateroom if they can't fill that other half.

Choose Your Travel Agent

Once you've done your homework, perused the brochures, familiarized your-self with the cruise line, learned about the ship, gotten an idea of what cabin you want, and decided when you want to sail, it's time to book your cruise and start dreaming about your adventure.

But *you* can't book your cruise. You need a travel agent to do it. Actually, you *might* be able to book your cruise (I did it once by accident), but I wouldn't recommend it. Most cruise lines will not deal with passengers and it doesn't cost any more to go through a travel agent, so let them handle it. In fact, your travel agent can save you quite a bit of money.

The most important thing is for you to do your homework first. Most home-town agents book all sorts of travel options—airline tickets, hotel packages, Club Med reservations, African safaris and, of course, cruises. While they'll be happy to book your cruise and even make some suggestions, most have not memorized the fine print in a brochure to know which lines will give the solo cruiser the best deal. You, as the passenger, have read this book and investigated the brochures so that you know what to ask for. *You* have become the expert. *You* will be guiding your travel agent. *You* will be taking charge of your vacation.

If you have a travel agent with whom you have a pleasant relationship, inves-tigate your options through him or her. You'll have the advantage of face-to-face contact and someone to call if you have any questions.

Another option is to call a cruise specialist. These folks do nothing but book cruises and often offer big discounts because of the volume of booking they do. In addition, some of them specialize in serving the solo traveler. At the end of this chapter is a list of travel agents who are cruise specialists, some with sub-special-ties in discount or last-minute travel. All have assured me that the solo traveler is a valued customer and they specialize in knowing their needs and catering to that clientele.

To find other cruise specialists, take a look in the Sunday travel section of a major newspaper. Most cruise specialists have a toll-free number and can quote you prices over the phone. There is also a bimonthly magazine called *Cruise Travel* which annually publishes a directory of reputable cruise specialists, along with updated listings of ships and itineraries

For information on subscriptions to *Cruise Travel* magazine, write:

Cruise Travel Magazine
P.O. Box 342
Mt. Morris, IL 61054-7780

Choose Your Dining Arrangements

Once you've decided to book your cruise, your travel agent will inquire about your choice in dining arrangements. Unless you're traveling on a ship with single-seating open dining, you'll have to decide whether you want smoking or non-smoking, early or late seating, and, possibly, what size table you'd prefer.

The first choice is easy. If you're a smoker, you'll probably prefer a table with other smokers. Keep in mind that more and more cruise lines are reserving fewer and fewer smoking tables and some cruise lines are instituting a policy of total non-smoking in the dining room.

The second choice concerns the time of dining. On most cruise lines, the first seating for dinner is at 6 p.m. or 6:30 p.m., with the second seating scheduled for 8 p.m. or 8:30 p.m. The majority of solo travelers prefer the second seating. The first seating is preferred by older people and families with children. If, however, you're a very early riser and want your breakfast early, if you retire by 9 p.m. and are used to dining at 6 p.m., you might want the first seating. If you're determined to be hungry for each and every midnight buffet, you'll barely have finished your dinner at the second seating before it's time to queue up for the late buffet, so the first seating allows for one more meal for the truly hungry.

Your last selection concerns the size of your dining table. While couples vie for the coveted table-for-two-by-the-window, the solo traveler is best off at a larger table for eight or 10. You'll often find yourself the odd person at a table (and we're not even getting into your personality and habits yet), so a table for four might find you situated with a honeymoon couple and a vacant chair. A table for eight is ideal, as you might find yourself with three other couples and, perhaps, another solo traveler. Tables for 10 are fun, but often so large you can't converse with the persons on the end or way across from you on the other side of a round table.

Courtesy Costa Cruise Lines

An inviting table for eight awaits its congenial group of diners on the *CostaClassica*.

Choose Whether To Buy Trip Insurance

One more decision will have to be made: Do you want optional travel and cancellation insurance? Trip insurance covers a variety of potential problems, such as trip cancellation due to medical problems, reimbursement for lost baggage over and beyond the normal rate offered by the airline or cruise line, additional health and emergency medical coverage, legal assistance, lost document replacement and/or coverage of other unforeseen circumstances

Trip insurance is recommended by all the cruise lines but whether you wish to purchase a policy is up to you and your own sense of well-being. If you're booking very far in advance to take advantage of early-booking discounts, you might well discuss trip insurance with your travel agent, because you never know what could happen in the next year. The decision as to whether this extra expense is worthwhile must be a personal one.

Cruise Specialists

World Wide Cruises keeps tabs on hundreds of sailings and is constantly in touch with the cruise lines to find out what the best available policies for the solo traveler are, according to Tara Rogers, vice president of the agency.

Any solo traveler interested in a cruise vacation can call the agency and ask for the "Singles Desk." A travel consultant will inquire about the dates the passenger wants to sail, desired itinerary and cabin choices. The consultant will then check cruise availability and match the solo traveler with the appropriate ship.

World Wide Cruises also has a "Singles Registry"—if someone wants to share a cabin, the agency will attempt to match them up with another client.

In addition, the agency puts together "Singles Cruises," booking large amounts of space on a ship and passing the volume discount on to the traveler. Either guaranteed shares or single-occupancy cabins are available. Prices vary depending on the accommodation selected.

If you'd like to be placed on the mailing list to find out about discounts or special sailings, call the agency's toll-free number or send a self-addressed, stamped envelope to:

World Wide Cruises
8059 W. McNab Rd.
Ft. Lauderdale, FL 33321
(800) 882-9000

The Cruise Line, Inc. provides two services to the solo traveler, according to President Larry Fishkin. First, the agency offers free consultation to potential clients to determine what their needs are. Second, the agency offers "significant discounted rates on most major cruise lines."

Solo travelers who want an update on the current cruise market can call the "Singles Hotline" at the agency's toll-free number and ask for Extension 613.

For solo travelers who would like information or assistance in booking a cruise, the agency provides a staff expert to assist singles. Call the toll-free number and request Extension 218.

Fishkin said the agency handles requests for single rooms and guaranteed shares, and is often able to recommend ships that avoid the single supplement, and possibly pair up the agency's clients to share a cabin. For more information, contact:

The Cruise Line, Inc.
4770 Biscayne Blvd.
PH 1-3
Miami, FL 33137
(800) 777-0707

Cruise Holidays is one of the largest cruise-only agencies in the country, with 160 offices throughout North America. Because of the quantity of bookings generated, the agency is able to pass savings on to the customer, according to Lorrin Boyer, director of marketing and communications.

One advantage is that the cruiser will be matched up with a local office and local agent who can advise the solo traveler of the best ship available and the "best price possible," Boyer said.

All the agents are "well versed in how to assist the single traveler," Boyer added.

For more information, contact:

Cruise Holidays
9665 Chesapeake Dr.
Suite 401
San Diego, CA 92193
(800) 283-SAIL

The Travel Company is the largest independent cruise booker in North America run as a single operation, according to Herb Goodfellow, president of the agency. He said the organization puts about 40,000 people a year on cruise ships, many of them solo travelers.

Because the agency controls so much space on so many cruise ships, and can hold it until up to a few days before sailing, they can offer lower prices to the public, Goodfellow said. Therefore, when a solo traveler has to pay a supplement, it is a percentage of the discount rate offered to The Travel Company clientele, instead of the brochure price.

For more information, contact:

The Travel Company
3351 El Camino Real
Suite 250
Atherton, CA 94027
(800) 367-6090

The Solo
Traveler's Options

Down to Gehenna or up to the throne,
He travels the fastest who travels alone.

Rudyard Kipling

When Noah built the Ark, the animals lined up two by two, boarding passes in their paws. Things haven't changed much since biblical days; arks and boats are still built to hold us animals two by two and if, by choice or chance, we don't want to travel with another pig or snake, we're probably going to have to suffer the consequences. When we travel solo, there won't be hell to pay in the biblical sense, but there might be surcharges, supplements and inconveniences.

Despite this historic tradition, you *can* have a exciting, exuberant and economical vacation if you arm yourself in advance with information and take command of your cruise.

You've already decided, for the obvious reasons listed in the previous chapter, why a cruise is the ideal trip, and why cruising alone works for you. The next thing to do is to weigh your options and book your trip.

One of the most vital decisions you will have to make is deciding whether your personal privacy and convenience is more important to you than money. More and more cruise lines are allowing solo travelers to book a guaranteed share, which means the cruise line will match solo travelers of the same sex so that they only have to pay the double-occupancy rate. For those who are unwilling to share a cabin with a total stranger, the solo traveler must choose between paying a single supplement, finding a ship with a guaranteed single rate or booking a single cabin.

Single Supplements

On the majority of ships, the single supplement is a standard 150 percent of the double occupancy rate. More luxurious cabins, such as deluxe outside staterooms or suites with private balconies, usually go for 200 percent the double occupancy rate.

The mathematics on this is simple: If a cabin on a ship goes for $2,000 a week and two people occupy the cabin, the cruise line will take in $4,000. If a solo traveler occupies it, the cruise line will only take in $3,000, even with the 50 percent surcharge. It's been noted that the highest-priced and lowest-priced cabins fill up the fastest, so the cruise lines are even more reluctant to allow a deluxe cabin to go at even 150 per cent the per-person rate.

While 150 percent may be the standard single supplement, not all cruise lines use the same formula: some cruise lines are higher, some are lower.

Since most cruises are all-inclusive packages, with air fare included, you might consider using any frequent flyer miles you've accumulated and book your own transportation. Cruise lines will often allow passengers a reduction of $250 or more if they supply their own transportation. Therefore, the extra 50 percent or more you pay for a single supplement will only be added to the cruise tariff, but not the transportation allowance. If you've booked a cabin for $1,400 and have to pay the single supplement of 50 percent, you'll end up paying $2,100. If you take advantage of the transportation allowance of $250, that cabin drops to $1,150 and the supplement brings it up to $1,750, a savings of $375. Keep in mind, however, that when you make your own travel arrangements, the cruise line will not provide transfers from the airport, or accommodations if it's necessary to fly in the night before due to time changes and length of travel.

When you book a cabin and you pay the single supplement, you should know in advance what your cabin assignment will be. For many passengers, the extra money spent is worthwhile, if it is important to them to have an outside cabin, be on a certain deck, be situated away from noise and traffic, or be near an elevator.

All ships have some form of single supplement. Most post the single supplement in their brochures and a few advise interested parties to call for rates. Some have cabins within specific categories on which no single supplement is levied, but if you want a specific cabin within a specific category, you can plan on spending an average of 150 percent the double-occupancy rate.

Single Cabins

Many ships have single cabins, but not all ships do. Newer ships, it seems, are more likely to be built with quad berths, to accommodate traveling families, than they are to be built with only one berth in a cabin. Often, these single cabins are much smaller and are likely to be inside. Size of the cabin doesn't matter to many people, since you don't have to maneuver around a roommate, but many people would prefer a porthole.

Although single cabins may seem like a good deal for the solo traveler, you'll get a better idea of what kind of deal you're getting if you compare the price to that of a double-occupancy rate on a nearby cabin. Often, the rate for a single

Courtesy Classical Cruises

The *Aurora I* and *Aurora II* each feature six outside single cabins like this one.

inside cabin is the same as the double-occupancy rate of a nicer outside cabin in a better location.

On some ships, double-occupancy cabins have two posted rates: one for double occupancy and one for single occupancy. If the cabin can accommodate two people, it is not technically a single cabin—it is merely being made available for solo occupancy with the single supplement built into the price at a dollar amount instead of a percentage.

To figure out how much more you'll pay for a single cabin, compared to a double-occupancy cabin, take a look at the ship's deck plan. Find a cabin on the same deck, perhaps even next to the one you're planning on occupying. Divide the cost of the single cabin by the per-person rate of the comparable cabin and you'll come up with a figure over 100 percent.

For example: A single cabin lists for $1,475 while the double-occupancy rate for a similar cabin is $1,100. Divide $1,475 by $1,100 and you'll see that the single cabins costs 134 percent of a comparable double-occupancy rate

Single cabins can still be a bargain, since they may be higher than comparable double cabins but still lower than other available cabins on the ship in which you'd have to pay the single supplement. Often, though, single cabins are placed in the same categories as higher-priced deluxe cabins. You might still save hundreds of dollars by booking a cheaper inside upper/lower cabin and paying the single supplement.

Guaranteed-Single Rates

Guaranteed-single rates are gaining popularity among cruise lines. A guaranteed single rate assures you that you'll have a cabin to yourself at a set tariff. Usually, you won't know your cabin assignment until the time of embarkation, so you won't know if you have an inside or an outside or on what deck you'll be assigned.

The advantages of guaranteed-single rates are that you often will get a better cabin than you paid for, and early-booking discounts usually apply. Of course, not all ships offer a guaranteed-single rate. In addition, the rate is usually comparable to a mid-priced cabin. Some solo travelers would prefer to book a much cheaper inside cabin at hundreds of dollars less.

Guaranteed Share

If you're willing to share a cabin with a total stranger, the solo traveler can take advantage of the same rates as those who travel in twos. Many cruise lines will allow a solo traveler to book on a guaranteed-share basis, meaning the cruise line will match you up with another solo traveler of the same sex while charging the double-occupancy rate.

For the timid or budget-conscious solo traveler, a guaranteed share is an excellent way to enjoy a cruise. Many people have found they have a lot in common with their assigned roommate and end up discovering a new friend with whom to visit ports and wile away the on-board hours. However, you should not approach the guaranteed-share option as a guaranteed-friend situation. Roommates are assigned solely on a financial basis; no consideration is taken by the cruise line concerning the compatibility of two people sharing a cabin, other than that they be of the same sex and, possibly, both are smoking or non-smoking occupants. Often, two people will find that they vary considerably in life styles, ages, sleeping habits, even outlooks on traveling. Others find the idea of sharing the intimacy of a small cabin and limited washroom facilities repugnant. Before you book a guaranteed-share, you should carefully assess your flexibility and willingness to share.

Quad Share

The bottom line on quad share is this: They're the cheapest way to go, but also the most inconvenient.

A quad share means that you'll share a cabin with up to three other persons of the same sex. There are usually two berths on the floor, and two others that pull down from the wall. A cabin that seemed to be closing in on two people now has to stretch to accommodate four. Can you imagine four women all trying to shower or plug in hair appliances at the same time as they get ready for the captain's formal party?

In addition, quad share rates rarely include air fare, so you'll have to add that to what you had thought were your savings.

Of course, there are some advantages. Often four people start out as total strangers but, through adversity, close living quarters and a sense of humor, turn into the "Four Musketeers." And even without the air fare, the quad share rate can still translate into substantial savings.

And the last possible advantage is this: You may book and pay for a quad share but end up with only one or two other roommates—or none at all.

Singleworld

Singleworld has been in business for more than 30 years and has booked more than 300,000 solo travelers on ships over the ships. While the concept of a travel club is something that will be explored later in this book, Singleworld is such a leader in the solo traveler industry that it's an option in itself, bigger than all the other travel clubs combined.

Obviously, the organization is doing something right. While Singleworld also books some European land tours, the bulk of its business is dedicated to putting solo travelers on cruise ships.

Here's how it works: Singleworld books a block of space on a cruise line, then advertises it in their brochure. The more popular the ship and itinerary, the more Singleworld sailings are offered. Sailing dates are usually broken up into two groups—those for travelers in their "20s & 30s," and those for travelers of all ages.

Currently, Singleworld is only booking cruise vacations with Carnival Cruise Line, Norwegian Cruise Line and Royal Caribbean Cruise Line. Singleworld departures are not scheduled for every sailing, so you'll need some flexibility in your schedule and preferences if you want to join a Singleworld tour.

Once on board the ship of your choice, Singleworld provides their own cruise director to help facilitate interaction among the travelers. All Singleworld travelers dine together (usually at the second seating), the Singleworld cruise director hosts a cocktail party just for your group, and a variety of optional shore excursions are offered for the Singleworld people.

All in all, Singleworld is a good way to travel, particularly for people who still feel uncomfortable about cruising alone and want to be sure there is a camp counselor to watch out for bumps in the road. If you're a very independent traveler, you may end up feeling *too* protected and sequestered. Some people don't want to dine with a homogeneous group of other single people; they prefer a table of people with different backgrounds and different stories. Some people don't want to spend their entire vacation—dining, shore excursions, cocktail parties—with the same people.

While you're free at any time to go off on your own, it's sometimes hard to pull yourself away from the group. Just remember, this is your vacation and you have the right to do what you want when you want. Similarly, you've paid for half a cabin and are under no obligation to keep your roommate company because he or she isn't brave enough to venture out alone.

Don't book with Singleworld under the assumption that you're going to have a wild week among hundreds of fun-loving single people. The number of people who book on any one particular Singleworld cruise varies, but it's often a small group of 10 or 12, sometimes even smaller.

The advantage to Singleworld is that you'll be with a group of other solo travelers and you'll have your own personal guide, in the form of a Singleworld cruise director, to answer your questions, give advice, dine with you and generally help you find your way. The disadvantage is that Singleworld only works with three cruise lines, so your choice of ships, times and itineraries is limited. You might even be able to get just as good a deal by having your travel agent get you a guaranteed share or single room. Also, you'll have to pay a Singleworld fee, and you'll soon discover that in addition to the other tips you'll be handing out at the end of your cruise, your Singleworld guide expects to be remembered, too.

Membership in **Singleworld** is $25 per year. This fee must be paid before you can book a vacation with Singleworld. For more information, contact:

Singleworld
401 Theodore Fremd Avenue
Rye, NY 10580
(800) 223-6490

Solo Traveler Clubs

Solo traveler clubs specialize in two things: matching people up from their registry to avoid the single supplements, and offering special sailings with either a high percentage of solo travelers or a large block of space for group discounts. Solo traveler clubs often sponsor lectures on specific topics of interest, such as kayak cruising or exotic locales. If you're interested in getting involved in a travel club, either to find out what travel options are open to you or to meet other people who might make interesting travel partners, watch your local newspaper for notices of get-togethers. If you attend one of these lectures, you might find out about special tours or trips planned by the club and you'll get a chance to discover if there is anyone there who shares your particular philosophy of cruising.

Some people like the idea of a travel club because they can meet potential roommates in advance and find out what their habits are. Is he an early riser or a night owl? Does she smoke? Does he want to take tours or just hang out at the beach? In reality, though, few of these things matter if you're independently inclined. Your potential traveling partner is merely someone to share space with so you can avoid a single supplement. If you make it known in advance that that is your priority, there won't be misunderstandings once you're on the ship and you go off to meet new people or follow your own schedule on board or in port. There's little difference between sharing a cabin with a stranger on a guaranteed-share basis and sharing the cabin with a person from a travel club—if you both agree that the purpose is solely to save money.

There might be solo traveler clubs advertised in your area, either in the travel section of your local paper or in a singles-oriented publication. Below are three clubs that specialize in matching people or providing opportunities for the solo traveler.

Partners-In-Travel, serving the West Coast, and **Partners East**, serving the East Coast, function solely as a "contact service for the single traveler," according to Miriam Tobolowski, publisher of the organization's directory and pamphlets.

Members pay $25 a year, which gets them the directory, all updates, and a package of three brochures geared toward the solo traveler, including "Singles-Friendly Tour Operators" and "The Singular Traveler," along with "Traveling Smart" and "Ready To Go," a pre-trip planning guide. Members fill out a short questionnaire indicating their age range, travel style, and what they look for in a travel partner. They then construct a personal listing of no more than 50 words about themselves for the directory. Upon receiving the directory, it is up to the members to make contact with potential traveling companions and make their own plans.

For more information, contact:

Partners-In-Travel
Attn: Miriam Tobolowski
11660 Chenault St. #119
Los Angeles, CA 90049
(310) 476-4869

or

Partner East
Attn: Diane March
50 W. 57th St. #15D
New York, NY 10019
(212) 245-7288

American Singles, a nationwide non-profit organization, sponsors two cruises a year for singles and provides a non-smoking roommate of the same sex to share the cost of a double-occupancy cabin. American Singles also provides a tour guide and free on-board cocktail parties. Typical size of an American Singles group is 100, and the group dines together at the second seating and socializes throughout the week. Individuals may also choose the first seating, but will not be dining with the group.

Membership in American Singles is free to single people of all ages in all 50 states. Most members are aged 30 to 55 and more than 90 percent are non-smokers.

For more information, contact:

American Singles
Attn: Tom Andrews
4 Highland Ave.
San Rafael, CA 94901
(415) 459-3817

Travelin' Singles describes itself as a "travel organization devoted to providing vacation trips to active, fun-loving singles in the 30s, 40s and 50s." All of the tours provide a professional escort to accompany the group.

In addition to cruises, the group also offers land package tours to such places as China, Rio de Janeiro and Greece. In all, the organization provides about 14 travel opportunities a year.

To join the group, you pay a "postage fee" of $15 to receive the organization's news updates. This translates into a a credit on your first trip. If you don't travel within a year, you're expunged from the group's files, to ensure that all members are active travelers, according to John La Point, president of the organization.

For more information, contact:

Travelin' Singles
Attn: John La Point
P.O. Box 111
Artesia, CA 90702
(800) 748-6662

Special Interest Organizations & Tour Operators

Like travel clubs, special interest agencies provide the opportunity to travel, but they tend to specialize more in providing you that opportunity among people with whom you have something in common. Some organizations focus on the mature traveler. Other organizations provide travel opportunities geared toward people of a specific sexual orientation. Still others are simply tour operators who buy up space on a ship (or charter an entire ship) and pass the savings on to their customers. Below are a few travel organizations that appeal to special interest groups.

Saga Holidays provides cruise opportunities for the "mature traveler." Although Saga doesn't deny booking to any travelers of any age, except those under 21, people should be aware that the "bulk of those people traveling" with Saga are over the age of 50, said Ruth Davidson, manager of public relations.

Saga has been in business in England for the past 40 years, and in America since 1981. All Saga tours are fully escorted, Davidson said, and the organization buys in bulk so they can offer varied itineraries and savings.

While Saga doesn't offer guaranteed shares through the agency itself, they may be able to place the solo traveler on ships that do honor that policy. In addition, Saga often runs specials in which they can offer a single at the double occupancy rate.

Saga sends out cruise news and cruise catalogues to travelers on its mailing list. For more information, contact:

Saga Holidays
222 Berkeley St.
Boston, MA 02116
(800) 343-0273

Taylor Tours and Cruises is an organization that provides cruise opportunities through a number of lines, including Holland America, Regency, Costa and Cunard. The tour operator buys blocks of space on a ship and occasionally charters an entire vessel and then passes the savings on to its clientele, said Bill Taylor, president.

Although Taylor Tours doesn't cater exclusively to the solo traveler, Taylor said he considers the solo traveler a "valuable customer." He cited an example when the agency bought up a number of cabins with upper and lower berths and was able to offer low rates on solo occupancy to those traveling alone. In addition, Taylor Tours can pass on lower rates by giving their discounted double-occupancy rate to people who travel with them on ships that accept guaranteed shares.

For more information, contact:

Taylor Tours
3171 Los Feliz Boulevard, Suite 307
Los Angeles, CA 90039
(800) 282-4998

Olivia Cruises is an offshoot of Olivia Records, providing travel opportunities for gay women. In 1990, Olivia tried a concert fest at sea and sold out the cruise immediately. By 1993, the group had scheduled its 11th sailing.

Olivia takes over an entire ship, providing women with "safety and freedom and empowerment," said Babs Daitch, public relations and special events manager for Olivia, and the atmosphere is "a very safe environment for women traveling by themselves."

Olivia's cruise provide an activities coordinator, singles tables, a "Singles Schmooze" hour and even their own version of "The Dating Game" so people can get to know one another. Guaranteed shares are available and roommates are matched up on their indication of smoking/non-smoking, age group, and can even note whether they prefer to be with someone who's in a "12-Step" program.

Daitch added that women traveling with Olivia cruises "don't have to be lesbians—just comfortable in the environment."

For more information, contact:

Olivia Cruises
4400 Market St.
Oakland, CA 94608
(800) 631-6277

RSVP Travel was started in 1986 to provide travel opportunities to gay men. The organization has had such success that it has scheduled 32 cruises and now owns its own cruise ship, the *Sea Spirit*. The ship sails out of St. Thomas during the winter and along the East coast of the United States during the summer, with a primarily gay staff. According to Andy Schmeidel, director of advertising and sales, RSVP is the only gay travel group that does not sell its tours directly—your travel agent will book you with RSVP.

On the *Sea Spirit*, guaranteed shares are available, and a "Dine Around" program is provided so solo travelers can move around, without assigned tables in order to meet the other passengers. Certain tours aboard the *Sea Spirit* are designated "Singles Week" or "Leather Week."

In addition to voyages on the *Sea Spirit*, the organization also charters other ships to provide travel opportunities for its clients.

For more information, contact:

RSVP Travel Productions
2800 University Ave. S.E.,
Minneapolis, MN 55414
(800) 533-1482

Your Best Options

When trying to decide which cruise to take, have a conversation with yourself and see if you make any of the following statements:

I've never been on a cruise before and I'm nervous about being being totally alone the whole cruise.

By the very definition of the cruise experience, there's little need to worry about feeling lonely. But if this is foremost on your mind, you have a number of options. First, you can choose a tour operator, such as Singleworld, that provides a social director to smooth things along. Second, choose a smaller ship that has more of a feeling of a cozy inn than a large resort. Third, select a guaranteed-share basis so at least there'll be another warm body in the cabin.

I want my own cabin but I don't want to pay any more than anyone else.

A number of cruise lines offer cabins to the solo traveler at the same rate as double occupancy. On Cunard Crown's *Cunard Princess, Cunard Countess, Crown Dynasty, Crown Jewel and Crown Monarch,* single occupancy is guaranteed with no surcharge, subject to confirmation 30 days prior to departure in Categories C through F. On Seawind's *Seawind Crown,* there is no surcharge for solo occupancy of Category M, cabins that have upper/lower berths and fall in the least expensive category. On American Hawaii's *Constitution* and *Independence*, there is no surcharge for solo occupancy of cabins in Categories C and G.

I want my own cabin and I don't mind waiting until I'm on the ship to find out what cabin it is.

Any ship that offers a guaranteed-single rate will give you a cabin to yourself at a set price, usually equivalent to a mid-priced stateroom with cabin assignment at the time of embarkation. Often, you'll end up with a better cabin than you had paid for. Lines that offer guaranteed-single rates include Star Clipper, Norwegian Cruise Line and Royal Caribbean Cruise Line, as well as Celebrity's *Meridian*.

I'd prefer a stateroom that's specifically a single cabin.

A number of cruise lines have ships with some single cabins available. Cunard's *QE 2* leads the pack, with 145. Single cabins are also available on American Hawaii's *Constitution* and *Independence*, Classical Cruises' *Aurora I* and *Aurora II*, Cunard's *Danube Princess, Sagafjord* and *Vistafjord*, Fantasy's *Amerikanis*, Holland America's *Rotterdam*, Ivaran's *Americana*, Norwegian Cruise Line's *Norway* and *Southward*, OdessAmerica's *Adropov* and *Columbus Caravel*, Princess' *Island Princess* and *Pacific Princess*, Royal Cruise Line's *Royal Odyssey*, Royal Viking Line's *Royal Viking Sun*, Swan Hellenic's *Nile Monarch* and *Orpheus*, and World Explorer's *Universe*.

I don't mind sharing with one other person in order to save some money.

What you've just described is the typical guaranteed-share program. Lines that accept guaranteed shares, either advertised in their brochure or accepted at the cruise line's discretion, include American Canadian Caribbean Line, American Hawaii, Cunard's *Countess, Princess* and *QE 2*, Delta Queen Steamboat Company, Metropolitan Touring's Galapagos Cruises, Holland America, Ocean Cruise Line, OdessAmerica, Princess Cruises, Royal Caribbean Cruise Line, Royal Cruise Line's *Crown Odyssey* and *Golden Odyssey*, Royal Viking's *Royal Viking Sun*, St. Lawrence Cruise Lines, Star Clipper, Sun Line, Swan Hellenic, Tall Ship Adventures, and Windjammer Barefoot Cruises.

I don't care about the cabin or the number of people I have to share with, I want to save money.

The more people to a cabin, the more you're going to save. It's simply a matter of economics. If you're willing to share the cabin with up to three— or even five—other people of the same sex, you can have yourself a pretty inexpensive vacation.

Cruise lines that offer quad shares include Carnival and NCL. Windjammer also offers quad shares but takes it one step further—some of the ships have "bachelor/ette" quarters, with six bunks to a cabin. You can also book quad shares through Singleworld.

I want to be pampered, and I'm willing to pay for it, but I don't want to pay an arm and a leg more than everyone else.

Seabourn, an ultra-deluxe cruise line, has instituted a policy of charging only a 10 percent surcharge for solo occupancy of a suite on many of its itineraries on the *Seabourn Pride* and *Seabourn Spirit*. Still other itineraries on that line are available at only a 25 percent surcharge. The standard single supplement on the unique *Radisson Diamond* is only 25 percent.

I want to meet a lot of other people who are traveling alone.

The best rule of thumb to meet the most people traveling alone is to find the cruise lines that have the best policies for the solo traveler. Look for a cruise line that advertises guaranteed shares and guaranteed-single rates, along with those ships that are preferred by Singleworld.

I love to dance but hate sitting on the sidelines watching.

If you are a woman who likes to dance, particularly to such traditional dances as the waltz or jitterbug, choose a cruise line that features a "Gentleman Host" program. Otherwise, there usually is a shortage of mature single males who like to dance. If you're very young and energetic, don't expect these men to be boogying in the disco. Also, do not expect to spend every dance on the dance floor with a gentleman host—he has to dance with all the ladies, who probably outnumber him five or 10 to one. Cruise lines that offer a "Gentleman Host" program on some or all of its ships or itineraries include Cunard, Crystal Cruise Line, Delta Queen, Holland America, Royal Cruise Line, Royal Viking Line, Sun Line and World Explorer.

Alternative Cruising

Two roads diverged in a wood, and I—
I took the one less traveled by,
And that has made all the difference.

Robert Frost

You're sitting by the fire, contentedly sipping a glass of herbal tea and watching an old black-and-white classic movie on TV, when a cruise commercial appears on the screen. The set comes alive with color, as you view semi-naked dancers laden with feathers and sequins go through intricate motions on a giant stage. A tuxedoed gentleman gallantly lifts his glass of champagne in homage to a beautiful woman in a slinky dress, after which they head up to the rough-and-tumble action in the casino.

Sound like your idea of a heavenly vacation?

What's that you say? The answer is NO?!?

You like the idea of a cruise, but your idea of entertainment leans more toward informative lectures than scantily clad dancers. You like the idea of traveling to different spots of the world instead of staying in one place, but you'd prefer to see exotic historic ruins instead of white-sand beaches ad nauseum. You like being with a group of people while still maintaining your independence, but you'd prefer to be with some people who share your same interests in nature, history, music, exploration or other esoteric hobbies.

Perhaps you're best suited to some form of alternative cruising. Traditional cruising is immensely popular around the world, with the number of cruisers growing with each passing year. But alternative cruising is gaining fans who travel the globe enjoying a type of vacation that seems made exactly for their needs.

The majority of people who experience a cruise do so on the major cruise lines within a relatively short distance of the United States. In fact, the latest statistics indicate 56 percent of all cruising occurs in the Caribbean market alone. Add in Western Mexico and Hawaii, and the figure jumps to over 65 percent.

But if your idea of a vacation means a more remote itinerary or a different type of vessel, there's a ship out there for you. You may give up exciting night life and gourmet French cuisine, and that would suit you fine. Cabins aboard many of these ships may feel like they'd fit into the closet of other mainstream vessels, but you're more interested in the lectures and experience you get *outside* your cabin. You may find that formal clothes have no place in your suitcase, and that's probably your preference. Devotees of alternative cruising swear it's the only way to go, at least for them.

One-Day Cruises

If you want to get a taste of cruising—feel the motion of the ocean without a big investment of time or money—you might try taking a one-day cruise.

One-day cruises don't give you the total cruise experience, but they do give you a sample of what cruising could be like. Cost for a one-day cruise includes meals and entertainment and usually runs less than $100 per person—and often that price includes a night in a hotel before or after your cruise. Of course, if you live in Boise, Idaho, it's not worth it to fly to the ocean for a one-day cruise. But if you live near or will be traveling to a port city, such as Miami or San Diego, you can take advantage of this unique opportunity.

On many one-day cruises, the price of the fare does not include use of a cabin. Cabins are priced per facility, not per person, so if you get aboard ship and meet a bunch of new friends, you can all rent a cabin together to use as a place to stash your belongings and clean up. You'll be spending most of your time lounging by the pool, eating at the buffets, gambling in the casino and enjoying the various live bands, so you won't be spending much time in the cabin anyway. And since this is a one-day cruise, not a one-night cruise, you won't be sleeping.

In other parts of the world, one-day cruises are common both as simple excursions and as methods of transportation. Ferry boats serve as transfer vehicles for cars and people between, say, England and Scandinavia, while providing comfortable accommodations and entertainment to make the time pass. Trips around the Grecian isles are extremely popular, providing different sights and sites, depending on the day of the week.

If you're planning a trip to Europe or other parts of the world, ask your travel agent about the possibility of adding a day or more to your trip to include a short cruise.

Freighters

Freighters are gaining popularity among cruisers in general and solo cruisers in particular because they offer a unique opportunity to travel at a leisurely pace and feel almost like a crew member instead of a passenger. Many freighters carry only a few passengers and have a limited itinerary, while others seem almost like luxury ships while they roam the globe. One advantage to sailing on a freighter is that these cargo ships are working ships. A stop at a port is not so much for the enjoyment of the passengers as it is to load and unload cargo. There-

All accommodations aboard CAST's *Husky*, *Muskox* and *Otter* are outside staterooms or suites with portholes or windows.

fore, there is more time in port to see the sights and get a feel for a foreign country. Some vessels even stay in a port for days. In addition, most freighters have reasonable prices for the solo traveler. When there is an additional surcharge, it is usually not the 150 percent often charged by the major cruise lines.

Freighter travel is not for everyone. Many voyages are lengthy, running 45 to 60 days. Many of the ships carry 12 passengers or less, so travelers must rely on their own devices for company and entertainment. Many ships go days between ports. And, because of the length of a cruise, a more substantial financial outlay is required. While the per-day cost of a freighter might be half of a regular cruise line, it starts to add up when you're booked for 15, 25 or 50 days.

Here are two major organizations that list and book freighter cruises. Both publish notices of availability on an assortment of freighters with a variety of itineraries.

Freighter World Cruises is the North American Passenger Representative for a number of international freighters. The organization publishes a newsletter which features current availability on a number of international freighters.

To inquire about the current newsletter, contact:

Freighter World Cruise, Inc.
180 So. Lake Ave. #335
Pasadena, CA 91101
(818) 449-3106

TravLTips, a travel association specializing in freighter accommodations, boasts a membership of 28,000. The organization publishes a bimonthly newsletter featuring articles about freighter experiences, ports of call, and vessels, as well as freighter listings and availability by itinerary.

Membership in TravLTips is $15 for one year or $25 for two years. For more information, contact:

TravLTips
163-07 Depot Road
P.O. Box 188
Flushing, New York 11358
(800) 872-8584

If you're already curious about freighter travel, here's a sample to whet your appetite.

Freighter World Cruises lists a 70-day cruise with *Mineral Shipping* (Singapore Registry). The vessel leaves from a southeastern U.S. port, travels to Brazil, then over to an assortment of Mediterranean ports. The ship carries 12 passengers and includes a swimming pool. Rates for double occupancy are $5,775 a person, while the single occupancy rate is $6,300. The per-day rate works out to about $90 a day for single occupancy, just $7.50 per day more than double occupancy.

TravLTips lists a 70-day cruise with the Blue Star North America Ltd. line on a 10-passenger ship. The vessel leaves from Jacksonville, Florida, travels through the Panama Canal to ports in Australia and New Zealand and returns to Florida or Philadelphia. Off-season double-occupancy rates are as low as $5,400 while single occupancy rates are as low as $6,100.

CAST Freights offers the opportunity to sail to Europe instead of flying there. The CAST freighters sail round trip between Canada and Belgium, carrying a maximum of 12 passengers. One way fare between Montreal and Zeebrugge is $2,120 for either a double or single. Two segments can be combined for a round-trip itinerary of 32 days for $3,890, double or single. CAST is handled by TravLTips.

For those looking for a slightly more luxurious freighter experience, Ivaran Lines offers the *Americana*, an 88-passenger cargo liner. There are 20 single cabins on board, and many of them actually cost *less* than comparable double-occupancy cabins. The ship features a swimming pool and whirlpool and follows an itinerary that leaves the United States to travel down the coast of South America and back again. Ivaran has even added a gentleman host to keep things lively.

Tall Ships And Sailing Vessels

Some people long for the beauty and simplicity of a tall ship, slicing through the ocean with sails blowing in the breeze. Tall ships are often geared more toward water sports than sightseeing in major ports. Because they are smaller, with a shallower draft, they can go to islands where the large cruise ships don't stop.

Life on board a sailing vessel is usually very casual, relying more on the whim of the sea to plot the itinerary than a rigid schedule adhered to from week to week. Some vessels, however, maintain the sense of elegance found on the mainstream cruise lines, complete with a captain's dinner with formal dress.

Many people are under the impression that they will be assigned chores aboard a tall ship and must earn their keep, in addition to paying their fare. While passengers are allowed to participate on some ships, no service is ever required. The approach is more one of openness—the willingness of a crew member to explain what he is doing when he hoists the sail or the accessibility of visiting the bridge at almost any time during the cruise.

Courtesy Ivaran Lines

The *Americana* features many of the amenities of traditional passenger ships, including a swimming pool, whirlpool, trap shooting, ping pong and shuffleboard.

While some tall ships are earthy and replicate the early experience of explorers and settlers, others are downright luxurious, calling at exotic ports of call with some of the most comfortable staterooms afloat.

If you want to stay close to home and feel almost like you're camping out, consider the summer tours of the Maine Windjammer fleet. The ships are small, accommodating a few dozen people, bathrooms are often shared, and food is good old American fare, including a traditional New England clambake.

The *Mandalay* is only one of the six ships in the Windjammer Barefoot Cruises fleet that provides tall-ship cruising adventures in the Caribbean.

Tall ships are more commonly found in the Caribbean, where they visit islands far from the madding crowd. Tall Ship Adventures' *Sir Francis Drake* holds 28 passengers and stops at various Caribbean islands for diving, snorkeling and water sports. The ships in the Windjammer Barefoot line hold a larger contingent of passengers in the same relaxed atmosphere. For a more mainstream tall ship experience, choose the Windstar or Star Clippers lines. While there definitely are sails on the Windstar ships, they're computer operated to unfurl in under two minutes, a grand sight to behold.

Inland And Coastal Cruising

Inland or coastal cruising is a totally different experience than a traditional ocean-going vessel. When cruising down a river or along a coast, passengers are stationary as they watch the scenery go by. Many vessels that cruise along the coast or down the waterways have cabins with balconies so passengers can enjoy their privacy while observing the scenery.

Courtesy Delta Queen Steamboat Company

The *Delta Queen* is the only authentic, fully restored steamboat in the United States to still carry overnight passengers. It has been designated a national historic landmark.

If you're looking to cruise close to home, there are a couple of options available. You can travel aboard an authentic paddlewheel steamboat with an historic tour of the American South aboard the Delta Queen vessels, or experience the Canadian culture on the St. Lawrence Cruise Line's *Canadian Empress*, a replica steamboat with an intriguing itinerary.

River cruising is even more popular farther from America, where a variety of vessels are waiting to take you along Europe's famed rivers. KD River Cruises and Cunard EuropAmerica offer tours down the Danube, Rhone, Elbe, Mosel and Main Rivers. There are also a number of cruise lines that will take you along the Nile River, with stops and shore excursions to the country's glorious temples and tombs.

Another inspiring route is along the coast of Norway. A number of popular cruise lines make sure they include this dramatic coastline in their itineraries, but the adventurous traveler can also cruise like the natives on the Bergen Line's mail and supply ships. Check with your travel agent about other coastal cruising opportunities.

Courtesy Bergen Line

A steamer in the Bergen Line travels along Norway's Trollfjord, stopping at 35 different ports along the coast 365 days a year.

There are, of course, many other rivers, coastlines and travel opportunities that await the creative cruiser. Look into a floating hotel along the Thames or a barge through France's wine country. Combine a transatlantic-crossing cruise with a land tour and a river exploration. Brush up on a foreign language as you chat with the natives on a German riverboat.

Scientific And Nature Expeditions

The opportunity to see fantastic scenery, to learn about the history and culture of a country, to explore the flora and fauna of a locale close up, is the main reason some people choose a cruise. Tours of the Galapagos Islands are available for those with an interest in reproducing Darwin's historic expedition, while the chance to go to the ends of the earth—literally—is available for those who seek the ice-bound regions of Antarctica and the North Pole.

Courtesy Clipper Cruise Lines

The *World Discoverer*'s shallow draft allows the vessel to almost touch the shoreline, while the zodiac landing craft affords passengers the opportunity for "up-close" nature exploration.

Cruises that focus on history, nature, and science have increased in popularity over the years, and the cruise lines have sought to accommodate this interest. Most cruise lines that offer exotic itineraries do more than just offer a place to sleep—included in the tour package are lectures by professors and experts on topics of interest to the passengers; tours and shore excursions to museums and botanical gardens; huge scholastic libraries on board the ship; and entertainment geared toward the culture of the countries and areas visited.

Special Expeditions' three ships include the *Sea Bird* and *Sea Lion*, which stay close to North and South America, and the *Polaris*, which travels over to Europe, too. The ships lead expeditions around South and Central America and Mexico, as well as the northwest United States and Alaska.

For those interested in those unique islands off the coast of Ecuador, Galapagos Cruises and Metropolitan Touring both offer tours of the Galapagos Islands. The opportunity to explore the wildlife and fauna indigenous to these islands lures

The 18,000-ton *Universe* is dwarfed by the magnificence of Alaska's Inside Passage.

passengers from all over the world. While itineraries featuring Alaska's icy exterior are extremely popular among cruise passengers, some lines take the search for glaciers one step further by offering cruises to the North and South poles. Using ships that are specially tempered and certified for safety among ice floes, these lines offer exploration of the extreme areas of the world, such as Antarctica and Greenland, even providing the appropriate clothing of boots and parkas, when necessary. And OdessAmerica's *Columbus Caravel* and World Explorer's *Universe* both feature a respectable number of single cabins to make these voyages accessible for the solo traveler.

If this type of travel seems a bit extreme but you still want to steep yourself in history and academia, look into Clipper, Classical, Swan Hellenic or Royal Viking lines, where the emphasis is on discovery but the experience is a little less extreme.

Whatever you choose to do, creativity is the key and adventure awaits you.

Chapter 4: Alternative Cruising 53

Pack It Up

The heaviest baggage for a traveler is an empty purse.

English proverb

The old adage concerning packing for a vacation goes something like this: "Take half as many clothes and twice as much money." In most cases this makes sense, because a typical vacation is filled with spontaneity and unexpected opportunities, requiring unthought of clothing and unheard of expenses.

The traveler to Europe might plan on spending his or her time visiting museums, churches, cafes and restaurants and thus pack accordingly. But most of us like to be prepared for any situation and are tempted to throw in a slinky black dress or a business suit in case the opportunity arises to visit Monte Carlo. Or we might stash away hiking boots and other outdoor gear in case the urge to go tramping the French countryside becomes overwhelming.

Then, too, you usually plan to spend a set amount of money and, prior to the trip, buy an established amount of traveler's checks. Once in Europe, however, it becomes apparent that those cute little cafes are a bit more pricey than anticipated, those four-star restaurants are more exorbitant than anything you've experienced in the United States, and trying to cash a personal check in Europe is a waste of your precious vacation time.

Cruise vacationers, take heart! This problem does not occur on a vacation aboard a ship. In fact, because of the logistics and intrinsic nature of a cruise, you may feel free to pack more clothes and accessories than you could possibly wear or need, and never fear that you'll run out of money (as long as you have a checkbook and a credit card!).

Prepare Your Documents

Getting your documents in order belongs under the chapter of packing because it is something you should have with you but should *never* pack in your suitcase. You will be asked to show your documents at many points throughout your trip, starting with your arrival at the airport and continuing on through embarkation and disembarkation.

Sometime before you leave for the airport or the cruise ship, fill in all the required documents. It is very annoying to wait in line behind people who didn't think to answer the questions on their embarkation forms, despite special notices in the cruise packet advising them to do so.

You do not want to be one of those people, do you? I didn't think so.

While you're loading up your suitcase with everything you think you could possibly need, you'll want to streamline those things you actually carry on your person. Take a few moments to clean out your wallet or purse before leaving on your trip. There isn't a lot of sense carrying all the credit cards and junk you usually tote along when you won't be making any major purchases at Sears or J.C. Penney. If you only carry the bare necessities, you'll have less to worry about if you lose your wallet or it falls overboard on some shore excursion.

Before you leave your house, make sure you have the following documents

Documents Checklist

- ☐ Airline tickets
- ☐ Cruise documents
- ☐ Embarkation form
- ☐ Cruise brochure
- ☐ Cruise baggage tags
- ☐ Immigration form
- ☐ Passport/identification
- ☐ Credit card
- ☐ Blank check
- ☐ Traveler's checks
- ☐ Money
- ☐ Business cards

and necessities filled out and with you. It will save you a lot of time, trouble and heartache in the long run.

Know What To Plan For

When you plan your cruise, you'll pretty much know exactly what you'll need for every day and every occasion. You'll know in advance what days you'll be in port and what you'll need to wear there (obviously, clothing needs are different for an Alaskan cruise than for a Caribbean vacation). You'll also know in advance what will be expected for evening wear.

You'll generally find that on a seven-day cruise, there will be two semi-formal nights, two formal nights, and three casual nights. This will give you a sense of what is expected for dress for the dining room, and will help you decide what to pack. Although definition of terms may vary from cruise line to cruise line, and the number of nights of each variety will vary based on the ship and its itinerary, you can get a feeling for what to expect clotheswise by following guidelines provided by the cruise line. Often, this information will be conveyed to you in your cruise documents before you even leave home, and the appropriate dress for the evening is almost always included in the daily program listing the day's events.

Your first night, the night of embarkation, is very casual because people have been traveling all day and usually don't feel like getting dressed up. In addition, there is a slight chance some passengers might not have received their luggage in their cabin by the time dinner is served, so it's unfair to expect cruisers to change into fancy clothes. Casual means sport shirts and slacks for the men, pants or skirts for the women. Shorts are never appropriate or permitted in the dining room for dinner on most cruise lines.

The second night, the first full day at sea, is usually the captain's cocktail party and is the first formal night. Formal means your absolutely best, most dazzling clothes. For women, that means the sequined number you paid a fortune for but only got to wear once, on New Year's Eve. For men, that means a tuxedo or dinner jacket. If you don't have a sequined dress or a tuxedo, *do not go out and buy one!* Any fancy dress (such as you'd wear to a wedding) is appropriate for the women, and a dark suit is standard for the men. In fact, while a tuxedo always looks great on a gentleman, the majority of men do not own one and will not wear one on the formal evenings, so you won't feel out of place. On some ships, there is even a tuxedo rental shop on board, so men who do not own a tuxedo can rent one, as well as providing convenience for men who don't wish to drag along their formal wear.

The third and fifth nights might be semi-formal, which means dresses for the women and sport coats and ties for the men, and the fourth night might once again be casual.

The sixth night will probably be the final formal night and the last night, the night before disembarkation, will be casual.

In general, just keep in mind that you will need to have something to wear for seven days of fun and sun, and seven evenings of dining and entertainment. And, yes, it is perfectly permissible to repeat an article of clothing, as long as it's clean and you don't wear the same thing *every* day.

Visualize Your Days

I use the information about the ship's schedule to plan my wardrobe. I lay out all the clothes I think I might need based on the ship's daytime itinerary and the demands of the evening dress. I take everything that I plan to pack and lay it on the center of the bed.

Let's take a typical day, such as the day we arrive in St. Thomas. I say to myself:

"Well, today is Tuesday. We're going to be in St. Thomas today, so I'll be shopping in the morning, then going to the beach in the afternoon. First, I'll need something to wear to breakfast and shopping. *(Then I take the pair of red flowered shorts, yellow tank top, and a pair of comfortable shoes, and lay them aside, or into the suitcase.)* In the afternoon, I'll be heading to the the beach. *(I take my bathing suit, cover-up, beach bag and beach toys, and lay them in the suitcase.)* That should do me until evening, when it's Caribbean night. *(I take the flowered dress and remember that I also want the necklace with the parrot, the fish earrings, and the green shoes and green purse.)*"

I progress in this manner until I've covered every day and evening of the entire cruise. Anything left over is put back in the closet.

I've found it very helpful if, while I'm visualizing each event and outfit, I visualize the *entire* outfit—not just the clothes, but everything that goes with it. How frustrating to remember the tuxedo, but forget the cummerbund or tie. How annoying to put on that gorgeous new dress, only to realize those rhinestone-studded shoes are still sitting at home on the shoe rack. Visualize the entire outfit, down to the lingerie and jewelry, and you'll have less of a chance of that happening.

Establish A "Vacation Box"

If this is the first time you've ever been on a cruise, you probably don't have a "vacation box." After my first cruise, I created one that I keep on the top shelf of my closet and now I've cut my packing time considerably. Once you return from your cruise, you too can create a "vacation box" and be prepared for your next time at sea.

In my vacation box are all the things I seldom use throughout the rest of the year but need access to while getting ready for a trip. I never have to search for my travel alarm or sewing kit, because I know it's right in that vacation box. I also keep my travel toothbrush and small samples of shampoos, conditioner and other personal necessities in there. This is also a good place to keep your beach toys, travel diaries and things you'll want instant access to when packing for your next cruise.

Prepare Your Carry-On Bag

After you've packed your main suitcase, you'll need to pack a carry-on bag. In fact, you may prefer to pack this first, so that you don't pack necessities into your main suitcase and then have to drag them out again for your carry-on.

In almost all instances, your luggage will be delivered to your stateroom after you board the ship. You can imagine what a nightmare it would be if 1,000 people tried to lug their suitcases up an inclining gangway and then down the narrow hallways of a ship. Therefore, the ship officials take over the responsibility of getting your luggage to your stateroom.

While you might embark the ship at, say, 2 p.m., your luggage may not arrive for a few hours. So keep in mind that it's important to pack a few essentials in your carry-on. See which of the following scenarios apply to you, because it could make a difference in what is packed in your carry-on luggage:

- ⚓ The ship's port of embarkation is near where you live, so you simply get to the port, drop off your luggage with a porter, and get on the ship.
- ⚓ You fly to the ship's port of embarkation and are transported to the ship by the cruise line.
- ⚓ You live a long way from the ship's port of embarkation, so the cruise line arranges to fly you in the night before and put you up in a hotel. You then get on the ship the next day.

In the first situation, all you really need in your carry-on bag are a few things that you'll want for the first couple of hours before your luggage arrives: a few toiletries, perhaps a change of clothing.

In the second situation, you will probably arrive at the airport and be asked to identify your luggage. The ship's representatives will then ensure that it, along with you, will be transported to the ship. Once again, you will probably only need a few of the basics.

The third situation is the most complicated. If you fly in the night before, the cruise line might take you to your hotel and take your luggage to storage. This eliminates the need to find it, identify it, load it and unload it two times. If this is the case, you will need enough in your carry-on bag to get you through your pre-cruise evening, the morning before you get on the ship, and the few hours on ship before your luggage finds its way to your stateroom.

In most cases, your luggage will arrive shortly after you find your cabin. Ship personnel do not indiscriminately leave bags on shore, like lost teddy bears forgotten by children. If your luggage is lost, chances are it was lost by the airlines. Chances are, also, it will be found by the airline. The question is: When will your lost luggage be located, and when will it find you on the ship?

Because the first full day after embarkation is usually a relaxing day at sea, you might be in a bit of trouble if your luggage doesn't make it onto the ship. Assuming the airline finds your luggage, but finds it after the ship sails, you won't get your baggage until the next port. In all probability, this will be after the captain's cocktail party, and you will be limited to the clothing and supplies in your carry-on until your baggage arrives in the next port.

For this reason, some veteran cruisers carry a rather heavy carry-on that includes a change of clothes for the first evening, a bathing suit, shorts and t-shirt for the next day, and a spare outfit and shoes for the captain's cocktail party the next night.

Someone who prepares for the possibility of lost luggage might be called paranoid when, in fact, the vast majority of people have never, ever had a problem. I have, however, talked to dozens of people who had had this happen to them (none of them Americans, you'll be glad to note).

In one case, the unfortunate woman had flown from Canada to Manaus, Brazil for an Amazon cruise. She wasn't concerned that her luggage hadn't arrived until the ship actually sailed, and the next stop wasn't until three days later. The stop was a Brazilian settlement populated by a few Indians, and the locale had no telephone, electricity and certainly no shopping. The poor woman attended the formal evening wearing the slacks she had on for embarkation day, along with a black sweater borrowed from the cruise director. The worst part was that she never did get her luggage during the cruise, had none of her clothes for the trip, and her suitcase was never found, even after the cruise had ended. While trying to maintain a positive attitude and make the best of it, she did break down once and forlornly wail, "But I had a different outfit and a different pair of shoes for every night of the week!"

Pack Anything You Want!

The wonderful thing about packing for a cruise is that from the time you arrive at the airport to start your trip to the time you arrive home at the end, you'll barely have touched the actual suitcase. Unlike people who take whirlwind trips of three European countries in one week, you'll see three, four, or more places in seven days and only have unpacked once. With that in mind, you can go a little crazy bringing along a few extras. Want to bring that boom box? Go ahead! Can't decide which bathing suits to wear? Bring them all along! Think you might like to go horseback riding along the beach in Jamaica? You don't have to decide now—just bring along the jeans and shoes, and change your mind later. After all, you only have to pack and unpack it one time, but after you're there, you might decide you *have* to have certain things. A little extra weight in your luggage never hurt, especially when you don't have to drag it every couple of days.

Bring Along The Unusual

The most popular cruises these days are those to the Caribbean, followed by other warm spots. A few cruise lines are even including stops on their own private beaches, where passengers laze the day away on beautiful white sands while being spoiled with good service and fresh fruit. If you're one of those people who enjoys the sun and surf, you may want to bring along a few essentials for making your beach time more enjoyable.

⚓ **Spray Bottle**
You can buy a spray bottle in most stores near home, and some ships and resorts even sell them (at inflated prices) for your convenience. Or you can dump out the window cleaner and use the bottle, filled with water. The wonderful thing about spray bottles is that you can lie on your lounge chair and never have to get up to escape the heat. A few spritzes, and your skin is once again moist and cool. Spray bottles are also great conversation pieces and are good for sharing.

⚓ **Inflatable Raft**
When you're on the beach, you'll probably see people bobbing in the ocean on rafts they've rented for the day. I like to bring my own inflatable air raft along so I have one in case it's not available at the beach (plus I don't have to pay a rental fee). The raft, when not in use, folds up to the size of a book and can be taken with you to every beach you visit. Plus, it's also good for sharing.

⚓ **Extra Band-Aids**

You might have remembered to bring along a first-aid kit but it seems nobody ever has enough Band-Aids for those blisters that inevitably develop from the mammoth shopping tour, or that irritating sand in your shoes after a day at the beach.

⚓ **Swiss Army Knife**

If you have a good Swiss army knife, bring it along. The corkscrew is extremely handy for that nice bottle of wine your travel agent might have sent, and you never know when you'll need that scissors, file, tweezer, toothpick or magnifying glass.

⚓ **Travel Diary**

I started keeping a travel diary and found it to be very helpful when returning to ports on future cruises. I jot down a few notes about good restaurants, the cost of a taxi to a certain beach, or the weather at different times of year in a port. I find it interesting to note the increase in prices over the years, and it's a good reminder of what I want to do again in the same port...or avoid in the future. Just about any type of small spiral-bound notebook will do, although I've invested in a lovely leather-bound version with my initials embossed in gold. I always have the feeling that I might like to return to a port city for a week's vacation, so it's nice to know I can refer back to my travel diary for recommendations.

⚓ **Address Book**

There are two types of address books you can bring with you. The first type is your own personal book with the addresses of your friends already entered, so you can send postcards and, in general, make your friends and family wish they were there. I also like to bring along a small, blank address book so I can record the names and addresses of new friends I've met on the cruise. It's easier than saving a bunch of torn napkins with scribbling on them, and I can write the name of the ship and the date of the cruise on the inside cover for recall later.

⚓ **Batteries & Film**

You may overpack in terms of clothing but one thing you never seem to have enough of is film and batteries. Forget to turn off the flash on your camera, and you've just burned out four new batteries. Misjudge how fresh the batteries are in your personal tape player, and you'll be without music. Shoot photos like crazy, and you're out of film. While batteries and film are available in port and in the ship's stores, you might end up paying two or three times what they cost at your local discount mart. You can always use extra batteries and film later in the year, so it's better to have too much than too little.

⚓ **The Cruise Brochure**

Bringing along the cruise brochure gives you instant access to the ship's deck plan and reminds you of the week's route and docking plan. And if you have the good fortune of getting an unexpected upgrade, you can instantly revel in how much money you have just saved by booking a lesser cabin but getting one much nicer.

Packing Checklist

EVENING ATTIRE

- ☐ Formal evening clothes
- ☐ Semi-formal evening clothes
- ☐ Casual evening clothes
- ☐ Dress shoes
- ☐ Socks/hose
- ☐ Jewelry
- ☐ _______________
- ☐ _______________
- ☐ _______________
- ☐ _______________

DAY/SHORE WEAR

- ☐ Shorts
- ☐ Slacks
- ☐ T-shirts
- ☐ Blouses/shirts
- ☐ Comfortable shoes
- ☐ Socks/hose
- ☐ Workout clothing
- ☐ _______________
- ☐ _______________
- ☐ _______________

BEACH/POOL WEAR

- ☐ Bathing suit
- ☐ Beach cover-up
- ☐ Beach shoes
- ☐ _______________
- ☐ _______________
- ☐ _______________

BEACH FUN

- ☐ Beach mat
- ☐ Spray bottle
- ☐ Suntan oil/sunscreen
- ☐ Snorkel/mask
- ☐ Beach bag
- ☐ _______________
- ☐ _______________
- ☐ _______________
- ☐ _______________

ACCESSORIES

- ☐ Jewelry
- ☐ Hair accessories
- ☐ Scarves
- ☐ Belts
- ☐ Ties
- ☐ Sunglasses
- ☐ _______________
- ☐ _______________
- ☐ _______________
- ☐ _______________

PERSONAL CLOTHING

- ☐ Lingerie/underwear
- ☐ Sleepwear
- ☐ Bathrobe
- ☐ Slippers
- ☐ _______________
- ☐ _______________
- ☐ _______________

Packing Checklist continued

PERSONAL ITEMS

- ❑ Toothbrush
- ❑ Toothpaste
- ❑ Dental floss
- ❑ Deodorant
- ❑ Shampoo
- ❑ Conditioner
- ❑ Hair spray
- ❑ Blow dryer
- ❑ Hot rollers
- ❑ Makeup
- ❑ Contact lenses/glasses
- ❑ Nail polish
- ❑ Nail polish remover
- ❑ Nail file
- ❑ Razor
- ❑ Cologne
- ❑ Vitamins
- ❑ Aspirin
- ❑ Medicines
- ❑ Birth control/protection
- ❑ _______________________
- ❑ _______________________
- ❑ _______________________
- ❑ _______________________
- ❑ _______________________
- ❑ _______________________
- ❑ _______________________
- ❑ _______________________
- ❑ _______________________

FUN AND GAMES

- ❑ Books
- ❑ Playing Cards
- ❑ Backgammon set
- ❑ Personal tape player
- ❑ Cassettes
- ❑ Portable video games
- ❑ _______________________
- ❑ _______________________
- ❑ _______________________
- ❑ _______________________

MISCELLANEOUS

- ❑ Travel alarm
- ❑ Swiss army knife
- ❑ Sewing kit
- ❑ First aid kit
- ❑ Camera
- ❑ Film
- ❑ Batteries
- ❑ Travel diary
- ❑ Address book
- ❑ Calculator
- ❑ _______________________
- ❑ _______________________
- ❑ _______________________
- ❑ _______________________
- ❑ _______________________
- ❑ _______________________
- ❑ _______________________
- ❑ _______________________

⚓ Calculator

You may not have to deal with foreign currency. Or you may not *want* to deal with foreign currency but find you *have* to. A simple calculator will do the trick. Many people have currency converters, which is merely a calculator that doesn't force you to figure out the formula of whether to divide the foreign currency into the American currency or vice versa. I prefer my calculator watch. It's cheap, handy, easy and multi-functional.

⚓ $1 Bills

Almost anywhere you find yourself in the world, you'll also find American currency recognized and probably accepted. But how many foreigners will have, or admit to having, the appropriate change for your American currency? A taxi ride to a secluded beach in Mexico might run you $7 but when you try to pay with a $20 bill, the driver either has no change or gives you a basketload of pesos in return. Bring *lots* of $1 bills with you...they're great for paying exact fares and they're handy for tips both on the ship and on shore.

Included is a general list for packing for your cruise. Of course, everybody doesn't need everything on this list (men, for example, can ignore the notation for nail polish and makeup, unless that happens to be their personal preference), but the list should help you remember those items that seem to slip through the cracks.

It's handy to photocopy this list and write in the items that you want to add. That way, you can reuse the list every time you take a cruise.

Finalize All Last-Minute Details

The pre-cruise checklist following this section lists the items that have to be taken care of at different times, depending on your schedule and rate of doing things. Obviously, you can't wait until the morning you're heading to the airport to cancel your newspaper, but you can start getting ready about a week in advance and double check all items before leaving the house. You might want to make a photocopy of this list and place it by your front door so you can check last-minute details before you finally leave

And now, as you leave your home, your adventure is about to begin. Bon Voyage!

PRE-CRUISE CHECKLIST

- ❑ Cancel newspaper
- ❑ Put vacation hold on mail
- ❑ Arrange feeding/boarding of pets
- ❑ Leave ship's emergency phone with friends/family
- ❑ Pay bills that will become due
- ❑ Do banking/get traveler's checks
- ❑ Water house plants
- ❑ Adjust sprinkler system
- ❑ Set answering machine
- ❑ Program VCR
- ❑ Throw away perishables
- ❑ Leave appropriate lights on
- ❑ Check coffee pot and all appliances
- ❑ Turn off/adjust heat/air conditioning
- ❑ Set burglar alarm
- ❑ Lock doors
- ❑ ______________________________________
- ❑ ______________________________________
- ❑ ______________________________________
- ❑ ______________________________________
- ❑ ______________________________________
- ❑ ______________________________________
- ❑ ______________________________________
- ❑ ______________________________________
- ❑ ______________________________________
- ❑ ______________________________________
- ❑ ______________________________________
- ❑ ______________________________________
- ❑ ______________________________________
- ❑ ______________________________________

Your First Day

The first step...which one makes in the world,
is the one on which depends the rest of our days.

Voltaire

I've heard it said that half the fun is getting there. I'm assuming that quote applies to vacations, although, taken in the broad sense, this could be applied to any situation.

I don't think I'd give such a high percentage as "half" of the fun you're going to have on a cruise being attributed to "getting there," but you can and should enjoy almost every moment and every experience leading up to the sailing and the adventure of your first day.

Once you step off the plane in a foreign city and set foot on the ground, you'll probably feel like your vacation is finally about to get *off* the ground. As you walk into the airline terminal, you'll most likely be greeted by one or more smiling faces belonging to cruise ship employees wearing uniforms and holding signs indicating which cruise line they're with. These are your on-land hosts who will pave the way to your embarkation.

Once at the airport, you might have to claim your luggage, or at least identify it to the cruise personnel. This is often a reassuring process, because it lets you know that your possessions have actually arrived at the same destination you did. Once you identify your luggage to the cruise line employee, you'll never see it again until it mysteriously arrives at the door of your cabin. The cruise people will ensure that it is loaded onto ground transportation for conveyance to the ship, loaded onto the ship, and placed at your cabin.

When the luggage transport has been arranged, it's time to go to the ship and begin embarkation proceedings. By this point, you've been conscientious enough to have filled out all the appropriate forms, so embarkation should run quite smoothly.

Embark The Ship

The cruise ship employee will drop you and the other passengers at the pier and point you in the right direction. You might pass through security, just like at an airport, and then you'll probably see a number of tables with signs such as these: "A-F," "G-L," "M-R," "S-Z." Despite your excitement, you'll probably be able to remember what letter your last names starts with, and you should stand in that line so an employee can check your documents, give you a boarding pass and allow you to begin embarkation.

Another very important piece of business will take place next, either on the pier or on ship: You must establish credit so you can charge purchases. Most ships nowadays run on a cashless basis. Bar charges, gift shop purchases, photos and shore excursions can all be put on your on-board charge account. In most cases, handing over a credit card will do the trick. If you don't have a credit card, you can pay a cash deposit and the difference will be refunded.

With the business settled, you're ready to embrace your new home.

As you board the gangway, you'll see a smiling person with a big camera. This is one of the ship's photographers, waiting to take the first of many pictures of you enjoying your cruise. Avoid the temptation of refusing to have your photograph taken. Despite the fact that you may feel conspicuous posing alone, this could be one of your favorite photos later. There's another reason for taking this photo—and you'll find out about it in the chapter on meeting people.

When you set foot on the ship that is to be your new home for the next few days or weeks, you'll once again see a smiling person who will be more than happy to direct you to your cabin. No matter how many times you've scanned the cruise brochure in an attempt to memorize the location of your stateroom and the other amenities, it does take a while to become oriented. Some cruise lines recognize this and, instead of merely pointing you in the direction of your cabin, will assign a steward to help you with your carry-on bags and lead you to your stateroom.

Settle Into Your Cabin

Now comes the shock: You still have visions of the "Love Boat" suites in your mind so when you see this living quarter that's not much bigger than a walk-in closet, a feeling of dismay may descend. Of course, by the end of your cruise you'll realize there was more than enough closet and drawer space, and that all you did was shower and sleep in your room.

Take a few minutes to get accustomed to the cabin. If there's a safe in the room, you can familiarize yourself with its operation and either program the security code or arrange to pick up a key from the purser. Flick on the lights. Run the shower. Look over the telephone numbers for services and amenities on board. Open and close your curtains and catch the view from your porthole.

If your timing is really good, your cabin steward will find you and introduce himself to you. This is the man who will see that you're comfortable for your stay on board, and you can let him know if you have any special preferences: an extra pillow, a bucket of ice every evening, additional towels or anything else he can do to make your stay a little better.

Assess Your Roommate Situation

If you booked a guaranteed share, now is the time to discover if you have a roommate or whether you'll have the room to yourself. Obviously, if you walk into the cabin and there's someone already unpacking, it's safe to assume that you have a roommate. Sometimes, though, it's not as easy to discern. Your plane may have arrived first and, since luggage often takes a couple of hours to be delivered, your cabin could be in virgin condition when you arrive.

The first dead giveaway is the dining-assignment cards. If you look on the dresser and find your dining arrangement next to one for someone you've never heard of, you can pretty well be sure that you're sharing the cabin. If the card is there, it's a good time to check out the name of your roommate and whether he or she has first or second seating.

Lack of a dining-assignment card is not a sure-fire indication that you have no roommate, however. Your new buddy-for-a-week might merely have taken the card with him or her to confirm the arrangements. Try looking in the closet. If there's a sweater or jacket hanging up that you didn't place there yourself, you can assume that the previous occupant of the cabin didn't just leave it there in case you got cold.

Of course, the absolutely easiest way to discover whether you've been assigned a roommate is to check either with the purser's office or with your cabin steward, the people who know who's in which cabins and when they'll be taking their meals. But what's the challenge in that?

Confirm Your Dining Arrangements

If you did not receive your dining room assignment with your documents or during embarkation, there will be a card with your table number and an indication of whether you have first or second seating. (This is the same card that helped you snoop out whether you had a stranger sharing the cabin with you.) If you are unhappy with your seating assignment, you'll need to see the maitre d'. The man who holds control over your gustatory pleasures is often situated in one of the lounges, ready with his table plan and grease pencil to make any necessary changes. Even if you received the seating you requested, it's not a bad idea to drop by his location to check things out. If you're traveling solo, you'll want to make sure you're at a larger table. Take the case of Maria: A young, attractive single woman on her first cruise, she had flown up from Brasilia to experience her first vacation alone. Her English was limited, but she was friendly and could certainly speak more English than anyone around her could speak Portuguese. When she arrived at her table, she discovered it was a table for four: Maria, an elderly couple and an empty chair. Maria was unaware that she could have requested a table change and spent most meals smiling painfully as the conversation flew around her head.

Explore The Ship

If you've determined that your seating arrangement is satisfactory, it's now a good time to explore the ship, because you don't have any luggage and you don't know anyone.

That's right! You don't know a single person on the ship and that cold reality is starting to set in. It can be an intimidating thought, but don't succumb to the temptation to shut your door and take a nap until dinner time. If you don't know anyone now, you still won't know anyone by dinner time, so get out there and make it your goal to meet people.

Courtesy Tahiti Tourist Board/Windstar Cruises

Passengers acquaint themselves with the layout and amenities of their ship as they prepare to set sail through French Polynesia.

You'll probably have a couple of hours between the time you embark and the time you go to dinner, so grab your copy of the ship's deck plan and walk, walk, walk!

During the time between embarkation and sailing, the cruise line might have a few tricks up its sleeve to keep you moving and make you feel welcome. Bar waiters will be walking around with exotic drinks in tall glasses with outlandish names like "Blue Hawaii" or "Yellow Bird." Before you happily accept the waiter's offer to take one off his tray, be aware that they are festive but not free. On various parts of the ship, different music will be playing—perhaps a steel band by the pool, dance music in a lounge or classical music in the ship's lobby. Relax and enjoy the sounds as you get a feel for your new home.

Try The Treasure Hunt

If you need a motivation or purpose for exploration, try taking the "Cruise Ship Treasure Hunt" near the end of this chapter. There's no winners or loser here, but you might even be able to interest a new-found friend in walking the ship with you.

If you do this treasure hunt correctly, you'll find the different amenities and areas of the ship that you hadn't thought to look for before. Although you still won't have memorized where everything is located, you'll get a general idea of where to go when the entertainment in the showroom starts, and you might even have an interesting piece of trivia to throw into conversation with people you've just met. ("Did you know," you might casually interject, "that there are 127 slot machines in the ship's casino?")

Meet The Cruise Staff

As you wander, blue drink in hand, you might hear an announcement that there will be a show in the main lounge to introduce the cruise staff to the passengers. There's a dual purpose to these shows and you can take it for what it's worth. On the one hand, it lets the passengers know who does what on board. On the other hand, it's a thinly veiled excuse to expose you to (read: sell) the services on the ship. Your cruise director will introduce you to the cruise and sports staff, the shore excursion people, the beauty shop and massage folks, the gift shop managers and anyone else under his or her jurisdiction. As a solo traveler, you'll get a chance to scope out the personnel and learn their names, because you'll be seeing them all week.

Sign Up, Enroll, Commit

Certain activities and services are nabbed fast, so now is a good time to decide whether you want to commit your time, energy and money to any of the services offered on the ship. You probably received information about shore excursions when you received your cruise documents. The prices on these shore excursions are not going to go down as time goes by. The only thing that will go down is the available space left. If there is a shore excursion that you're looking forward to, whether it's a submarine ride, a cooking tour or an underwater diving expedition, sign up at the earliest opportunity before space and equipment is already spoken for.

Other services also go fast. There are a limited number of hours in the day, so there is a limited number of appointments available with the masseuse. The night of the captain's cocktail party is the busiest time at the beauty salon, so if you know you're going to want a manicure or other treatment that day, sign up at the earliest opportunity.

Wave Bon Voyage

Somewhere in the midst of this wandering and discovery, you'll hear the blare of the ship's horn indicating your cruise will begin soon. One-half hour before departure, you'll hear an ear-piercing blast. Then, 15 minutes before departure, your hearing will be assaulted by two blasts. Finally, you'll hear three

Courtesy Royal Caribbean Cruise Line

Bon Voyage is more than a phrase—it's an attitude.

blasts, meaning the ship is ready to leave. Depending on the time of day, this can be a very festive event or the ship will just slip quietly away from the pier. Usually, an afternoon departure is accompanied by hoopla, confetti, live music, tropical drinks and great merriment. A late-evening departure, such as one scheduled for 11:30 p.m., is more subdued, since many people are either inside watching a show or have already turned in for the night.

You may not know anyone to wave good-bye to; you may not know anyone to wave good-bye with. Take this as an opportunity to *meet* someone to share your cruise experience. Look around at the people getting into the festivities. If you see someone standing alone, chances are he or she is either a solo traveler or the spouse is in the cabin unpacking.

Either way, it's nice to share the big send-off with a new friend.

Muster At Your Station

One other thing that occurs on the first day after the ship sets sail (or sometimes during the morning of the second day) is the muster drill. Inside your cabin, you'll find a bright orange safety vest and a notice placed on the door or wall about where to report in case of emergency. A muster drill is required by law and passenger attendance is mandatory. If it didn't have such serious connotations, the drill would actually be funny, as hundreds of people swarm to their muster stations or lifeboat locations to be inspected by the ship's personnel.

As you leave your cabin accompanied by your safety vest, you'll get a feeling for the passengers as a community. Carefully note the number of your muster station and, once you hear the signal for the muster drill, proceed along with your fellow passengers to line up for inspection. The drill takes about 15 minutes but is a necessary routine done on every cruise ship.

Greet Your Tablemates

By the time dinner comes around, you should be famished, what with all the walking, talking, discovering and exploring you've done. When the cruise line says dinner is at 8:30 p.m., that really means 8:30 p.m. If you're a few minutes late, you won't get be forced to stand in the corner with a dunce cap on, but try to be considerate of your table mates as well as your dining room staff. On most ships with two seatings, the dining room doors are closed 15 minutes after the seating begins, so bear in mind that fashionably late means no more than 5 or 10 minutes.

You might already know what size table you've been assigned, but there's no way you could anticipate what your table mates will be like. The first night is always a little tense, as everyone at the table tries to find their common bonds and loosen up with each other. You may feel that you're a fish out of water with the other people at the table, but don't give up so easily. Often, it's the differences among people that make for lively conversation. A homogeneous group of people is often a dull group of people. Variations in age, sex, and countries make for a stimulating week of dining.

Acknowledge The "WO-POs"

At the end of your first day, after a day of traveling and facing new experiences, you'll likely feel invigorated and excited about the coming week. Then again, you may have hated your first day and wonder why you're on this stupid ship to begin with. You know that every day that passes will just make you feel lonelier and, given it to do over, you probably would have preferred to stay home and clean out the linen closet.

CRUISE SHIP TREASURE HUNT

1. **To start things off swimmingly, locate the largest pool. What's the maximum depth?**

____

2. **Travel to the Purser's desk. How much is a stamp for a postcard mailed in the first port of call?**

____

3. **Gambol on over to the casino. How many slot machines are there?**

____

4. **This ought to whet your appetite: What's the highest number used in the dining room for table assignments?**

____

5. **Quiet, please! In the ship's library, look at the books whose authors' last names start with the letter "M." What's the title of the book by the first author?**

____

6. **Say "cheese" when you locate the photo display of the ship's senior officers. Who's the chief engineer?**

____

7. **Show you know your way around and find the show lounge. What brand of piano or keyboard is used?**

____

8. **When your credit cards star vibrating, locate the souvenir/sundry shop. What do you think is the most inexpensive item in the window?**

____

9. **Going to the other extreme, there's probably a jewelry display near there. What's the most expensive item in the window?**

____

10. **Speaking of expensive, locate the deck with the luxury suites. What's the name of the cabin steward who works there?**

____

11. **Dance your way up to the disco. How many bar stools are there?**

____

12. **Make yourself at home in your own cabin and write down your muster station number.**

____

13. **Stumble over to an open bar inside the ship and find out what *tomorrow's* drink special is.**

____

14. **Now lumber over to the health club and find the scale. What was the weight of the last person who used it?**

____

15. **And still on the subject of health, locate the masseuse and find out the cost of a one-hour massage.**

____

16. **Continue your tour at the shore excursion office. What time does it open up tomorrow?**

____

17. **Sail on over to the lifeboats and write down the maximum capacity listed.**

____

18. **Last assignment. Find an officer with at least three stripes on his shoulder and have him sign on the dotted line.**

● ●

Welcome to the world of the WO-POs. WO-POs are a common condition that every seasoned traveler has experienced at least once. A person taking his or her first cruise alone is almost guaranteed to get the WO-POs.

WO-PO is short for "Woe, po' me." That, in itself, is short for the entire gamut of self-pity. "Woe, po' me...I spent all this money on a vacation and I'm all alone. Woe, po' me...I have this stranger sleeping across from me who snores...and I'm paying money to listen to it. Woe, po' me...this ship is rocking and creaking and I'll never be able to get to sleep without my own pillow. Woe, po' me...I miss my dog and I put him in the kennel and it's costing more to feed him than I usually spend on myself. Oh, WOE PO' ME!"

If you get the WO-POs, relax and indulge yourself in them. Realize that you're tired and alone and, as bad as you feel now, you'll wake up to a tempting breakfast and a week that promises adventure. Indulge in the WO-POs while you're alone and have the chance because, believe me, no one else wants to hear them. And indulge in them the first night so you can get them out of your system and, at the end of the cruise, look back on those WO-POs and laugh at how far you've come in just one week.

Getting To Know...Everyone!

The only way to have a friend is to be one.

Ralph Waldo Emerson

With all the excitement of getting to the airport, getting to your flight, getting to the ship, getting settled in your cabin and getting to know your way around your new home, you'll be kept pretty busy and the excitement level will stay pretty intense.

Then, all of a sudden it might hit you: You're all alone on this floating hotel and you don't know another living soul. Rather than hiding out in your cabin until you feel it safe to come out, view this as an opportunity and a challenge to make friends. In fact, set a goal of meeting and learning the names of at least three new people, then write their names down at the end of the day. As unbelievable as it seems now, you will meet so many new folks that you may forget which names go with which faces.

Although you may have convinced yourself that the whole reason you're on this trip is to relax and be left alone, you might discover that it really is much more fun to develop a group of friends with whom you can share your experiences both on board the ship and on the shore. It's a very gratifying feeling to walk into a lounge or a showroom and have someone shout your name across the room. You instantly are transformed from feeling like a lost sheep to a person with a connection to the cruise experience. Meeting new people is a personal growth experience that allows you to feel like some sort of success has been achieved.

In addition, every new person you meet is not only a new opportunity for a long-time friendship, it's also an opportunity to meet potential friends for exploring the ports.

Treat Yourself To The Right Attitude

The most important thing to keep in mind is that no matter what your age or gender, it's important to meet *everybody*. If you limit yourself to meeting only those people of the opposite sex who fall within the appropriate age range, you'll deny yourself one of the greatest pleasures of travel and cruising. That wizened little lady in the beach chair next to you might come up with the most outrageous stories to keep you amused by the pool; the couple from Vancouver, with their warmth and openness, will beckon you across the dining room to join them at their table; the young newlyweds from Salt Lake City are so outgoing that they make new friends wherever they are, and, in fact, could be responsible for inadvertently introducing you to the love of your life a few days from now.

Break Down Your Defense Barriers

Most of us go though our daily lives comfortable in our place in society and work. Occasionally, we meet new people through friends or activities but rarely do we turn to a stranger on a bus or a restaurant and start a conversation. We wrap ourselves in a protective cocoon and question the motivation of strangers who attempt to initiate a conversation. "Why is he talking to me?" you might think. "What does he want?" "Is she after me for my money?" "What if he asks me out and I have to say no?" "How do I get rid of this bowser?" "If he finds out where I live am I putting myself in a position of danger?" "Could this stranger turn into a case study of 'Fatal Attraction?'" "Is he an axe murderer?"

These questions do not exist on a cruise. Everyone is there to have a good time. Everyone there can afford to be on a cruise. And everyone there soon finds it natural to speak with the people near them. Many people on your cruise are life-long travelers and the act of getting to know the people around them is the norm, not the exception. If you drop your defense mechanisms, you'll surprise yourself at how outgoing and even charming you can be.

Look For Baggage Tags

Your opportunity to meet new people actually begins before you even board the ship. If you're flying in from a major city, chances are there will be a whole slew of people on the same flight as you. Although it's not required, many people put the ship's baggage tags on their carry-on luggage. Scan the people waiting at the airport and locate those familiar baggage tags. Talking about the cruise line or cabin selection is a natural beginning to a friendship.

Wear Identifiable Clothing

Bill, a chemical engineer from Boston, always wears his favorite Red Sox t-shirt when he goes on a trip out of town. The logo and city identification is usually enough to start a conversation. It seems everywhere he goes, someone is either a Red Sox fan, or wants to know if Bill is a Red Sox fan. From there, the conversation moves to where the other person is from, and a casual friendship is started.

Sarah, a secretary from Toronto, wears a pin that says, "I Love My Cocker Spaniel." This seems to attract other dog lovers, and soon strangers are comparing pictures of their beloved pets, much like doting grandparents do.

Many people simply wear something nautical, even if it's just a pair of earrings. Whether anyone notices or not is irrelevant; the wearer feels in the swing of things. It's easy to turn to another person and comment,"Gee, you're certainly in the spirit!" and once again, a passing acquaintance is born.

Hand Out Streamers

Unlike many television and movie scenes, casting off at the pier does not involve hundreds of people at the dock waving goodbye. More likely, there'll be hundreds of people on the ship waving goodbye to a deserted stretch of cement. There's still the chance to throw streamers, whether anyone is waving back or not. On some ships, the cruise staff hands out streamers to everyone, but on others, leaving the pier lacks the proper party equipment. I always bring a couple of rolls of streamers, just in case. You can break them into smaller rolls and pass them around to people you haven't met yet. You'll instantly have a small party going, and folks will remember you in the next few days as that nice person with the streamers and the fun attitude.

Courtesy Royal Caribbean Cruise Line

Streamers add to the festivity of any send-off.

Flaunt This Book

Whenever Melanie, a paralegal from St. Louis, travels to Europe, she uses this trick: She pulls a map out and looks around to get her bearings. She may not be confused, but if a friendly person comes over to help her, she certainly doesn't object.

Mark, a waiter from Chicago, has a different little ploy: He sits down at a sidewalk cafe and pulls out his guidebook. He assiduously studies the choices the book recommends, intent on enhancing his European experience. He knows however, that sitting at a bistro reading a guidebook will do more than get him to the right places—it sends a message that he is a a stranger in a strange land, looking for the native experience or fellow countrymen with whom to share it.

On a cruise ship, *everybody* is a stranger in a strange land. You can sit there staring at a deck plan of the ship and no native, other than a crew member, will offer advice.

Ah, but read this book, with its title prominently displayed, and savvy people will instantly start a conversation. Why else would you be reading a book called *Cruising Solo* unless you were living the title? Some people will want to protect you, some will want to coddle you, some will want to latch on to you, some will want to wine and dine you, and some will just want to discuss your choice of reading material. You may even meet a like spirit reading the same book.

Initiate Conversations

Most of us wear our own particular cloak of cynicism and mistrust. Because of this, we don't really know how to start a conversation with a stranger. Believe it or not, the most banal and innocuous questions are the best conversation starters.

Courtesy Cunard Line

A stranger can't become a friend unless you talk to each other.

Try these trite little questions and see how amazingly well they work:

- ⚓ Is this your first cruise?
- ⚓ So, where are you from?
- ⚓ Why did you choose this cruise line?
- ⚓ Have you been to any of these ports before?
- ⚓ How are you enjoying the cruise so far?
- ⚓ What's your cabin like?
- ⚓ Are you taking any shore excursions?

Meet The Crew

If you're on the ship but can't force yourself to walk up to a stranger and start talking, go directly, and do not pass go, to a bar. Bartenders are always gracious and friendly and you'll have made your first friend. The bartender will remember your name and make you feel welcome every time you return. Even if you don't drink alcohol, the bartender will be glad to serve you a soda with a side of valuable advice. In addition, the atmosphere of a bar, such as the pool bar when you're waiting to sail, is very casual and, while you may not be comfortable starting a conversation, the person next to you might.

You can also meet the working crew and personnel by attending the get-acquainted show that the cruise staff puts on. This show is usually on the first night and is designed to familiarize you with the people and amenities aboard. Sometimes, it seems like only a hard sell of the ship's products, services and excursions, but take it with a grain of salt and focus on the people and their functions—you'll be seeing them a lot over the week. Often, the dancers in the night-time revue double as bingo callers; the masseuse might also be the aerobics instructor. All the cruise staff will be friendly and willing to answer any questions you might have if you see them walking around deck. If you remember their names, they'll make a special effort to remember you.

Attend Lectures

Before you arrive in port, the cruise staff will sponsor a lecture on the ports, shopping and shore excursions. If you attend these lectures, you'll benefit in a number of ways: You'll have information that will help you get around; you might meet a similar-minded person sitting next to you; you'll get more details about a shore excursion you're interested in; and you'll have information to pass on to other people who didn't attend the lectures.

Mug For The Ship's Photographer

As you board the ship, as you meet the captain, as you go about your daily activities, the ship's photographers will be there to record it on film. Many people traveling alone try to weasel out of getting their picture taken with the rationale that they don't want to be alone in the photo, and because they're not going to buy a photo of themselves, anyway.

Courtesy Harvey Lloyd/Windstar Cruises

Take a scuba lesson in the ship's pool and you might discover a water aficionado for exploring the depths once you get to a port.

Resist the temptation to shy away from the camera. When the photos are posted at the photo gallery, it's a perfect opportunity to scan the prints and find *other* people who also are traveling solo (as well as twosomes of the same sex who might later be fun shore partners). There is absolutely no obligation to buy any of these pictures, but you might find you absolutely *must* have that picture of you with the iguana.

When the photographer comes strolling by, you might try grabbing the nearest body and pulling him or her into the picture. Nancy from Boston always asks the nearest man (married or single, old or young) to be in the picture with her. Rarely does she buy that picture, but she makes a new friend every time.

Take Pictures Of Others

As you stroll around, you'll see lots of people with cameras taking pictures of their spouses or traveling companions. They'd probably like the picture better if they could both be in it, but one has to pose and one has to shoot. Be helpful and offer to take a picture of both of them. Your kindness will be appreciated and they might return the favor for you sometimes. Conversely, you're traveling alone and, unless you have *really* long arms, it's difficult to take a picture of yourself. Position yourself against the railing, with the beautiful horizon as a background, and ask someone to take your picture, too.

Go To The Singles' Party

Unlike singles' parties back in your home city, the singles' party aboard ship is not a meat market—it's a meet market. Some cruise lines have even moved away from calling it a Singles' Party and have dubbed it a party for People Traveling Alone. This is a great way to meet unattached people of both sexes who might want to explore the ports with you or share an espresso after dinner. (You'll hear more about this later.)

Enjoy Early-Morning Coffee

If you're the type who likes to greet the day early, take the opportunity to have early-morning coffee out on deck. You'll see a number of people relaxing over their first cup and it's a terrific chance to find a new friend. Often, people who travel together have different internal schedules, so one will sleep late while the other jump-starts the day with caffeine. It doesn't matter about the person's sex or marital status—just get out there and meet a new acquaintance.

Attend The Muster Drill

Muster drills are not meant to be social experiences. Muster drills are important life-saving exercises and are required by law. But just because it's serious doesn't mean you can't make it fun. As you leave your cabin and head to your muster station, you'll get a general idea of who else is in the cabins near you. These are the people you will be greeting and nodding to as the week goes by. You'll see people of all sizes and shapes wearing those funny-looking life vests and that, in itself, is worth the effort of the drill. For the women, it's also a great opportunity to check out the officers, as they strut around making sure that everything is functioning properly and acting important for your benefit as well as their own.

Participate!

Every cruise director I've ever spoken with emphasizes that the way to have fun on a cruise is to participate. Whether it's the beer-drinking contest, the horse racing, the masquerade or the trivia quizzes, you'll have a much better time and a more memorable vacation if you participate in the activities. If you feel too shy to actually participate, at least watch. You'll have something to talk about with your dinner companions and a heart full of memories when your trip is over.

Are You Hungry Yet?

"**G**ood Morning! It's 6:30 a.m. and this is your wake-up call." At first, you sit up, bleary eyed, wondering what ever possessed you to try to face the day this early and then you remember:

This is the day you're going to spend eating non-stop!

As your brain starts to join the world, you hear a discreet knock at your door, letting you know it's time for your first meal.

Continental Breakfast

Last night, before you went to bed, you put a hanging tag on your door telling your room steward what you wanted for breakfast, and what time you'd like it served. Sure enough, there's your meal, right on time.

The good, strong coffee begins to perk you up, as you sip the freshly squeezed juice and nibble on the still-warm croissant. Soon, you feel awake enough to venture out on deck for your next installment.

Early-Morning Coffee

As you leisurely stroll up to the open-air cafe, you see a few brave souls sipping the bracing coffee, although a few have chosen tea. While this little meal is billed as "Coffee for Early Risers," you do see dishes of assorted pastries and decide a Danish won't ruin your appetite for the breakfast buffet ahead.

Grabbing your tray, you see an interesting-looking older gentleman dining alone and ask if you can join him. "Why?" he says. "Am I coming apart?" It's a little early for jokes, but you sit down anyway, and a lively conversation ensues. You exchange names and hometowns and the talk moves on to last night's entertainment, the magnificent costumes of the dancers, and the anticipated activities of the day.

Breakfast Buffet

By now, it's 7:45 a.m., the perfect time to head outside for a bracing walk and the opportunity to chow down again. Up on the pool deck, you see people relaxing at patio tables as they enjoy their first meal of the day. You smile smugly, knowing you're literally one up on them. In fact, you're two up on them, but who's counting.   You keep that smug smile to yourself, however, because you know this is a great way to make a couple of new friends, early birds though they may be. As you go through the buffet line, you pass up the coffee and rolls for a bit heartier fare: scrambled eggs, sausage, and some nicely done potatoes. The woman in front of you is piling up the same assortment of foods, and you jokingly compare tastes. She motions to a table where she's placed her beach bag and you both sit down to a delicious meal.

Dining Room Breakfast

By the time 8:30 a.m. rolls around, you're afraid you might, too, but you're determined to make it to the main dining room. After all, this is where they have all those exotic things you only get at home when you go out for Sunday brunch. You locate your regular table and settle in for an eating extravaganza. You greet your table regulars and trade information about what you all did between dinner last night and breakfast this morning.

Instantly, your waiter, Joaquim, stands at your side, a smile on his face, as he adroitly places your napkin on your lap, inquires how you slept, and sets a menu in your hands.

Decisions, decisions, decisions! Yesterday you had a masterpiece of Eggs Benedict, beautifully arranged with a slice of orange and a sprig of parsley. What'll it be today? You consider the corned beef hash, but decide that with two breakfasts under your belt already, perhaps you should eat light. Then you see smoked salmon on the menu. (Back at home you call it Lox and Bagels, and you'd pay $9.75 for it in a deli, but here you can enjoy to your heart's content.) To round it out, you order some fresh cantaloupe, which your waiter deftly removes from the rind and slices for you.

Joaquim solicitously asks if everything is OK, since you didn't seem to eat very much, and you assure him you're just eating light so you'll have room for lunch. After all, there is tomorrow...and tomorrow...and tomorrow. Visions of future breakfasts dance around in your head as you imagine an aromatic kippered herring (you've never had kippered herring, but then, what are cruises for if not to experiment?). You noticed that there's also that good old Southern favorite, hominy grits, (which you never can seem to find except when visiting Dixie) and later in the week, you'll try the Belgian waffles. So many breakfast items, so little time.

By this time, you're feeling a little lethargic, but it's already 9:30 a.m., and the waiters are anxious to leave, so you waddle out of the dining room and head out toward the pool to let the sun sweat off some of those calories.

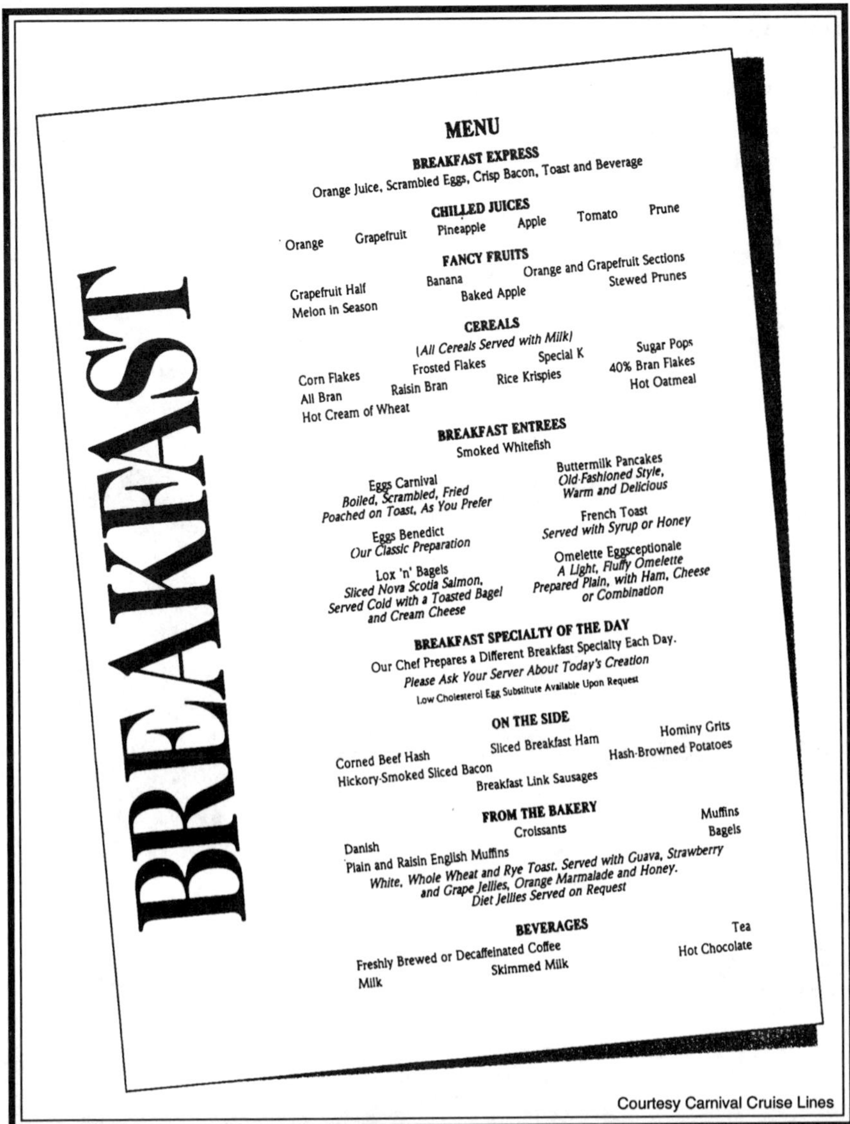

Courtesy Carnival Cruise Lines

Mid-Morning Bouillon

By the time 11 a.m. rolls around, you feel like you could uses some sustenance. After all, it's hard work oiling up and sipping a Bloody Mary. I mean, you actually had to move when the waiter brought you your drink and asked you to sign for it. Good thing it's time for the mid-morning bouillon break. You decide to only have a few of those creamy little crackers that go with the bouillon, because you don't want to fill up before lunch. You seem to be the only one asking for bouillon, but the waiter enjoys your enthusiasm as he pours the steaming broth into a cup.

Lunch Buffet

The smell of freshly cooked meat wafts over toward you, letting you know the kitchen staff is grilling up hamburgers and hot dogs. It's only 11:30 a.m., and you decide to see if you can hold off your raging appetite until noon. Finally, at 11:45 a.m., you can't take it anymore and move into the line for the lunch buffet. The woman in front of you piles her plate high with a nice, green salad but you go for the heartier fare, choosing a juicy hamburger, loading it up with lettuce, tomato, onions, and pickles. The fries look pretty good, too—hot and crisp—so you ask the chef to add them to your plate. By the time you get to the home-made chocolate brownies, you decide to pass. After all, you'll be eating again in just over an hour. As you near the end of the line, a group of people from yesterday's shore excursion spots you, waving and pointing to an empty seat at their table. You grab your tray and head on over to this convivial assemblage.

Courtesy Cunard Line

For those who don't want to miss even a minute of the sun, dining out on deck is the option of choice.

Dining Room Lunch

After going back to your stateroom to change (you already know that bathing apparel is not appropriate in the dining room and, anyway, you need the exercise of walking to your cabin), you once again sit down at your regular table. Some of your tablemates ate lunch outside, so it's a smaller, more intimate group now. Your dining mate to your left is up for a hearty meal, so he orders the soup, the roast chicken with little baby potatoes, and a key lime pie for dessert. The woman to your right wants to eat a little lighter, so she has a salad and grilled fish with fresh vegetables. Across the table from you, the couple from Vancouver is AB-SOLUTELY STARVING, so they both have an appetizer, soup, salad, pasta and,

Chilled Juices

CRANBERRY   TOMATO

Soups

·CREAM OF CHICKEN   CREOLE SOUP

Pasta

RAVIOLI PARMIGIANA

Eggs

SALAMI AND EGGS

Entrees

FISH AND CHIPS
HAWAIIAN BARBEQUED CHICKEN
♥*HUNGARIAN GOULASH*
Served with Noodles
SHRIMP AND GREEN PEPPER SALAD
With Jicama, Kidney Beans, Corn, Lettuce
and Avocado, in Lime Spicy Vinaigrette

Sandwiches

GRILLED HAMBURGER
Served with Lettuce, Tomato, Onion, Pickles,
and your choice of Cheese or Bacon and French Fried Potatoes.
PRIME RIB SANDWICH
Served on Garlic Bread.

Vegetables

CALIFORNIA MIXED VEGETABLES   CREAMED CORN
PARSLEY POTATO   FRENCH FRIED POTATOES

From the Ship's Oven

SLICED FRENCH LOAF, WHITE AND WHOLE WHEAT

Desserts

GRASSHOPPER PIE   GERMAN CHOCOLATE CAKE
BANANA PUDDING WITH RASPBERRY SAUCE

Ice Cream and Sherbets

CHOCOLATE, VANILLA AND STRAWBERRY
PINEAPPLE, LIME OR ORANGE SHERBET

Beverages

COFFEE   DECAFFEINATED COFFEE
TEA   HOT CHOCOLATE   MILK
♥ **Indicates reduced calorie and cholesterol selection**
Also see our Special Lite Cuisine Menu

L7/691RF

Courtesy Commodore Cruise Line

lo and behold, not one but TWO desserts. You ask for some papaya juice and a slice of quiche. A simple bowl of vanilla ice cream sounds refreshing for dessert, but your waiter cajoles you into allowing him to add chocolate topping and whipped cream. You fear you'll never make it to your afternoon snack. It's 2:00 p.m., and you start to wonder how Dom DeLuise does it.

Afternoon Tea

It sounds so civilized to partake of afternoon tea, doesn't it? It evokes images of pinkie fingers lifted in the air, delicate sips of sherry and watercress sandwiches. That's actually pretty close to the truth on this ship, but other ships have Americanized the routine into another food chow-down opportunity. Nibbling daintily on a cucumber sandwich with the crusts cut off, you turn to the couple next to you and ask them how they're enjoying the food. (You can tell by their girth what the answer is, but you ask anyway.) They are very happy with tea and sandwiches but tell you about the last ship they were on in which the 4 p.m. feeding frenzy had a different twist every day: Monday it was frozen yogurt; Tuesday it was tacos; Wednesday it was egg rolls; Thursday it was guacamole and chips. Interesting concept, and you relish the bit of education to go along with your sandwich.

Snack Restaurants

After eating more meals before dinner than you can count on one hand, you're enjoying this opportunity to sit down in a quiet lounge and sip tea with civilized people. But you remember the last ship *you* were on, too, where every day, at 5 p.m., people would be lured into the ship's pizzeria by the smell of fresh-baked dough. On the ships catering to people with children, the ice-cream restaurant was constantly busy. It was always a fun place to meet a boisterous group of people, but your stomach tells you "thank you" for passing on that get-together now. Of course, if there were a caviar bar here like on some other ships (cost additional, naturally) you might park yourself on a stool and fight anyone else who wanted to usurp your place.

Room Service

There's absolutely no reason to order room service except that it's there. Luckily, the choice is limited to sandwiches and accompaniments, so you order a B.L.T. on toast and, what the heck, some macaroni salad, too. When the tray arrives, the room service staff has graced it with a chocolate eclair that looks too good to pass up.

Dining Room Dinner

Tonight is a formal dinner, so everyone at the dining table is dressed to kill, including you. At this point, you wonder how clothes bought pre-gorge are able to fit now, but you're thankful for small favors. To go along with the formal attire, the dinner menu features the specialties of the house. When it's your turn to order, you can't decide between the shrimp cocktail and the Sevruga caviar, so you order both. Since you want to savor each little caviar egg slowly, you decide

IN-SUITE MENU
AVAILABLE AT ALL TIMES.
DIAL 555 FOR SERVICE.

APPETIZERS
Smoked Norwegian Salmon with Cream Cheese
Prosciutto Ham and Sweet Melon
Shrimp Cocktail

SOUP
Clear Chicken Broth with Vegetables

SANDWICHES
Corned Beef, Rare Roastbeef
Ham, Swiss Cheese, Turkey
on White or Whole Wheat Bread
Served with Pickles and Cole Slaw

HOT ENTREES
Hamburger or Cheeseburger, Traditional Garnish
American All Beef Hot Dog with Chopped Onions and Sweet Relish
Grilled Minute Steak, Herbal Butter
Sautéed Chicken Breast with Rosemary
All Dishes are Served with French Fried Potatoes

SALAD
Mixed Garden Greens with Sliced Tomato
Assorted Cheese Plate with Fresh Fruits

DESSERTS
Caramel Custard
Chocolate Cake with Whipped Cream
Vanilla, Chocolate or Strawberry Ice Cream

BREAKFAST
For in-suite breakfast, please
complete the menu form in your portfolio
and place it outside your door before retiring.

Captain's Gala Dinner Menu

Appetizers

Marinated Grilled Peppers Calabrese

Gravlax and Quail Eggs, Bagnarotte Sauce

Supreme of Chicken Terrine   Escargots a la Bourguignonne

Soup

Cream Caroline   Consomme Mogador   Chilled Madrilene

Salads

Panachee
Mixed Lettuce with crisp Vegetables

Regis
Garden Greenery topped with Bacon Bits and Croutons

Roquefort, Thousand Island, Champagne Vinaigrette or Italian Dressing

Entrees

*Tropical Red Snapper
A lightly seasoned Fillet, broiled and offered with Capers and Herbed Butter

Duckling A L'Orange
*Crisply roasted Long Island Duckling
complemented by the traditional Orange Sauce*

Lobster Thermidor
*A classic seafood preparation, chunks of Lobster in a creamy Sauce with Mushrooms
and a touch of Cognac, topped with grated Cheese and baked golden brown*

Rack of Lamb Provencale
Rack of baby Lamb roasted with a blend of Herbs, Garlic and Mustard

Tournedos Rossini
Filet of Beef with Madeira Sauce

Buttered Broccoli Isigny   Leek Flan

Potatoes au Gratin   Boiled Potatoes   Wild Rice

Desserts

Apple Tart Tatin, Calvados Sauce   Cherries Jubilee

Gateau Grand Marnier   Creme Brulee

Burgundy Cherry, Chocolate Almond or Strawberry Ice Creams   Today's Sherbet

Fruit and Cheese
An assortment of fresh seasonal Fruit complemented by fine Cheese
Roquefort   Camembert   Jarlsberg   Saint Paulin

*Lean and Light

Courtesy Celebrity Cruises

THE CHEF PRESENTS

We take pride in presenting Chef Michel Roux's recommendation
for this evening's meal, foods especially designed
to complement each other and provide a fine dining experience.

SUPREME OF CHICKEN
*A Terrine of Breast of Chicken
with Alpine Mushrooms and Pistachios*

CREAM CAROLINE
A smooth creamy Corn Potage

PANACHEE SALAD
*A crisp variety of mixed Lettuces, topped with Carrots
and Cucumber, the Chef suggests a Champagne Vinaigrette Dressing*

TOURNEDOS ROSSINI
*Tenderloin of Beef sauteed and crowned with Pate de Foie Gras,
enhanced by a light Madeira Wine Sauce*

APPLE TART TATIN
*A delicious French style preparation
with a carmelized top and delicate Pastry bottom,
served with Calvados Sauce*

THE WINE STEWARD SUGGESTS

The following Wines are recommended to complement the Chef's Selection

St. Francis Chardonnay, Sonoma, 1988, California $15.00

Château Malescot, St. Exupery, Margaux, 1982, France $35.00

BEVERAGES

Freshly Brewed Regular or Decaffeinated Coffee   Iced Coffee

Tea, Herbal Tea and Iced Tea   Hot Chocolate   Milk

Celebrity Cruises menus and service have been designed
under the personal supervision of international chef, Michel Roux.
He is unrivalled in Europe as one of the most innovative
and exceptional of restaurateurs.

Courtesy Celebrity Cruises

Courtesy Royal Caribbean Cruise Line

to pass on the Avocado Cream Soup, but look forward with anticipation to the Caesar salad, prepared personally at your table. You follow this up with the broiled lobster tail, while covetously eyeing the luscious-looking Beef Tenderloin chosen by a few others at your table. You know that if you really wanted to make a spectacle of yourself, you could finish your sweet lobster and Joaquim would disappear into the kitchen to present you with your own Beef Tenderloin, too. But there's still dessert, so you hold off.

As soon as your plates are cleared, your waiter disappears and the lights are dimmed as you all await the big meal-ending extravaganza. A hush falls over the room, the music starts and from both main doors of the dining room, dozens upon dozens of waiters stream down the aisle, each one bearing a lighted Baked Alaska. The waiters ham it up, moving to the music and nodding in acknowledgment to the special applause each receives from the tables he serves.

After the excitement dies down a bit, your waiter carefully slices the masterpiece and serves each person a piece. Coffee is being poured, but you decide instead to try the cappuccino. It is promptly brought, steaming and foamy with just a touch of cinnamon on the top. A perfect end to an amiable meal. You wonder how you'll have room for the midnight buffet, but you're so close to success in your eat-it-all mission, you know you'll go the whole nine yards (which is what your waistline will be by the end).

Midnight Buffet

It was hard to leave the gambling tables, especially when you were winning, but you convinced the two people on either side of you to take a walk down two decks to view a better scene.

For the first time since this morning, you're excited about food—not to eat it but to *photograph* it! It's the Gala Buffet and, although the dining starts at midnight, the doors open at 11:30 p.m. for shutterbugs.

There's something therapeutic in taking pictures of food instead of ingesting it. Besides, you get some exercise as you walk by the display, focusing and snapping.

It's hard to decide what to shoot first: the impressive ice sculpture; the five-pound block of butter molded into a mermaid; the watermelons carved in bas relief; the oranges, lemons and grapefruits with their rinds sliced into variegated chrysanthemums; the carved radishes, beets and onions; the tomato roses. The list goes on endlessly and so, seemingly, does this buffet.

The array of foods is stunning. Chefs in tall white paper caps are slicing juicy roast beef, and there's a lovely assortment of petit fours beckoning you. But the fresh fruit is so artistically arranged, looking so succulent, that a plateful and a cup of coffee is all you need at this point. Besides, you and your former gambling companions are headed to the disco to dance off your calories. (However, at the rate calories are burned off during active dancing, you'd have to work full-time the next four years as an exotic dancer just to break even).

Late-Night Mini-Buffet

Fernando, the D.J., keeps you moving with song after song that requires more energy than an aerobics routine. You know you don't have to keep dancing, but every song has such a great beat your feet have a mind of their own. By the time 1:30 a.m. rolls around, you actually feel some rumblings and grumblings emanating from below the neck but above the hips. You and your current dancing partner take a break and move over to the corner of the disco where the mini-buffet is set up. After a few bites of a ham and cheese sandwich and a handful of potato chips, you're ready for one last dance to end this eating orgy.

If you want to add it up by the numbers, you could have had the opportunity to indulge in 13 different dining experiences, eaten or viewed hundreds of foods, and consumed thousands of calories. You might have met dozens of new people and greeted scores of other friends. Most important, you might have learned that eating is more than consuming—it's experiencing the delights of sight, smell, taste, color, texture, ambiance and friendship.

Shipboard Activities

Enjoyment is not a goal,
it is a feeling that accompanies
important ongoing activity.

Paul Goodman

"I could never go on a cruise," friends or newly made acquaintances have commented. "I'd go stir crazy! There's nothing to do on a cruise but stare out at the sea!"

I smile and politely hold my tongue for two reasons: First, they're absolutely wrong; and second, this comment almost always comes from someone who has never been on a cruise ship.

The reality of the situation is actually just the opposite of what these people imagine. There is *too much* to do on a cruise ship, and that doesn't even include going ashore and seeing the town. Most likely, the decision is not whether to relax by the pool in the afternoon, or simply take a nap, as much as it is whether to try your luck at bingo, learn how to play bridge or shoot some hoops on the basketball court. It always seems as if all your favorite activities are all happening at the same time and, perhaps, this is more than imagination. The truth is, there's so much to do, you can run yourself ragged trying to do it all. One person even commented that there were so many activities happening simultaneously on Cunard's *QE 2* that it would take five weeks of continuous cruising to experience it all.

For the person traveling alone, participating in the ship's activities does more than fill the time between meals. Happenings around the ship help you get acquainted with the cruise staff. The woman who leads the morning exercise may well be the person who also conducts the horse racing. With the amazing ability that cruise staffs possess, there's a good chance that by your second or third participation she'll be calling you by name and you're feel connected to the ship and the cruise.

Every time you participate in an activity, you meet a wider circle of friends with whom you'll have something in common every time you run into them later. Congratulating someone after he's won the ping pong tournament will probably win you a friendly smile; remembering him later in the week and reliving his victory will win you not only a friendly smile but also a friend. Every time you meet people by participating, you have made a potential friend for later in the cruise, someone who will hail you over to a seat in the showroom, invite you to join her at the bar for cocktails, or make room for you for at a lecture or by the pool.

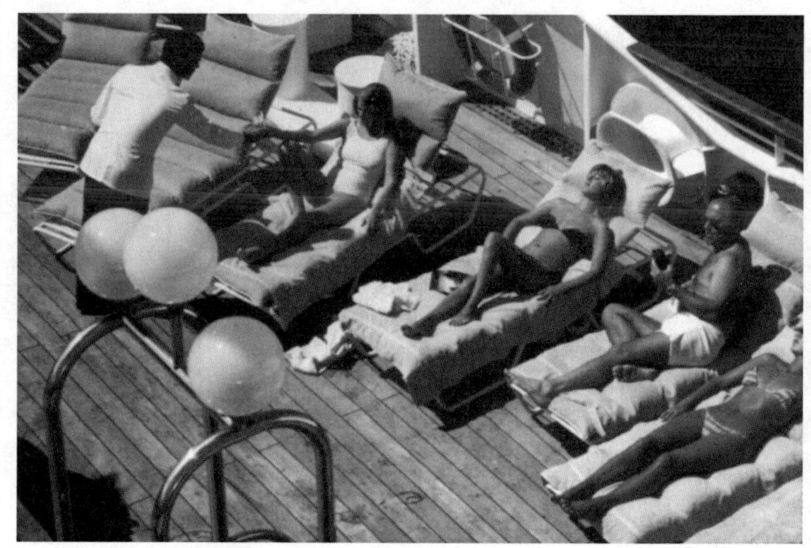

Courtesy Cunard

You can do it all...or have it done for you. These people choose to relax by the pool on the *Sea Goddess*, relegating more strenuous activities for later in the day.

Of course, there's another, more mercenary reason for participating: PRIZES! Gambling activities, such as bingo and horse racing, can garner you money, but other activities, such as trivia contests and pool games, can get you a slew of prizes. Over the course of just a few cruises, I have amassed a collection of the following (most with the cruise line logo): beach bags, beach towels, sunglasses, pens, pencils, ashtrays, lighters, coasters, fanny packs, travel diaries, umbrellas, playing cards, jigsaw puzzles and a wide assortment of mediocre to bad champagne.

Often, it's difficult for the solo traveler to get in the swing of things and boldly push his or her way into this no-man's-land of participation. The best advice I can give you will sound like an athletic-wear commercial: JUST DO IT! And in the interest of helping you do it, here's a brief run-down of some of the activities usually found on board, and how they're usually run. Hopefully, a little knowledge will demystify the process and encourage you to join in the fray.

While not every ship does every activity the same way, use this guide as a jumping off point and then jump right in. All you really have to lose is that empty space around you.

Attempt Aerobics

There's a very real reason to get involved in the aerobics and exercise classes: It has something to do with the multiple meals and snacks available on most ships! Exercise activities don't mean you have to work yourself into a frenzy, however. There are all sorts of classes at different times of day geared to different levels of exertion and fitness.

Courtesy Royal Caribbean Cruise Line

It doesn't matter what shape you're in—the right exercise class can get you into shipshape shape.

Take a few moments for non-stress stretching. Join a group-walk around the deck. If you're up for it, do a step class or a heart-pounding aerobics routine. Or just spend a little time in the on-board gym, walking the treadmill. Or not. Lay by the pool instead, sipping a Mai Tai, as you watch the athletically inclined grunt their day away.

Attend Arts & Crafts

For the artistically gifted or interested, there's a host of creative opportunities aboard most ships. Find out about the art of batik dying. Develop your skills at needlepoint and stitch a replica of the ship on which you're sailing. Paint yourself a t-shirt or hat. Most of these activities require a small payment for materials, but at the end you've got a hand-made souvenir to take home with you.

Battle At Backgammon

You don't have to be an expert in the game to participate in a backgammon tournament, but it certainly helps if you've played before. Sometimes, there is a beginner's backgammon lesson earlier in the week, followed later by a tournament with prizes (such as the much sought-after coaster set). More importantly, as you move through the ranks, you might find a backgammon partner for fun and non-tournament play.

Bet On Bingo

For whatever its reasons, bingo is one of the most popular activities aboard a ship. People rush back from shore to get a good seat in the lounge. People buy two, three and four bingo cards. People bring good-luck charms with them. And people have been known to win thousands of dollars on a single game. Could that be its lure?

On some ships, the bingo cards are paper and you punch out the numbers. Some ships have hard cards with sliding windows to mark the numbers. Some ships have paper cards that are marked with crayons. Whatever the card, the important thing is to listen to the instructions ("This bingo is the four corners, and the four corners only!") and listen to the numbers called.

Prizes at bingo depend on the number of people playing but run into several hundred dollars a game. Most ships have "Jackpot Bingo," in which a set amount of numbers are called the first day, such as 45, with a prize of, say $500 available if anyone fills up the whole card in the first 45 numbers. The amount of numbers increases at each session, while the prize money accumulates and increases, as well.

"Jackpot Bingo" is rarely won until the final session, but it is *always* won then. Some people have paid for their entire cruise with a $5 or $10 investment.

Be On The Bridge Tour

A bridge tour is the opportunity to visit the life-center of the ship. This particular activity seems to appeal to men more than women, which brings up an interesting point for the solo female: Whether or not you care how the ship is run, take the bridge tour. It's one way to ensconce yourself in a group of men. In addition, it's an opportunity to observe this bastion of male officerdom, with these proud sea representatives in their cute white uniforms sharing their work quarters.

Check Out The Casino

The casino is technically a shipboard activity since it is scheduled for specific times and there's lots of games to play. But while other shipboard activities require little investment, the casino can be quite costly if you don't know what you're doing.

Obviously, bigger ships have bigger casinos with more games. Smaller ships might have slot machines, blackjack and, perhaps, roulette, while the larger ships will have more of these tables and also include craps, Caribbean poker and Red Dog.

Courtesy Royal Caribbean Cruise Line

Will luck be a lady tonight? You won't know if you don't try...

The casino is never open while the ship is in port and the slot machines are open for more hours than the tables.

The ship often schedules gambling lessons for those who are neophytes. If you're unsure of what you're doing, spend a few minutes taking instruction before you lose your tropical shirt. It almost Murphy's Law that you can slowly and steadily win $60 over an hour's time but you can lose hundreds in just a few minutes.

Go Golfing

You won't find a full 18 holes on the top deck of the ship, but for those with a penchant for golf, activities are available. Whether it's putting around a 3-hole course, driving golf balls off the back of the ship, or even participating in a high-tech, computerized golf simulator, there's something for the links enthusiast.

Have Fun At Horse Racing

Like bingo, horse racing is one of the most popular activities aboard a ship. Unlike bingo, horse racing is a bit more entertaining for the viewer who doesn't want to put up a financial investment.

There are usually six wooden horses placed on a track that's divided into a set number of spaces, or furlongs. Two dice are rolled, and every time a horse's number comes up, the horse moves a space. If a double comes up, the horse gets to move two spaces. First horse to the finish line wins.

Sounds simple, doesn't it? Ah, but there are a myriad of layers and a number of opportunities to participate in the horse racing.

Start off a duffer, end up a pro after a little practice at golf aboard the *QE 2*.

First of all, the horse needs a jockey. While the cruise director is rolling the dice, someone has to move the horse. If you're chosen or you volunteer and your horse wins, you could also win money, prizes or just fame.

Secondly, you can bet on your favorite horse. Depending on the odds, a mere $2 bet could net you a healthy return on your investment, if you're lucky and the dice are with you.

Thirdly, and the most fun in horse racing, you'll have the opportunity to buy a horse for the owner's race.

For the owner's race, the horses are put up for bids. Depending on the munificence of the crowd, a horse may sell for as little as $30 or $40 to as much as several hundred. The winner usually gets to keep *all* the money collected for *all* the horses.

It's much more fun to form a "consortium" to buy a horse. A consortium is simply a social corporation to own and control your horse. You can gather people in advance and agree on a set price to spend, or you can get caught up in the frenzy of bidding and convince the total strangers next to you to join you in this venture. While individuals do buy horses, consortiums of 20 or more people have been formed. (Of course, while your initial investment is limited, so is your split of the winnings.)

Once you've bought your horse, you'll have to name it and then decorate it. Some people use ship-provided materials, such as crepe paper and balloons, to dress their horses, while others join in a group and roam the shores searching for esoteric foreign materials to adorn their nag. Still others use materials found in their suitcases.

Here's an example: Kira enticed Rich and Sue, people she had met just an hour earlier, to join her in a consortium. They bought horse Number 1 for $45. They named the horse "Rented Meat," dressed "it" in gold lame lingerie and sunglasses, and attached a condom, because they practiced safe riding. Their horse was cheated out of the "best dressed" award, and their steed came a lot closer to the glue factory than it ever did to the finish line. But what fun they had for a mere $15 each!

Indulge In Ice Carving

Ice carving demonstrations are not only unique to a ship but also perfectly suited to it. When you see those magnificent ice carvings at the gala midnight buffet later in the week, you'll know how they were done. And you can watch this bit of craftsmanship, a true artist working with a freezing block of ice, while sunning yourself in your bathing suit.

Ice carving is done outside by the pool. Where else would you put a massive 300-pound block of ice that will be chipped away and melted?

The ice carver lays out his tools and sets to work. Over the course of 20 minutes or so, that gelid square will turn into a creation of beauty. As the carving is going on, the cruise director will probably keep your interest piqued by asking you to guess what the final form will be, and the answers range from the amusing to the absurd. Chips will fly and hunks will fall and finally, a Pegasus, a stately bird or a bevy of cherubs will emerge.

I've been told that on Alaska routes, chunks of glaciers are netted and brought on board for the ice carving demonstration. As if nature weren't beautiful enough, humans can enhance it even more.

Learn At Lectures

All ships have some kind of lectures, whether they're designed to sell their tours or designed to enrich you culturally. Some people attend every single lecture available; after all, that's what they're on the cruise for. Others avoid lectures like a bad case of the flu; after all, that's not what they're on the cruise for.

The type of ship on which you're sailing will determine the type and number of lectures you'll find offered. Most ships offer lectures on ports and shopping. Here is where you'll find out what sights to see and what sites to visit; what bargains you'll find and where you'll find them; where town is and whether you can walk in on your own; how much a cab should cost to certain places and what the local customs are.

Port and shopping lectures are very helpful, usually including a map of the surrounding areas and a list of reliable shops. Often, the ship will encourage you to visit these shops, fill out a raffle form and later be eligible for a prize.

These stores may, indeed, have the best prices. The staff on the ship may, indeed, have checked them out. But don't feel obligated to only visit those stores recommended by the ship. Keep in mind that there is often a reciprocal relationship between the stores in port and the ship, and there will be a definite bias to recommend those stores.

There is another type of lecture found more commonly on expedition and nature cruise ships. Most people take these cruises because of the uncommon itineraries and unusual wildlife and flora found on these routes. These cruise lines almost always provide naturalists, historians and cultural experts to discuss the past and future of the area. If you've chosen one of these ships, you have the opportunity to steep yourself in interesting knowledge.

Notice Napkin Folding

Every night when you come to dinner, you might find your napkin folded in a new and unique way. Well, if your waiter can learn to do it, so can you. The cruise staff is ready and able to help you turn your dining room table into a work of art that will rival the cruise ship's.

Play Ping Pong

If you didn't think ping pong was challenging enough already, try doing it in the middle of the ocean when the high seas are rocking and rolling. Almost every ship has a ping pong table located somewhere on deck (often outside but in an area protected from the wind). Paddles and ping pong balls are usually available during specified hours. Grab a partner and practice your serves and spins, because you might end up the champ during the ping pong tournament.

Participate In Pool Games

Pool games are silly. Pool games are stupid. Pool games are mindless. And pool games are absolutely hilarious. Whether you choose to observe or participate, get yourself out to the pool and prepare to laugh.

Pool games aren't necessarily *in* the pool. Some pool games are *by* the pool. Some pool games don't require a pool at all—they're played *on* the beach when the ship docks at a private island. Whatever the preposition used, the adjective might be *wacky*.

Pool games take real people and ask them to do ridiculous things in a non-threatening manner. Everyone has fun, but no one is made fun of. People forget that they're in their bathing suits and they never did lose those last 10 pounds. Nobody notices or cares because the person's sense of humor and sportsmanship comes through. Some people say they're too shy to get up in front of people and participate, but every "shy" person I've talked to who's been convinced to do it has had the time of his or her life and admitted to feeling part of a group instead of on display.

Some pool games require teamwork and some are individually competitive. None is dangerous and all are funny. There's always a winner, but never a loser.

No matter how many cruises you go on, some classic pool games will prevail and some new variations will creep up. I really hate to spoil the fun by describing each one, so let me just give you the names of a few. Don't be misled by the name—there are usually a few twists that make it even more interesting.

- Ping Pong Ball Stuffing
- Beer drinking
- Balloon Bursting
- Hairy Chest
- Best Tan
- Knobby Knees
- Spoon Diving
- Pillow Fighting
- Team Numbers

Search Out The Scavenger Hunt

Scavenger hunts are sometimes conducted in the main showroom and sometimes conducted outside; they usually require a team of up to six people. The cruise director might instruct you that he will shout out an item and, as soon as it is located, a team member must race up to the the cruise director with that item. The items start out simple: a postage stamp, a cruise bulletin from that day. Beware, though! The items get more creative, more intimate and more outrageous. Here's an opportunity to get two forms of exercise: running your legs off as you race up with your items, and laughing your head off as you try to comply.

Sample Shuffleboard

No, shuffleboard is not just for old people. It's actually a complicated, strategic game that can be played right there in the beautiful sunshine. If you've never played shuffleboard, grab someone and ask for the equipment. If you have no one to challenge, go watch someone who's playing. Offer to keep score. If you don't know how to play, ask for explanation as the game progresses.

Try Trapshooting

Like the bridge tour, trapshooting is mainly a man's domain. Unlike the bridge tour, there's probably a physical reason for this: Those guns give off quite a kick! That's still no reason not to try it.

Trapshooting is usually held a couple of times a week, often culminating in a trapshooting contest. Many people are terrific at trapshooting because it's a popular sport back home. For others, shooting skeet is a unique event, and taking part on the ship is a perfect way to experience this sport.

There is usually a minimal charge for trapshooting, often $1 per shot, to cover the cost of the clay pigeon and the ammunition.

Test Your Trivia

You may think trivia is nothing but a bunch of useless knowledge. You may think useless knowledge is an oxymoron. But if you don't know what an oxymoron is, you don't have enough useless knowledge.

Trivia contests attract a devoted and passionate group of people. Don't be dissuaded from participating just because you don't think you're "*Jeopardy*" material. Some trivia contests test your general knowledge; others ask questions that are sheer guesses.

There are actually a couple of types of trivia contests. On many ships, a sheet of trivia questions or puzzles are posted in a designated area. Individuals are encouraged to fill them out and turn them in as early as possible. On some, the winner is the person with the most correct answers and the earliest entry time. On others, the winner is chosen by random drawing. These contests often have themes, such as world capitals or famous people, but sometimes they're rebuses or picture puzzles that require logic instead of information.

The other type of contest is team trivia. Groups of two to six are formed to answer the questions. The larger the group, the better your chances because, obviously, six heads are better than two. This is a terrific way to meet people of different ages, different professions and different countries, because what you don't know about World War II, that widow from New Jersey might be able to fill in. That guy from Australia will certainly know the Ayers Rock answer, while someone else remembers that a rhinestone was once used for the eye on a poodle skirt. If you win a bottle of champagne, open it immediately and celebrate with your new friends.

Witness Wine Tasting

And speaking of champagne, get ready to sip the bubbly at the ship-sponsored wine tasting. Wondering what wine goes with tonight's rack of lamb? They'll probably offer it at the wine tasting and tell you what other dishes to serve it with. In between, you can clear your palate with an assortment of cheese and crackers, while the sommelier takes you on a journey from appetizer wines to those served for desserts.

There is usually a slight charge for the wine tasting, perhaps $3, but you'll get to sip some exclusive wines and you might end up with a souvenir to take home, such as an engraved wine glass or a replica of the cup the sommelier uses to taste the wine.

GOOD MORNING SUNRISE: 7:00 AM		WEDNESDAY, DAY 4 SUNSET: 6:02 PM
6:30 AM	Coffee & Danish	Panorama Grill · Lido
7:00 AM	Walk-A-Mile	Olympic Track Sun Deck
7:30 AM	Stretch & Relaxation	Aerobics Studio
7:45 AM	Breakfast Main Sitting	Both Dining Rooms
8:00 · 10:00 AM	Light Deck Breakfast	Panorama Grill · Lido
8:00 AM · 6:00 PM	Pools are Open. Jacuzzi's Open.	Lido Deck
8:00 AM · 8:00 PM	Shuffleboard Available	Sun Deck Forward
8:00 AM · LATE	Ping Pong Available	Verandah Deck Forward
8:00 AM · 8:00 PM	Purser's Office Opens	Empress Deck
8:00 AM	Slot Machines are Open	Crystal Palace Casino
8:00 AM · 8:00 PM	Nautica Spa Salon Opens	Sports Deck Forward
9:00 AM	Breakfast Late Sitting	Both Dining Rooms
9:00 AM · 10:00 PM	Galleria Shopping Mall Opens	Atlantic Deck
9:30 AM	Bridge Walk-Through	Meet Portside Lido Deck
10:00 AM	Horseracing	Blue Sapphire Lounge
10:00 AM · 11:00 AM	Coffee, Tea & Bouillon	Panorama Grill · Lido
10:00 · 11:00 AM	Library is Open	Explorer's Club
10:30 AM · 1:00 PM	Snorkel Rentals & Video Diary Desk Opens	Empress Deck
10:30 AM	Aqua Aerobics	Verandah Deck Aft
11:00 AM	Senior Aerobics	Aerobics Studio
11:00 AM · 2:00 PM	Photo Gallery Opens	Empress Deck Grand Atrium
11:00 AM	Travel Talk · Grand Cayman & Jamaica	Blue Sapphire Lounge
11:30 AM · 2:00 PM	Specialty Sandwiches	Lido Deck Poolside
11:30 AM · 2:30 PM	Light Lunch & Salad Bar	Panorama Grill · Lido
11:50 AM	Captain's Bulletin from the Bridge	
12:00 NOON	Lunch Main Sitting	Both Dining Rooms
12:00 NOON	Beauty Demonstration	Lido Deck
1:30 PM	Lunch Late Sitting	Both Dining Rooms
2:00 PM	"New Image" Seminar	Aerobics Studio
2:00 PM	Trapshooting	Promenade Deck Aft
2:00 · 3:00 PM	Library is Open	Explorer's Club
2:00 PM	Pillow Fighting Contest	Lido Deck
2:15 PM	Grandma's, Grandpa's & Honeymooner's Party	Blue Sapphire Lounge
2:45 PM	Dr. Ruth Sex, Love & Romance Trivia Quiz	Blue Sapphire Lounge
3:00 PM	Bingo Supreme	Blue Sapphire Lounge
3:00 PM	Low Impact Aerobics	Aerobics Studio
4:00 PM	Galley Tour	Meet at Blue Sapphire Lounge
4:00 PM	Multi-Impact Aerobics	Aerobics Studio
4:00 · 5:00 PM	Ice Cream & Cookies	Lido Grill · Outside
4:00 · 5:00 PM	Frozen Yogurt	Lido Grill · Inside
4:00 · 5:00 PM	Tea Time with "Scott" in Piano	Society Bar
4:30 PM	Trapshooting	Promenade Deck Aft
5:00 · 11:00 PM	Photo Gallery Opens	Empress Deck Grand Atrium
5:00 · 6:00 PM	Guacamole & Salsa Party	Promenade Deck
6:00 PM	Dinner Main Sitting	Both Dining Rooms
6:00 · 8:00 PM	Snorkel Rentals & Video Diary Desk Opens	Empress Deck
7:00 · 8:00 PM	Guacamole & Salsa Party	Promenade Deck
7:15 · 8:00 PM	Dance to the ECSTASY Orchestra .	Blue Sapphire Lounge
8:00 PM	Dinner Late Sitting	Both Dining Rooms
8:00 PM	Bingo Supreme	Blue Sapphire Lounge
8:30 PM	Showtime (Main Sitting)	Blue Sapphire Lounge
9:15 PM	Piano Bar Opens with "Peter"	Neon Bar
9:30 PM	Dance with the "Sea Breeze"	Starlight Lounge
9:45 PM	Dance with the "Music Society"	Chinatown
10:00 PM · 2:00 AM	"Mike" Performs for You	City Lights Boulevard
10:00 PM	Stripes Disco Opens with "Jeff"	Promenade Deck
10:30 PM	Showtime (Late Sitting)	Blue Sapphire Lounge
12:15 AM	Midnight Special	Starlight Lounge
12:30 · 1:30 AM	Dessert Buffet	Wind Star Dining Room
1:30 · 2:30 AM	Mini Buffet	City Diner · Promenade Deck

DRESS FOR THE EVENING: Casual

MOVIE: "The Doctor" 7:30 AM, 10:00 AM, 12:30 PM, 3:00 PM, 5:30 PM, 8:00 PM, 10:30 PM, 1:00 AM, 3:30 AM

It's Ashore Thing

Praise the sea; on shore remain.

John Florio

One of the most thrilling sights for any traveler is to watch from the deck of the ship as an exotic port slowly comes into view. The anticipated pleasures turn into a reality as the vessel glides up to the pier, expertly docked by the pilot. Down on the wharf is the hustle and bustle of local people, ready to serve you, transport you, give you information and, in general, find some way to separate you from your much-desired American money.

Before arriving in port, you might have armed yourself with enough information to make you feel like a local expert. You've read other guidebooks that outlined the geographic splendors. You've asked around to find out where the best beaches are. You've conferred with the crew to discover where they go for fun. You've perused the encyclopedias to get a grasp of the local history and culture. You might have even read a few cookbooks to learn some local recipes.

Arm Yourself With Information

No matter what you decide to do—go exploring on your own, take a tour, pal around with other passengers or just walk around—the most important thing you can take with you is information.

You can find out most of what you need to know from the port lectures given aboard ship. Many guidebooks are helpful in highlighting points of interest. Cruise lines often provide maps into town, complete with street names and shopping information.

In general, though, you can find out what you need just by asking other passengers or the cruise staff.

Make sure you know these vital facts:

⚓ What is the exchange rate? Can money be changed on the ship? What times are the banks open?

⚓ How far is it to town? Is it walking distance?

⚓ Where are the best beaches? What is the best way to get there? Are there hotels there that welcome cruise ship passengers? Is there any charge to use the facilities or to gain entry to the beach?

⚓ Is there a set rate on the cabs? What is the average price to get to various locations in town? What is the average price to book a cab for a half day?

⚓ Is there any standard rate for certain sports or amenities, such as the rental of jet skis, parasailing equipment or lounge chairs? Where are the best bargains?

⚓ What is the policy on tipping in this locale? Is there a service charge built into the restaurant prices or is a gratuity expected?

⚓ What time do passengers have to be back on board?

⚓ Did I remember to bring everything I need? Do I have my boarding pass, money and, perhaps, credit card?

Now all you have to do is determine how you're going to accomplish everything you want to do and see everything you want to see in the one day you have in port. You may know exactly what you want to do, but you have to decide how you want to do it and with whom you want to do it.

Sign Up For A Shore Excursion

The cruise line, of course, is more than willing to help you achieve all your travel goals in port. Cruise ships offer a variety of port excursions in relative comfort at reasonable prices. Since the cruise lines know the likes and needs of their passengers, you're likely to find some sort of excursion in each port that will appeal to you.

Some people look forward to shopping. Others want to spend the whole day lounging on a beach, drinking rum punch. Others enjoy the beach but prefer a more active excursion, including snorkeling or scuba diving. Still others want to discover the heritage and culture of an area, visiting ancient sites and historic monuments.

Whatever you choose to do, the cruise line can help you do it. Or you can do it on your own.

Before the cruise, or perhaps once you board the ship, you'll receive information on available shore excursions offered by the line. You will be advised to sign up early to avoid disappointment, as space is limited. Prior to arriving in port, the cruise director might give the previously mentioned port talk, discussing not only the available shore excursions but also giving shopping hints, distributing maps into town and recommending stores and restaurants.

If there is a shore excursion that intrigues you, or if you feel you don't want to explore the town on your own, or if you haven't met enough other people to organize a group, by all means select one of the ship's shore excursions. Often, they are unique and unavailable through any other source than the ship. You will be treated with care and your comfort will be attended to. You'll be accompanied by an English-speaking guide who will keep you entertained with little bon mots about what you're seeing. You'll know in advance how much you're going to spend and exactly how long it'll take. And, chances are, you'll still have time after the shore excursions to do a little exploring on your own. You'll travel in air-conditioned comfort, and your guides will probably arrange for a short break and a cool refreshment.

Here's an example of some types of shore excursions offered on Caribbean routes:

SPECIAL-INTEREST EXCURSIONS

Here is a sampling of our Special-Interest Excursions.

Caribbean Dining

Take advantage of your cruise to sample Caribbean cuisine. The following excursions include lunch and offer local dishes as part of their menus:

St. Lucia—Tour A—Grand Island
Martinique—Tour F—St. Pierre and Plantation de Leyritz
Montego Bay—Tour F—Dunn's River Falls and Ocho Rios
Montego Bay—Tour G—Croydon Plantation in the Mountains

For excursions that offer a more casual lunch or barbecue, there's also:

Barbados—Tour H—Jolly Roger Sailing Party
St. Lucia—Tour B—Northern Island and Reduit Beach
St. Lucia—Tour C—St. Lucia By Land and Sea
St. Lucia—Tour S—Tall Ship West Coast Spectacular
Grand Cayman—Tour F—North Sound Spectacular
Mayreau—Tour F—Grenadines Sailaway and Palm Island
St. Maarten—Tour B—Explorer Cruise to Marigot
San Juan—Tour R—San Juan Surf and Saddle

Caribbean History

From the amazing civilization of the Mayans to the "Discovery of the New World" to pirate ships and lost treasure, the history of the Caribbean is rich, varied, and absorbing. These tours offer you a glimpse into this history:

Barbados—Tour A—Barbados Island and Villa Nova Plantation
Barbados—Tour B—Barbados Heritage and Sunbury Plantation
Cozumel—Tour A—The Lost Civilization - Tulum and Xel-Ha
Martinique—Tour A & B—Island and St. Pierre

Montego Bay—Tour A—Rose Hall and the White Witch of Jamaica
San Juan—Tour B—Old and New San Juan

Walking Tours

Martinique—Tour L—Walking Tour of Fort-de-France
San Juan—Tour L—Walking Tour of Old San Juan

The Caribbean from Above and Below

If you're looking for a unique experience don't forget our Helicopter and Submarine Excursions.

Helicopter Tours

Barbados—Tour J—Bajan Helicopter
St. Thomas—Tour J—Virgin Islands Helicopter Odyssey
San Juan—Tour J—San Juan by Helicopter

Atlantis Submarine

Barbados—Tour I
St. Thomas—Tour I
Grand Cayman—Tour I

Nature Tours

Here are our favorite tours for nature lovers:

Barbados—Tour G—Harrison's Cave and Island Vistas
Martinique—Tour G—Balata Tropical Gardens
Montego Bay—Tour G—Croydon Plantation in the Mountains
San Juan—Tour G—El Yunque Rain Forest; Tour K—Hiking in El Yunque

Also, don't forget all of our New Waves and other outdoor excursions.

Caribbean Party Time

It's party time in the Caribbean and these excursions are well-known for their unlimited rum punch, music, and fun:

Barbados—Tour H—Jolly Roger Sailing Party
St. Thomas—Tour H—Kon Tiki Party Raft
Cozumel—Tour H—Fiesta Boat and Beach
Martinique—Tour H—Calypso Beach and Party Cruise

Courtesy Princess Cruises

Decide Whether To Change Money

Just about anywhere you go in the world today, it seems, American dollars are understood, accepted, even preferred. You'll have to decide if you want to deal in the local currency of a port or stick with American money.

A little research into the exchange rates can save you some anxiety, time and money, but only you can decide whether you're more comfortable dealing with local currency or American dollars.

The first thing to consider is where you'll use your money. If you're traveling to a popular Caribbean or Mexican port, you'll find that many of the prices in the stores, as well as the bargaining on the street, will be in American currency.

If you do decide to deal in local currency, you might be able to exchange money right on the ship. Your other option is to visit a local bank to change money.

There are, of course, advantages to be said for both sides. If you exchange your money for the local currency, you'll lose a little bit on both ends of the deal—when you change dollars, you'll pay one rate and when the bank buys it back at the end of the day, you'll receive another rate. On the other hand, most haggling and buying tends to be in round dollar amounts, the price of a soda from a street vendor will be $1, while in local currency you might pay the equivalent of 60 cents. Only you can decide if the additional 40 cents here and there is worth the thrill or hassle of changing money.

Just so you at least know what currency you're going to be dealing with, there's a chart at the end of this chapter that will get you started in the right direction if you decide to change money. Keep in mind that a lot of countries use the dollar as its currency, but it's not the U.S. dollar—they use the Eastern Caribbean dollar, or the Australian dollar, or the dollar of their country.

Walk Into Town

In many ports, the main section of town is walking distance from the pier. Never trust your sense of direction to go into town—make sure you check a map and then double check by asking someone which way you should go. Often, the beaten path looks like it will lead right to the main area when this is only an illusion. It's frustrating to walk 15 minutes, only to realize you must walk that same 15 minutes back and then proceed in the opposite direction for another 15 minutes. Sometimes you can see the town from the deck of the ship and this will give you an indication of where you should go.

If you're the adventurous sort, a solo walk through the streets of a strange city can be an exhilarating experience. You'll be able to mingle with the locals, stop at intriguing shops, outdoor markets and cafes, and wander off into areas that aren't included in the guided tours offered by shore excursions.

Board A Tender

If you can't walk off the ship onto the pier, you're probably anchored off-shore and will have to take a tender onto the land. Tenders are smaller boats that shuttle people in groups between the cruise ship and the pier. There are usually a number of tenders running continuously to get the passengers into the port. After all, it's quite a task to get a couple of thousand people off a megaliner. On some ships, you simply line up at the gangway and board the tender. On others, you'll have to take a number and wait until you're called.

Waiting for tenders tends to be like waiting in line to board a plane. Despite the fact that it might be more inconvenient, boarding a tender gives you more time to make your shore plans because you might meet some interesting people aboard the tender who invite you to join them on their foray.

If you have to take a tender, make sure you allow extra time at the end of the day to get back on board. When the cruise line says the last tender leaves at 4:30 p.m., you shouldn't be sitting in a restaurant waiting for your check at 4:25. If you miss your tender, you miss your ship

Join A Group

If you get off the ship and know where you want to go but don't have anyone to go with, you can try and insinuate yourself into a ready-made situation. In most ports, there'll be a slew of cab drivers waiting at the dock to take the hordes of people to various locales around town. While standing on the pier waiting for transportation, you should chat with the people near you to find out where they're headed. Often, a cab to a location is based on a flat rate: a set fee of $10 to the beach on the south side of the island, for example. If a group of four people is going where you want to go, you can inquire if you can split the cab ride with them. Instead of paying $2.50 per person, the fare will work out to $2 a person and very few people object to an additional person sharing this form of non-committal transportation.

At other times, cab rides to specific locations are set at a per-person basis, particularly when the system has vans or minibuses lined up. Let the cabdriver or transportation chief know that you're riding alone and don't want to engage the entire cab. Many minivans accommodate 12 or 14 people at a time and don't start rolling until every seat is filled up. Let the driver or transportation head know where you want to go and he will probably stick you in a seat in a larger vehicle. Once the maximum number of people has been loaded in, your coach will take you to your destination.

Grab A Cab

If you still want to remain independent, there's nothing to stop you from taking a cab to wherever you want to go, except for the fact that it'll cost more. If you want to walk into town in the morning, go back to the ship for lunch, and then head out on your own to another part of the port in the afternoon, you might find your own personal cab the ideal way to go. Whether you're going with a group or alone, make sure you agree on the price of the ride *before* you get into the cab. Getting into a cab and asking the driver to simply take you to a location is an invitation to be overcharged. Also make sure you agree on what currency you're talking about.

Courtesy Holland America Line

Many passengers find they start off on their own but wind up in the same place, soaking up the same sun.

Just because you might have to pay the price of an entire cab to a beach or location is not a reason to give up on a port and sit alone on the ship. If you take a cab by yourself, there's a good chance you'll run into other passengers wherever you go and, as the time to reboard gets closer, you'll probably be able to split a cab with others on the return trip.

Form A Group

One of the nicest ways to enjoy your day in port is to hook up with some congenial people with the same interests as you. You might consider hiring a cab for a half day or even the whole day at a set rate.

Since competition for transporting passengers is fierce, you'll be able to get a good package deal on a tour of the area. Cab drivers will offer to take you wherever you want to go (or show you the highlights of the area, if you leave it up to him) based on an hourly or specific rate. You can set your own itinerary, and the cab driver will wait as you browse among shops, sip a soda in a cafe, or lounge on the beach.

Because the field is so competitive, you might be able to bargain on the price of the cab driver's services. If you do engage a cab for a half day, don't pay him the money upfront. While most cab drivers are honest, there's nothing to stop the cabbie from dropping you off at your first destination and hightailing it out of there in hopes of picking up another fare.

Also, make sure your cab driver speaks English. If the cab driver has learned enough English to entice you into his cab with promises of a guided tour, you'll be expecting tidbits of information for the price. Many a passenger has been disappointed to head out to the countryside only to find out that the cab driver's English is limited to "I'll give you a guided tour. I speak English."

Simply asking a cabbie, "Do you speak English?" is not enough to determine his language skill. Most cab drivers know that question well enough to know to answer yes. Instead, ask him a question like, "When was the last time it rained here?" and see how he does. The real advantage of an English-speaking cab driver is that he'll be able to provide information that the cruise line personnel probably don't know, such as how much the banana boat ride costs for the natives or where a local beach is that's not infested with tourists.

However, take certain recommendations with just a slight bit of wariness. If you ask the driver to take you to a restaurant that he recommends, you might end up at his wife's cousin's brother's kitchen.

One more caveat: I've often heard rumors of cab drivers who will recommend visiting a beautiful sight, such as a flowering garden or mountain waterfall. You'll enjoy yourself until it's time to leave to get back on the ship, and then the cabbie will require you to pay more than you'd agreed upon up front. You're held hostage for money with the fear that you'll miss the ship. I've never spoken with anyone to whom this has happened and think it might be in the same category as an urban myth, like alligators in the New York City sewers. There is also some speculation that this sort of rumor is put out by cruise personnel who would much rather sell you their safe shore excursions. If you like your stories salty, you can supply a few grains here.

WORLD CURRENCY

There are too many countries in the world to list the unit of currency for each one, but this chart should at least orient you to the currency of some countries where many cruise ships visit.

Country	Currency
Antigua and Barbuda	Dollar
Argentina	Austral
Australia	Dollar
Austria	Schilling
Bahamas	Dollar
Barbados	Dollar
Bermuda	Dollar
Brazil	Cruzado
China	Yuan
Costa Rica	Colon
Denmark	Krone
Ecuador	Sucre
Egypt	Pound
Finland	Markka
France	Franc
Germany	Mark
Greece	Drachma
Grenada	Dollar
Guatemala	Quetzal
Hong Kong	Dollar
Iceland	Krona
India	Rupee
Indonesia	Rupiah
Ireland	Pound
Israel	Shekel
Italy	Lira
Jamaica	Dollar
Japan	Yen
Martinique	Franc
Mexico	Peso
Monaco	Franc
Morocco	Dirham
Netherlands	Guilder
Netherlands Antilles	Guilder
New Zealand	Dollar
Norway	Krone
Panama	Balboa
Poland	Zloty
Portugal	Escudo
Russian Republic	Ruble
St. Kitts-Nevis	Dollar
St. Lucia	Dollar
Seychelles	Rupee
Spain	Peseta
Sri Lanka	Rupee
Sweden	Krona
Thailand	Baht
Trinidad and Tobago	Dollar
Turkey	Lira
United Kingdom	Pound
Venezuela	Bolivar
Vietnam	Dong

Spice Up Your Language

*Slang is the language that rolls up its sleeves,
spits on its hands and goes to work.*

Carl Sandburg

You can pepper your conversation with the salty talk of the sea (and sound like a seasoned sailor) by simply adding a few appropriate words and phrases used on cruise ships.

Passengers don't usually employ all the taut terminology used by the officers and crew, but knowledge of a few ocean-going words will help you understand what's happening and let you get in the swing of things.

You may never have the chance to casually display your grasp of a bollard or a davit, but some words are so basic to sailing that you might feel lost at sea without them.

If your daily cruise program tells you that skeet shooting will be held on 6 Deck, Aft, Port side, you'll know where to muster.

In truth, you're probably more savvy to sea-going terms than you give yourself credit. Take the simply quiz below, checking off the appropriate answers to the questions, and you might surprise yourself by getting every one right!

Abeam
❑ What's glowing from E.T.'s finger
❑ At the middle of the ship's side

About
❑ What Evander Holyfield fights
❑ Onto a new course, direction

Above Board
- ❑ Where diver Greg Louganis stands
- ❑ Located above the waterline

Aft
- ❑ About fifty per cent
- ❑ The back of the ship

Aground
- ❑ How you like your a coffee
- ❑ Stranded on a sandbar, land, or in shallow water

Ahoy
- ❑ Sound made when you spit overboard
- ❑ Word used to hail another ship

Alleyway
- ❑ Style of boxing used by the former Cassius Clay
- ❑ A narrow passageway or corridor

All hands
- ❑ Clumsy person who's worse than all thumbs
- ❑ Everyone who works on the ship

Aloft
- ❑ Living space for a artist
- ❑ At a great height, often in the riggings or the mast

Amidships
- ❑ Standing at the pier
- ❑ In the middle of the ship, halfway between the front and back

Ashore
- ❑ Cowboy's affirmative response to a question
- ❑ Where you go when you leave the ship

Astern
- ❑ Controversial radio host AHoward
- ❑ Toward the back of the ship

Athwart
- ❑ A thwing you get when you strwoke a toad
- ❑ Across the ship

Backwash
- ❑ What's left in the last sips of a soda pop bottle
- ❑ Water thrown back by the ship's propeller

Ballast
- ❑ Opposite of Ballfirst
- ❑ Heavy material carried to provide desired stability

Bar
- ❑ What Davy Crockett killed
- ❑ A shoal or reef

Barge
- ❑ Simpson mother of Bart, Maggie and Lisa
- ❑ A flat-bottomed boat, often used for carrying cargo

Batten Down
- ❑ Type of collar on men's shirts
- ❑ To fasten down, or make watertight

Beacon
- ❑ Breakfast meat served with eegs
- ❑ Beam of light on shore for direction and navigation

Beam
- ❑ Lima, kidney or string
- ❑ The width of the ship at its widest point

Bearing
- ❑ Jewelry for a grizzly or a Kodiak
- ❑ The direction of the ship

Bells
- ❑ Scarlett O'Hara and Melanie Hamilton
- ❑ A system of time-telling aboard ship by the ringing of bells

Below
- ❑ When the drone is sad
- ❑ Any deck on ship lower than the main deck

Berth
- ❑ Where a similar sounding event nine-months later might originate
- ❑ Your bed on board ship; also, where the ship is docked

Bollard
- ❑ Actor Michael J.
- ❑ A post on the pier where the ship's mooring lines are fastened

Bon Voyage
- ❑ A trip to the former capital of the former West Germany
- ❑ Term used to wish you a happy sailing; from the French meaning "good trip"

Bow
- ❑ To bend at the waist when meeting the captain
- ❑ The front of the ship

Bridge

- ❏ The captain's dental work
- ❏ The captain's navigational command post

Bulkhead

- ❏ The feeling you get from one too many Pina Coladas
- ❏ A wall inside the ship

Buoy

- ❏ Alamo hero who inspired a knife
- ❏ A floating object that marks the water's channel

Cabin

- ❏ Term used to indicate the taxi is not out
- ❏ Your room on board ship

Cable

- ❏ Tone found between Jayble and Ellble
- ❏ The chains that hold the ship's anchor

Cable Length

- ❏ Duration of an HBO special
- ❏ A nautical unit of length roughly equal to 600 or more feet

Capstan

- ❏ Place to hang your bonnet or beret
- ❏ A mechanical device for winding in rope or cable

Chart

- ❏ How your steak comes when you order it very well done
- ❏ A map of the bottom of the ocean

Coaming

- ❏ The act of arranging one's hair with a toothed utensil
- ❏ A raised frame around an opening to keep out water

Companionway

- ❏ New charity formed by United Way
- ❏ A stairway inside the ship

Compass

- ❏ Two betting options on a Craps table
- ❏ A navigational instrument for determining the ship's direction

Conning

- ❏ The act of selling "real" Rolex watches for $20
- ❏ A low observation tower

Course
- Describes that yokel at the table who keeps telling dirty jokes
- The ship's route

Crow's Nest
- Popular brand of bourbon
- An elevated lookout area

Davit
- Curse uttered when you stub your toe on the coaming
- A crane used for hoisting and lowering the lifeboats

Deadlight
- What you've got if you forgot to put in fresh batteries
- A heavy shutter on a porthole to keep out light or water

Debark
- De coating on de tree
- The same as disembark, it means to leave the ship

Dock
- The "Love Boat" physician, played by Bernie Koppel
- The pier where the ship anchors

Doldrums
- Barbie and Ken's bongos
- A series of winds north of the equator

Draft
- What many politicians avoided during the Vietnam War
- The depth a ship is immersed when carrying a load

Drill
- What the dentist uses while asking about your family
- A training exercise, such as testing lifeboat safety

Embark
- What 'em dogs do when they see 'em mail carriers
- To go on board the ship

Even Keel
- Brother of dancer Ruby
- The upright steadiness of the ship

Fair Wind
- Smell in the ship's duty-free perfume shop
- A wind blowing in the same direction the ship is going

Falling Glass
- ❑ Result of one too many umbrella drinks
- ❑ Dropping barometric pressure

Fantail
- ❑ Request shouted when someone gets a hot seat
- ❑ A part of the stern that overhangs the rear of the ship

Fathom
- ❑ Broadway character who hangs out in an opera house
- ❑ A unit of depth measurement equal to six feet

Flags
- ❑ What your energy does at the end of a day on board ship
- ❑ An international system that communicates cargo, registry, etc.

Flotsam
- ❑ Rabbit brother of Mopsam and Cottontail
- ❑ Floating debris from a shipwreck

Fore
- ❑ Not agin
- ❑ The front of the ship

Forward
- ❑ Attitude of the crew toward a woman in a low-cut dress
- ❑ Also the front of the ship

Free Port
- ❑ Complimentary sweet wine
- ❑ A port where goods are free of customs duty

Funnel
- ❑ Festive adornment on Laverne DeFazio's sweater
- ❑ The ship's smokestack

Galley
- ❑ Female looking for a Guyley
- ❑ The ship's kitchen

Gangway
- ❑ Cry heard on deck when the crew finally gets leave
- ❑ The entrance and exit of the ship.

Gross Registered Tonnage
- ❑ Your weight at the end of the cruise
- ❑ A measurement unit of the ship, with 100 cubic feet equalling one gross registered ton

Gunwale
- ❑ New type of corduroy fabric
- ❑ The upper edge of a ship's side

Hand
- ❑ What you give the ship's entertainers
- ❑ A member of the ship's crew

Harbor Master
- ❑ What one does with a fugitive captain
- ❑ The official in charge of the harbor

Hatch
- ❑ What one wears on one's headtch
- ❑ An opening in the deck

Hawser
- ❑ Young doctor Doogie
- ❑ A rope for securing the ship

Head
- ❑ Not 'hind
- ❑ The bathroom on a ship

Helm
- ❑ Where your angry wife tells you to golm to
- ❑ The steering apparatus of the ship

High Seas
- ❑ Where drug smugglers sail
- ❑ Open ocean outside a country's territorial limits

Hold
- ❑ What you are as a result of hadding years to your hage
- ❑ The cargo area of a ship

Hook
- ❑ Peter Pan's enemy
- ❑ Another name for the ship's anchor

House Flag
- ❑ What's wrapped around a sailor buried at sea
- ❑ The cruise line's logo, often seen on the funnel or a flag

Hull
- ❑ Where you're going in a hundbasket
- ❑ The outside or body of the ship

Jetsam
- ❑ Last name of George, Jane, Judy and Elroy
- ❑ Extraneous material thrown overboard deliberately to lighten the ship's load

Keel
- ❑ Last name of Broadway star Howard
- ❑ The spine of the ship that runs the entire length

Knot
- ❑ Phrase made popular by "Wayne's World"
- ❑ A measure of the ship's speed, equal to about one nautical mile per hour

Landfall
- ❑ The traditional California cry after an earthquake
- ❑ The sighting of land

Latitude
- ❑ Opposite of lassitude
- ❑ North-South geographical measurement

League
- ❑ Where Madonna played ball
- ❑ Unit of measurement roughly equal to three miles

Leeward
- ❑ Medical floor for Lee patients
- ❑ Away from the wind

Let go
- ❑ What you say when the cat's got your tongue or a crab's got your toe
- ❑ To release the ship's lines or ropes

Lifeboat
- ❑ Short-lived "Love Boat" spinoff
- ❑ The vessels on a ship used in case of emergency

Log
- ❑ Constant companion of a strange lady on "Twin Peaks"
- ❑ The official record of the ship's daily details

Longitude
- ❑ The act of coveting
- ❑ East-West geographical measurement

Manifest
- ❑ Adjective describing your destiny aboard ship
- ❑ The listing of the the ship's passengers, crew and/or cargo

Master
- ❑ What Barbara Eden called Larry Hagman in "I Dream of Jeannie"
- ❑ Another name for the captain

Moor
- ❑ Othello
- ❑ To secure the ship at a port

Muster
- ❑ "Clue" game colonel in the library with a wrench
- ❑ To assemble for the lifeboat drill or other purpose

Nautical Mile
- ❑ The length you'd walk for an aquatic Camel
- ❑ Distance measurement, slightly longer than a land mile

Navigable Waters
- ❑ What Simon & Garfunkel's *first* bridge was over
- ❑ Water deep enough for the ship to safely maneuver

Out Of Trim
- ❑ When it's time to go to your barber
- ❑ Loaded improperly

Overhang
- ❑ Technique used by fancy wallpaperers
- ❑ Part of the ship that extends beyond the hull

Pelorus
- ❑ A distressing skin disease
- ❑ A navigational device for measuring observed objects

Pilot
- ❑ Where your park your Lemon Meringue or Boston Cream
- ❑ A specially trained captain who maneuvers the ship in or out of port

Pitch
- ❑ The spiel the travel agent gave you to get you to book this cruise
- ❑ The opposite of roll; the forward-backward motion of the ship

Port
- ❑ Decanted
- ❑ The left side of the ship

Prow
- ❑ The male version of "prowess"
- ❑ The front of the ship

Quarters
- ❑ Coins you endlessly feed into the slot machines
- ❑ The crew's living accommodations

Registry
- ❑ Where brides indicate their gift choices
- ❑ Where the ship's certificate of ownership is registered

Rigging
- ❑ Charges once levied during Chicago's elections
- ❑ The lines used to support a ship's mast and work the sails

Rising Glass
- ❑ Action of toasting the Captain
- ❑ Ascending barometric pressure

Roll
- ❑ Rock's companion
- ❑ The opposite of pitch, this is the side-to-side motion of the ship

Rudder
- ❑ What you keep getting if you don't use your sunblock
- ❑ Device at the ship's stern used for steering

Running Lights
- ❑ Handy gadget for nighttime joggers
- ❑ Lights illuminated at night so the vessel can be seen by other ships

Screw
- ❑ Oh come on now, do you really think I'd put that here?
- ❑ The ship's propeller

Scupper
- ❑ A baby skipper
- ❑ A drain for collecting excess water

Scuttlebutt
- ❑ Derogatory term for a flabby posterior
- ❑ Gossip aboard ship

Sidelight
- ❑ A hobby or avocation
- ❑ Either of two night lights carried by the ship; red on port, green on starboard

Skipper
- ❑ Athletic partner of Hopper and Jumper
- ❑ Slang term, not really used on cruise ships, for the captain.

Sounding
- ❑ What it means when you touch your ear in a Charades game
- ❑ Measurement of the water depth

Stabilizer
- ❑ Long-lasting battery to compete with that drum-banging rabbit
- ❑ Mechanical device on ship which provides for smoother sailing

Starboard
- ❑ What the entertainer is when you tell him about your grandchildren
- ❑ The right side of the ship

Stateroom
- ❑ Request of crew member when you tell him you're lost
- ❑ Your cabin

Stem
- ❑ Really backward Mets
- ❑ The forward part of the ship

Stern
- ❑ How the captain looks when you tell him he "drives a nice boat"
- ❑ The rear part of the ship

Stowaway
- ❑ Payment option if you can't afford layaway
- ❑ An unregistered passenger who is illegally on board

Swell
- ❑ Term made popular by Cole Porter songs
- ❑ A prolonged succession of waves

Taffrail
- ❑ What people say when Taf is ill
- ❑ The rail around the ship's stern

Tender
- ❑ After nineder and before elevender
- ❑ A small boat for carrying passengers or supplies to shore

Trade Winds
- ❑ What Thor and Odin do for fun
- ❑ Winds blowing in one direction, especially toward the equator

Under Way
- ❑ Not really an option after eating eight meals a day
- ❑ Moving; no longer in port

Wake
- ❑ A widdle body of wiquid
- ❑ Path of water behind the ship

Waterline
- ❑ Queue at the oasis
- ❑ The outside of the ship's hull above water

Wharf
- ❑ Sound little Orphan Annie's dog makes
- ❑ The dock or pier

Wharfinger
- ❑ Another James Bond nemesis
- ❑ The manager of the wharf, the wharfmaster

Windlass
- ❑ Girl in a gale
- ❑ A mechanical hoisting device

Yaw
- ❑ Opposite of Naw
- ❑ To deviate from the set course

Special Events

*Friendship should be surrounded with ceremonies
and respects, and not crushed into corners.*

Ralph Waldo Emerson

Even before you leave for the ship, you'll be preparing for some of those special moments that could easily turn into your favorite memories. Better yet, there are a variety of special events the cruise line doesn't even hint at that are waiting to delight and amuse you.

The special events on a ship are varied and appeal to all the different senses and needs of the crowd. Everything from casual participation to formal procedure is available, and, while you need not do everything and go everywhere, there are certain events that define and enhance the cruise experience.

To many people, the highlight of the cruise is the first formal night when the captain hosts the cocktail party. To other people, the more comical events, such as the men's lingerie contest, linger in their memories long after formality has waned. Either way, there are special events and special evenings to please a variety of tastes.

Of course, there is some sort of special event happening every night aboard a ship that prides itself on entertainment. On Monday, you might go to the showroom for a rip-rousing Broadway revue; on Tuesday, it's jazz in the lounge with some heavyweight talent; on Wednesday, the theme might be entertainment in Jolly Old England; and on Thursday, the dancers outperform any act you've seen in Las Vegas.

But in addition to performers entertaining the passengers, there are a lot of opportunities for the passengers to entertain one another, or just get to know each other and the people who work on the ship. For many, this is the best part of cruising, because it involves real people in real situations.

Courtesy Royal Caribbean Cruise Line

Entertainers on the RCCL ships combine talent, music, lighting, choreography and costume savvy to present a top-notch show.

Meet The Captain

For many passengers, the captain's cocktail party is the height of elegance and the high point of the cruise. The formality of the occasion, not to mention the free cocktails and hors d'oeurves, heightens the experience.

On most ships, there are two parties: one for each dining room seating. If the cocktail party for the second seating is called for 7:30 p.m., a line has already formed by 7:35 p.m. and continues to snake its way down the halllway and up the stairs. The line moves remarkably well, considering each passenger must be introduced to the captain and pose for a photograph. Often, portrait-quality pictures are taken outside the salon where the captain is, both to make use of the waiting time and to capture people on film when they're looking their best.

Just prior to stepping into the lounge, a member of the cruise staff might ask your name and then escort you up to the captain, at which time she will make the formal introduction. You'll smile at the captain and shake hands while you pose together for a photograph. You'll mutter something about what a beautiful ship he runs, and then you'll move on as he greets the next person.

From here, you'll either be escorted to a seat or you'll have to find someplace to park yourself. This is a great chance to meet some total strangers who will turn into friends. Find a group of people with an empty space on their couch and ask to join them. When people are dressed up and in the presence of the royalty of the captain, they tend to remember the manners and graciousness that is often lost in the everyday hustle and bustle of real life.

The captain's cocktail party is a slightly different experience for the solo traveler than for the other passengers. As you prepare to go to the cocktail party,

Courtesy Cunard Line

Passengers dressed in their best get to mingle with the officers.

you might feel a little isolated and unsure of the procedure. The best thing to do is find a public lounge and start talking to the people around you. Chances are, there's some other solo travelers there, too, who are feeling the same way and also want someone to go through the experience with. Or, as you stand in line waiting to meet the captain, make sure to start up a conversation with the people in front and back of you. After you shake hands with the captain, it's a natural transition for these people to ask you to join them, or for you to invite them to sit with you.

Go To The Singles' Party

The first couple of cruises I went on, I avoided the singles' party like a contagious case of the flu. I didn't like being labeled single, and I didn't like the implication that everyone at this party was there to pick up a member of the opposite sex. I soon learned how narrow-minded I was. The purpose of the singles party doesn't have to be to meet other single people; in fact, some cruise lines play down the singles aspect and play up the angle of meeting other solo travelers

When Richard, a production assistant from Los Angeles, went on his first cruise, he was accompanied by his parents. It was a college graduation present from them and it was his first real travel experience. I asked him if he had gone to the singles' party and he acknowledge that he had but only stayed for five minutes. "Why?" I asked. He replied, "I looked in there and didn't see anyone I wanted to dance with, so I split after a few minutes."

Richard never did meet someone to dance with but, more importantly, he lost a major opportunity to find some friends to pal around with. At that same party were a number of guys his own age who rented jeeps and water skis, went parasailing, and eventually hooked up with a great group of other people to party with. Richard went on a lot of bus tours with his parents.

Socialize With Other Past Cruisers

Many passengers swear by a particular cruise line and consistently book their next vacation with the same line, sometimes only days after leaving their last cruise.

Cruise lines rely on this passenger loyalty, and many reward their past cruisers with a special cocktail party, often dubbed the "repeater's party."

When you fill out your cruise documents, there might be a place to check whether you've sailed with the cruise line before. If a repeater's party is part of the on-board activities, you will find an engraved invitation slipped under your door asking you to join the captain and staff.

Repeater's parties are pretty low-key events—it's just a bunch of past cruisers who are being treated to an intimate cocktail party. There's a feeling of unity and uniqueness: the party is not listed in the ship's daily program; a sign outside the door indicates the lounge where it's held is closed to the public for a private party; the guests are often given a small token of the cruise line's appreciation, such as an enameled pin with the line's logo; it's easier to get a cocktail and canape than at the captain's party; and the captain might even say a few words to this exclusive group, expressing the cruise line's gratitude.

Repeater's parties are a great way to socialize with new people, since you all have something in common. It's quite natural to turn to the person sipping champagne next to you and inquire, "Which other ships in this line have you sailed on? What was your favorite cruise?"

Participate in Theme Nights

When you get your cruise documents or you read the cruise brochure, you might discover that there are various theme nights. Popular themes include Country & Western, Caribbean, and Fifties nights. Often, the entertainment goes along with the theme, with special bands, dance lessons and contests on the appropriate evenings.

Nobody is required to participate on theme nights, but if you really want to be a part of things, you only need to pack a few accessories to join in. No, you don't have to bring those heavy cowboy boots with you and try and cram in that aging cowboy hat—a checkered shirt and bandana will get the idea across just fine. Any flowered shirt or dress brings the feeling of the Caribbean to the ship, and that charm bracelet you never get a chance to wear is great for Fifties night.

Prepare For The Masquerade

Getting dressed up in masquerade costumes is not everyone's idea of a good time, but it sure is fun to watch. Some people bring elaborate costumes from home, while others take advantage of their spontaneous creativity and instantly fashion a costume.

There are very few rules about what costumes should be composed of, and the cruise director and staff have all sorts of props and supplies that will help you fashion a creative ensemble.

David and Robbie, two Los Angeles caterers, brought their costumes with them from home. It's little wonder that they brought 12 pieces of luggage with them—the hat for Robbie's Napoleon costume took up one piece of luggage, while the hoop and bustle for David's Josephine outfit took up another. They won a prize for "Most Elaborate Costume."

Janet's and Sam's costume took up very little space. They tucked in two large brown plastic garbage bags into their luggage. On the night of the masquerade, they cut out arm and neckholes and slipped the bags over their heads. Nobody could figure out what Janet and Sam were until they saw the signs on their backs: Janet's said "Hershey Bar." Sam's said "Hershey Bar With Nuts." They won a prize for "Most Humorous Costume."

Dinah from New York is an actress, so she felt perfectly natural parading around in her costume. While on shore in Puerto Vallarta, Dinah visited a record shop where she cajoled the salesman to give her a poster of a popular local singer. She affixed the singer's face to her own with a piece of string, stuck some silver earrings in the poster's ears and cut out the eyes and mouth. With a borrowed grass skirt, she hulaed around the dance floor while sticking out her tongue through the self-made mask. She won a prize for "Most Creative Costume."

Of course, you're welcome to be a clown, a tramp or a bunch of grapes. Or you can just sit back and cheer for those people who enjoy getting dressed up for your amusement.

Display Your Talent

After a few nights of glitzy and glittery entertainment, the passenger talent show is like a fragrant ocean breeze, full of warmth and reality. Sure, passenger talent is not the stuff found on "Star Search." Therein lies its charm.

On a recent cruise, the passenger talent show included a concert pianist, a clog dancer, a couple in their seventies playing harmonica duets and a German woman with a very strong accent singing her off-key rendition of "Under The Boardwalk."

If you have any type of talent—from lip synching "Achy Breaky Heart" to the last vestiges of those tap dancing lessons your parents scrimped to give you—give something back and entertain your fellow passengers. If you have no talent, or have no desire to display it, support your fellow passengers and root enthusiastically for those who do.

The ability to enjoy the passenger talent show brings out the best in all of us: It shows that we've matured to the point that we no longer smirk at people who display themselves as less than perfect; it shows a willingness to support another human being in their endeavors in life; it allows us to see beyond the superficiality of a performance and appreciate the person within.

For those who choose to participate, the talent show is an opportunity to break out of our mundane lives, ruled by convention, and share a part of ourselves with a non-judgmental audience. You'll discover you had more friends on board than you thought, as people you've barely met, as well as total strangers, compliment you on your performance. And if you're an audience member, take a moment to throw a kind word someone else's way. It'll make both of you feel good.

See (Or Be) A Man In Lingerie

One of the absolutely hootin'-hollerin'-hysterical good-time events is the Men's Lingerie Contest. Usually, a group of red-blooded All-American males line up on stage in their typical macho attire and then are given twenty minutes or so to change their appearance (with the help of a wife, girlfriend or female passenger).

Men who wouldn't be caught dead wearing a pink shirt at home suddenly show up in bras, slips, bustiers and nighties, often with tissues and balloons stuffed inside to enhance the image.

Men who usually are embarrassed by a smudge of lipstick on their cheek now appear with a full coat of gloss on their mouth, complimented by royal blue eye shadow, blaring rouge and thick mascara.

And men who normally make sure they strut in a studly way will now prance around the stage, hamming it up to the cheers of the audience.

After these men have displayed their feminine assets and womanly charms, the audience will vote by sound of cheers and applause. All the work and potential blackmail threats might yield the winner a bottle of champagne.

Party Out On Deck

A popular tradition on some ships is the Deck Party, held around the pool on a (hopefully) calm and mild night. Even though we might have lain out on deck all day, there's a kind of ethereal romanticism that surrounds a night-time deck party. Special decorations are hung, special lights are strung. A live band plays soft or rousing music, and the chef prepares a beautiful buffet, served out in the open.

Stars shine down as guests move around and mingle. Passengers who normally would have been in bed by 10 p.m. stay up for the deck party. The food tastes better alfresco and the motion of the ship feels gentler, more seductive, as the magic of the night takes over.

Create Your Own Special Events

All cruise ships have their own traditions. The cruise brochure may only hint at these, because each each cruise staff makes the tour memorable for the passengers in their own special way. Once on board the ship, you may find that there is a particular tradition that abounds, whether it's a special show performed by the cruise staff, a unique kind of party hosted on the fourth night, a Karaoke Contest for kids, or a Calypso Dance Contest on a private beach. You also have the opportunity to create your own special traditions. One I particularly enjoy is the "signing of the cork." While not necessarily a "special event" like a Talent Night, it is still something that makes an event (the sharing of a bottle of wine)

Courtesy Windstar Cruises

The lights aboard a Windstar Cruises ship compete with the lights of Monte Carlo.

very special. It's quite simple to initiate cork signing. When you order a bottle of wine that you plan to share with your table mates, ask the wine steward to return the cork to you. Take out a pen and write the date on the end of the cork and pass it around the table to your companions, asking each one to write his or her initials, name or a short message. In years to come, you can fish the cork out of a drawer and relive the happy times of your cruise again and again.

Isn't It Romantic?

*Romance is a love affair
in other than domestic surroundings.*

Sir Walter Raleigh

The starlit sky is broken only by the glow of a full moon. A soft Caribbean breeze wafts through the air, gently rustling your hair and the clothing of the person with whom you're holding hands. No one else is out on deck as you wonder at the wonder of two people from such different parts of the world finding each other—and it doesn't hurt that there's an overwhelming physical attraction, to boot.

Isn't it romantic?

Well, golly gee, yes it is. This is part of the reason why people go on cruises, and the cruise lines know it. They advertise the cruise experience that way because, gosh darn it, cruises *are* romantic. And while the cruise lines don't gear their advertising to solo travelers looking to make a match, matches do occur with predictable regularity.

There's a lot of reasons why romance is rife on cruise ships. You're in a situation where all stress is eliminated. Your biggest decision is not whether to pay the rent or the electric bill but whether to have rack of lamb or lobster. You've got an almost unlimited number of new people to meet and exciting new situations to encounter. Every need is catered to; boredom is not an option. Adrenaline is pumping and pheromones are drifting through the air.

Once you meet someone, you have almost everything in common but no disagreements to divide you. You're literally in the same boat. It doesn't matter whether you're from New Orleans and she's from Seattle. At this moment, right now, you're in the same place at the same time.

Unlike the ups and downs of a regular relationship, a cruise-ship romance that's going well is all up. While a couple at home might argue about one another's spending habits or leaving socks on the floor, people on a cruise ship don't have to deal with that. They can be together when they want to be together and still have the privacy of their own cabins when they choose.

Being on a cruise ship is a great social equalizer. There is no class distinction among passengers—after all, every one has paid his or her own way and, regardless of your cabin accommodation, you all eat in the same dining room, dance to the same music and are treated to the same entertainment. The bus driver and the janitor are equal to the lawyer and the doctor—better, actually, if they are kinder, more generous, have a better sense of humor.

Not surprisingly, there are many more single women than men on cruise ships. On some lines that appeal to a more mature traveler (read: widows and widowers), it's been estimated that single women outnumber single men ten to one.

The fact that single women outnumber men on almost every cruise ship should not be taken as a bad sign for members of either sex. Men: If you are reading this, start planning your next vacation and make sure it's on a ship. If you are friendly and considerate, you will find yourself appreciated and catered to, probably unlike anything you've experienced at home. If you're friendly, considerate and also good-looking, you'll be approaching deification status.

Women should not be disheartened by these statistics, either, because there is one hidden asset that most cruisers forget: For a cruise ship to handle 1,500 people, it takes about 750 people to run the ship. Except for a few female officers, that means there are 750 MEN—officers, bartenders, waiters and other personnel—who might appreciate your company.

There is, of course, some difference of opinion about who makes the best romantic target during your cruise vacation. Purists would argue that such a discussion is meaningless; love occurs when love finds you. Others would argue that love and lust are two different things and knowing the territory allows one to make informed choices.

The Officers

There are a limited number of officers on a ship and they are easily recognized by their white uniforms. The officers are the higher-paid, better-educated, more-respected denizen of the seas. Their job titles include captain, staff captain, chief engineer, radio officer, hotel manager and a variety of other jobs that keep the ship in ship shape.

Different cruise lines have different ways of noting the rank and jobs of their officers but, in general, the more stripes on an officer's shoulder, the higher up the evolutionary chain he is. Also, take a look at the symbols on his epaulets—they are a clue to what his job is. A propeller might indicate an engineer, while sparks might let you know he's a radio officer. I use the word "he" here because, save for a few pursers and other assorted officers, the world of the officer is a man's world.

It's always amazing the way women worship officers at sea. If the same thing were true back home, Ralph Kramden and Ed Norton would have women

Courtesy Cunard Line

Meet an officer and find out how the other half lives.

flocking around them continually. Ralph, as driver of a bus, is really not much different that the revered captain, driver of this boat. And good ol' Ed, as a sewer worker, got down and dirty taking care of things, not unlike an engineer tinkering with a faulty valve.

But there is a difference, isn't there?

First of all, officers have an international aura to them. Most cruise lines feature officers from Italy, Norway, Greece or other exotic countries. Americans don't know how to speak these languages, but these officers converse with us in our language with their cute, little accents. We immediately ascribe some form of intelligence to them because we know they're bilingual.

Second of all, officers are polite and have some sense of sophistication. They may have started as low-life seamen on a cargo ship, but by strength of character, intelligence and determination, they have risen to where they are. They represent the cruise line, so they cannot be crude or inconsiderate in public. They've traveled the world and usually have interesting stories to tell. The senior officers are introduced to hundreds of people at a time each week during the captain's cocktail party, so they are comfortable in social situations.

Third of all, there is an aura of power and authority around officers. They are part of that elite cadre. They run the ship. They sign for their drinks. They nod to one another. They speak their own tongue when they're together. And you want to be a part of it, to experience this society of the sea.

If you want to meet an officer in a social situation, the best way to do it is to find out where the officers hang out and then go there. It's usually a bar or the disco—look for a cloud of white jackets huddled together. It's often easier for a woman to simply approach an officer and ask him to dance than the other way around. Officers do not want to impose themselves on passengers. It would be the height of rudeness to ask a woman to dance, only to find out she's just killing time while her husband is playing craps. If you don't feel comfortable asking an officer to dance (and it can be intimidating breaking into a group of men huddled together), just try making eye contact and being non-threatening. Return to the same place each night. You might find a situation where the officer who strikes your fancy visits the disco alone that night. Or he finally realizes that the man playing craps is not your husband after all. Your best bet is to show up alone, so that adorable purser will not only know you're unattached but won't have to contend with a group of giggling females. Patience helps, but don't waste your entire vacation sitting on a bar stool, waiting, while you could be having fun in a different part of the ship.

Another way to meet the officers is at the captain's cocktail party and the repeaters' party. The captain usually introduces his staff at the party, so you can see what the officers look like and learn what they do. If there's time, the officers mingle and you might be able to ask a charming little question that will make you stick in his mind. At the repeater's party, senior officers often circulate among the passengers and you might have an opportunity for a brief conversation

One ideal opportunity to share time with an officer is if you're lucky enough to have one assigned to your table. On some lines, the officers host a table at each sitting. Unless his job duties interfere with his social duties, you can expect to enjoy this officer's company at dinner up to three times during the week. You can expect the red *and* white wine to be flowing along with the conversation. Everyone at the table is on his or her best behavior and you'll have the chance to ask all the questions about life at sea you've ever been curious about. The depth of your inquiries and the clever phrasing of your questions will root you in the mind of this charming gentleman. The officer, being a gentleman, will answer each of your questions politely, without giving any indication that these are exactly the same mundane questions he gets asked every single week by every single table of people he hosts.

While there is a lot of excitement and fun spending time with an exotic officer from a foreign country, there are problems that can get in the way of your vacation.

After all, this *is* your vacation but it's the officer's job. While you want to party in the disco until four in the morning, your new-found love has been up since 6:30 a.m. and will be up at that time tomorrow, too. You may want to see the show in the main lounge, but he's seen that same show every Tuesday for the past three months. You'd like to go gamble, but he's not even allowed in the casino. You'd like to have someone to explore the different ports with, but officers rarely get any time off. If they do, they grab a quick game of tennis with another officer and have to be back on the ship in a couple of hours.

If you do develop a relationship with an officer and want it to progress further, you have some decisions to make. Officers are the most privileged breed on the ship, so their living quarters are usually, but not always, more comfortable than the passengers and crew. Rules on every ship vary about where officers can and cannot go, but an officer might invite you to his cabin. If this happens, you can be pretty sure he doesn't want to compare the differences in the existential philosophies of John Paul Sartre and Soren Kierkegaard.

On some ships, officers prefer to visit in your cabin. On other ships, officers are not even allowed in your cabin but may invite you to their quarters. There are different reasonings behind this, but try this explanation on for size, rendered to me by a handsome, rule-adhering Norwegian: If an officer goes to a woman's cabin and there is a problem, the woman can say the officer forced his way in there. But if a woman goes to an officer's cabin, she has gone up there of her own free will, and the case for rape is harder to prove. This is an interesting theory, as theories go, but it doesn't account for the fact that a woman still has the right to say no, no matter what cabin she's in.

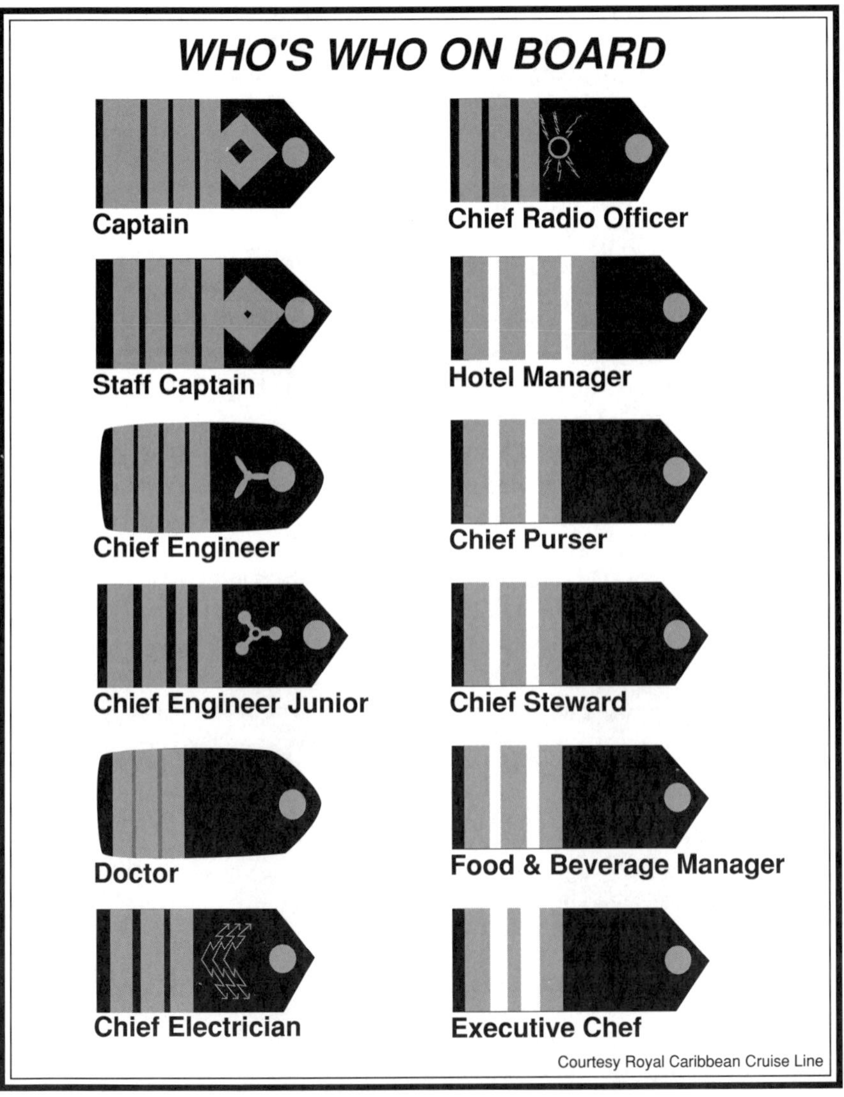

The Crew

Members of the crew are easy to spot: they're hard-working, they seem to be continually jovial and, in their spare time, they're surrounded by an almost totally male world. Crew members have few of the privileges of officers but have a great deal of exposure to passengers if they're waiters, bartenders or in other jobs in the public eye.

Crew members tend to be more flirtatious, warmer, and with a better sense of humor than officers. They're from countries around the world and honestly miss their families and cultures. So many passengers treat crew members like second-class citizens that any kindness shown to them by a female passenger is very much appreciated.

Regulations for crew members are much more strict than for officers. Not only are crew members usually not allowed in the passenger's cabins, passengers are usually not allowed in the crew members' cabins, either. Crew members often sleep two or four to a cabin, so if they do sneak you in, you might be lucky enough to have some quiet privacy, but more likely you'll have a raging party or (I've been told) the makings of an orgy.

Because of these stringent regulations, meeting with a crew member is more difficult than with other people aboard ship. A crew member can't just invite you to the Lido bar for a drink; more likely, he'll invite you up to an isolated deck from which he isn't banned, a bottle of champagne in hand. Once more, you're dealing with a situation where you might want to try the bingo or horse racing but your crew member is not allowed in that area. It takes much longer to finish a bottle of wine than a simple cocktail, so you might find yourself missing out on a lot of activities while you kill that magnum.

Most ships have a "crew bar," so that crew members can let off a little steam. There are women members working on the crew, often as room stewardesses, but like female officers, they are in the minority. The crew bar is usually reserved for crew only, but on some ships the crew are allowed to invite passengers down on, say, a Tuesday night. On some ships, the crew members just take their chances by sneaking passengers down for drinks and dancing.

Like officers, crew members have very little time off, so you won't find a ready companion for exploring the ports. If your favorite bartender or waiter gets any time off, most likely he heads to the nearest beach or bar for a couple of hours and then has to be back on the ship. Some forego time on land and simply catch up on their sleep.

The Staff

The staff aboard a ship are neither fish nor fowl—that is, neither officers nor crew. Their services are usually based on a contract, and their rules and regulations vary depending on their function and the cruise line.

The staff aboard a ship consists not only of the cruise director and his associates, but also the service personnel, such as the people in the beauty salon, the masseuse, the the gift shop people and the casino staff. Include in there the entertainers, and you've got a wide variety of people to meet.

Courtesy Royal Caribbean Cruise Line

At night the entertainers perform for the passengers, but when they're not on stage or performing, these hard-working folks often enjoy socializing with the ship's guests.

It's these folks to whom male passengers tend to become attached, primarily because this is where the very good-looking women often can be found. They're people-oriented service personnel who are attractive, helpful, friendly and outgoing. In addition, they have better schedules than the crew. When the ship is in port, for example, the gift ships and casino are closed.

This tale can be told about any person aboard ship, but it happened to involve a hair stylist. Jason from Atlanta was looking forward to his cruise because he'd been so busy at work he literally didn't have time to get his hair cut. Seizing the opportunity to take advantage of available services, Jason made an appointment at the ship's hair salon. Not only did Jason receive a great haircut, he hit it off with the stylist, too. They spent the rest of the week together in romantic bliss and continued to write to each other after the cruise ended. Jason went ahead and booked a return trip on the same ship. When he got there, his stylist friend informed him that they'd had a great week together before, but she had a boyfriend and couldn't repeat their past experience. It would have made things a lot easier if she had simply told him that when he wrote her of his plans to travel on the ship again, but she didn't. Of course, similar stories have been told by members of both sexes about different personnel on all ships.

The Gentlemen Hosts

On some of the more up-scale cruise lines and those that sponsor longer trips, both of which appeal to a more mature traveler, gentlemen hosts are a part of the amenities.

A gentleman host on Royal Cruise Line finds dancing the night away is one of the best parts of his job.

A gentleman host is a mature man who is traveling on the ship to provide companionship to single women. He is receiving his cruise free or at a great discount in exchange for his services. In essence, he is getting paid for having fun, although the fun is technically work.

Gentlemen hosts dance with unescorted ladies, fill in as a fourth at bridge, accompany women on shore excursions and generally keep the party going. Gentlemen hosts are screened carefully by the cruise lines and provide a little male ambiance in what could be a hen party among older women.

Putting gentlemen hosts in the romance chapter is, in a way, a contradiction because romance between passengers and hosts is not acceptable behavior. If a gentleman host is showing an undue amount of attention to one woman in particular, romancing her off her feet, so to speak, then he's not doing his job. The host's job is to provide attention to and entertainment for *all* the single women on the cruise, not any one lady in particular. Ignoring his job is grounds for terminating the relationship between the host and the cruise line.

If, however, you feel that an occasional dance with a witty urbane gentleman is your idea of romance, then go ahead and have a romantic time. If you feel that a pleasant conversation with someone other than your two-year-old grandson lends a little romance to your life, then more power to you. And if that charming story the gentleman host told at bridge will make your cruise seem more romantic to your friends when you retell later, then by all means do enjoy the romance of your cruise.

Besides, who's to say what kind of friendship or relationship will develop once you're both off the ship and back at home?

The Passengers

All in all, most passengers agree that the best person with whom to develop a romantic interest is another passenger. Most likely, you speak the same language and have the same cultural heritage. You're sharing the same cruise experience, so you can discuss the entertainment, the food, the ports and the sights. You can laugh at the cruise staff and critique the people you've met in common.

You can go to the same places together—gambling, the shows, shore excursions. You can visit the different lounges, loll by the pool, relax in the hot tub, stroll around the deck.

Courtesy Cunard Line

Passengers find they share many of the same experiences aboard the *Cunard Countess.*

You don't have to worry about any rules and regulations. If one of you has a single room, you're all set to spend quality time together. You can call each other whenever you want and drop silly little notes under each other's doors. You can have public displays of affection and not have to worry if someone is going to write you up or dress you down.

You can establish a whirlwind romance with exciting dates that would cost a fortune on land but are a mere pittance on the ship—because almost everything has been pre-paid in the price of the cruise. You can have a romantic dinner of caviar and lobster and not even pull out your wallet. You can see musical extravaganzas and truly funny comedians without shelling out for the tickets, and you can dance till dawn without a snooty doorman commenting on your attire and charging you an arm and a leg to get in.

After you disembark the ship, there's the potential of continuing your relationship. You may be from different parts of the country, or even different countries, but people have been known to relocate for love. If one of you has the type of job where location is unimportant (in the health-care field, for example, where jobs are plentiful around the country), you might be able to forge a new life together.

Advice Straight From The Hip (And Other Parts Of The Anatomy)

All in all, the opportunity for romance and excitement exists on any vacation, if you seek it out or let it find you. It doesn't hurt to enter into a romantic liaison with your eyes just a little bit open—in fact, it will probably hurt less in the long run if you do. While the purpose here is not to lecture like a mother, a little knowledge passed on from previous travelers might help make the romantic experience even more enjoyable.

⚓ Avoid romantic entanglements with other passengers on the first night.

During the first day or two, passengers are just starting to meet one another and get accustomed to the ship. If you become involved with someone on the first night and are seen dancing and exchanging intimate gestures on every deck, people will assume you're traveling together, perhaps on your honeymoon, and will leave you alone.

⚓ Avoid romantic entanglements with officers and crew on the first night.

There is a very well-developed sense of propriety and ownership among the crew and officers aboard a ship. If you are seen as involved with an officer, or the property of an officer, you will probably be left alone the rest of the trip. This is a bit less so among crew members, since there are so very many crew members and they can't keep track of each other's conquests all the time, but be careful of any involvement too early.

⚓ Avoid romantic entanglements with your dining room waiter (and even your busboy or cabin steward).

The dining room is an ideal time for your waiter to flirt with you and show you extra attention. It's probably one of the only places where he has contact with the female passengers and is the ideal opportunity for him to set up a date for later, to share a bottle of wine and a little conversation. The same goes, to some extent, for your busboy and, in the cabin areas, for your steward.

Consider the negatives carefully before becoming entangled. If your flirtation continues, it could get in the way of your waiter's job, affecting the service he gives to the other passengers, thus affecting his rating and his tips and, in effect, jeopardizing his job. While this is not necessarily your concern, consider another scenario: After one night of wining and romance, you find your interests lie elsewhere. You now have to face your broken-hearted paramour three times a day, and you, with the superior passenger status, must give your food order to this poor guy while he's in a subservient position. And then, at the end of the cruise, you have to tip him, too.

⚓ Be selective with whom you get involved.

The smaller the ship, the more important the above rule is. If you establish a romantic relationship with someone aboard ship and decide you want to move away from it, you'll spend a lot of time dissolving the ties. You'll might attempt to elude the other person (staying out of your room to avoid phone calls and staying away from public rooms to avoid confrontation), hoping the ties will lessen and the other person will find a new interest. Or you might have a heart-to-heart with the other person and once again spend energy avoiding one another if the ending is acrimonious.

⚓ Always use protection.

If you decide the romance should progress to an intimate level, use of a condom is the only logical choice. A week ago, you didn't even know the person you're about to sleep with *existed*. That also means you have no idea who or how many her or his sexual partners were in the last week. You may have been working 51 weeks out of the year and this is your one week to howl, but how do you know your partner hasn't been howling every night of the year already? Even if the threat of AIDS weren't so real, there are plenty of other insidious diseases that would be all too happy to find a new host. And we haven't even gotten into the ramifications of pregnancy and the whole menu of sexually transmitted diseases. Of course, it's your life...literally.

⚓ Don't even bother asking about marital status.

If you ask your romantic partner about his marital status during an intimate situation and he admits he's married, what type of person does that make him? And if you ignore his answer, what type of person does that make you? And if you ask him about his marital status and he lies and says he's not married, would you know the difference anyway?

⚓ Be considerate of your roommate.

If you're looking for a place to be alone with your new love, you'll end up in one of your two cabins. If you've got the cabin to yourself, then there's no problem. But if you've booked a guaranteed share, there's a big problem. True, the cabin is half yours but that's no excuse for being inconsiderate and ignoring the fact that the cabin is also half your roommate's, too.

The first thing you should do is work out some kind of signal that lets your roommate know you'd like some uninterrupted time in the cabin. Some people swear by a tie over the outer doorknob, but cruise ships are often pretty casual and there might not be a tie handy. Actually, a sock on the doorknob might present the same problem. Whatever you work out, you want to avoid someone walking in on you at the wrong moment.

Once you've established a signal, you should also be considerate of how long you banish your roommate from the cabin. A good roommate might be willing to disappear for an hour or so, but it's not fair to ask him to wander around on the deck until 3 a.m. It's also unreasonable to expect your roommate to find someplace else to bed down so you can wake up the next morning with your new love.

⚓ Don't expect eternal love.

I don't want to sound cynical, but if you want to have a good time on your cruise, take it for what it's worth at the moment and worry about the future later. Promises of undying love and devotion seem a lot harder to live by when you're separated by 2,000 miles, a couple of weeks of reality, and the demands of your daily life.

⚓ Don't plan on a future with a man (or woman) of the sea.

Once your cruise ends, you and your beau might promise to keep in touch, take another cruise together or visit each other when he's in a port near where you live. But the sea has a way of taking its toll: ships change itineraries, crew members get transferred, some people leave the cruise-ship life. An attempt at writing might last awhile, but a whole new slew of passengers get on the ship each week and, while the cruise might have been a high point in your year, it's just another Cruise Number 4217 to a crew member when enough time passes.

⚓ Don't equate the success of your cruise with the success of your sex life.

If you spend your entire cruise chasing after likely sexual partners, you'll miss out on the real romance and adventure of cruising—discovering new friends of all ages who, coincidentally, might also be potential sexual partners. You'll also be missing out on activities and events that shape the total cruise experience if all you want to do is bring back tales of sexual conquests. Worse yet, if you don't have a satisfying sexual experience, you might consider your week to be a waste of time and money. After all, you could have stayed home and not gotten laid, either.

⚓ Be wary of gold diggers.

OK, so this is a long shot, but it does happen. Some people aboard ships, even other passengers, have been known to take advantage of lonely passengers. Let me relate the story of poor Cathy, a young widow ripe for the plucking.

I wouldn't be telling this sad story and exposing Cathy to all of you rumor-hungry readers, except Cathy herself chose to go on *"Hard Copy"* and expose herself, so I'm only repeating her story.

It seems poor Cathy was widowed at the age of 38 and, after seeing her husband through a terminal illness, took a cruise with her mother to recover. The first night, she met a dashing officer who swept her off her feet. They fell madly in love and made plans to spend the rest of their lives together in romantic Norway. Her big mistake was disclosing her husband's life insurance settlement; her bigger mistake was writing check after check to her lover. Bottom line: The love of her life dumped her, scurried off to hide it out in Norway, and Cathy lost her faith and trust in men and love, not to mention a cool $77,000.

I did hear through the rumor mill that the dashing officer died recently of a heart attack. Cathy never did get her money back, but I guess there was some sort of justice administered.

Take A Tip From Me

Gratitude is the most exquisite form of courtesy.

Jacques Maritain

Have you ever tried to order a beer from a bartender who felt it more important to rub that last spot of dirt off a glass than to acknowledge your order?

Getting that beer becomes a game—the more you try to catch his attention, the more important shining that glass becomes. First you try catching his eye, but his eyes are cast upon that all-important glass. Then you try a non-threatening verbal signal: "Excuse me," you say. At that point, washing the rest of the glasses becomes his most important mission in life.

"I'll be with you in a minute," he deigns to say. Despite the fact that there is no one else waiting to be served, he absolutely MUST wash those two other glasses before drawing you your drink.

After you hand him a $5 bill, you get $1.35 back. You want to leave him no tip at all, but are overcome by guilt. You feel funny about leaving the 35 cents change, so you drop him the dollar instead. In the end, you've paid nearly $5 for a beer that you had to cajole. Hey! Who's the customer here?

Imagine that scenario, live it now, and forget it ever happened, because it will *never* happen on board a ship. If it does, it will not go uncorrected for long.

The point of this whole story is that you'll get terrific service despite the fact that your tip is a known quantity when you ask for service. True, a 15 percent gratuity is usually added to most bar bills, but this doesn't slow down the service; instead, it makes the bartenders and bar waiters hustle more, so they can increase the total bill and thus add up their total tip.

It's hard to tell who works hardest aboard ships—it seems that all the members of the staff are always working, always working hard and always doing it with smiles on their faces.

While you've had a week of relaxing and pampering, the crew has gone about its business to serve your every need in the most congenial way possible. At the end of your cruise, it's up to you to show your appreciation in the form of a monetary gesture.

Unless your gratuity is included in the price of your cruise, or the cruise information specifically states in advance that gratuities are not accepted, you'll have the opportunity to tip the personnel on your last night on board.

In general, cruise ship crews rely almost exclusively on tips. They might receive a small salary, perhaps $50 a month plus room and board, but the money to feed their families in their various foreign countries comes directly from you.

The unfortunate thing about tipping at the end of the cruise is that many people feel like they're tapped out financially after a week of paying for shore excursions, souvenirs in port, photos aboard ship, losses in the casino, and that rapidly mounting bar bill. Some people figure they're getting off the ship the next day, so it doesn't matter what they tip. Some people convince themselves that, actually, the service wasn't that great, so they don't have to tip much. These are excuses, not reasons, to penalize the people who have served you all week. One of the best ways to avoid this is to take $100, set it aside, and consider it untouchable until tipping time comes. The fact that people feel financially bereft at the end of the cruise may even be the reason some cruise lines allow passengers to cash personal checks of up to $250. It may also be the reason some cruise lines are now simply adding the gratuity into the cruise tariff.

Each cruise line will give you guidelines about tipping, printed in the daily program, left on a card in your room, or imparted during a final lecture. When in doubt, the cruise director and his staff will be happy to confirm what the appropriate tip is. In general, tipping is almost always done on the last night before disembaration. Keep in mind that if there is a problem, such as a broken light in your room or an overdone steak at dinner, the personnel will be happy to make things right. It's not fair to the crew if you live with the problem, never tell anyone about it, and then penalize the personnel with a lower tip because you were unhappy or inconvenienced. If the cruise line personnel are not aware of the problem, they can't make it right—and they do want to make it right for you.

Your Cabin Steward

You might have spent the whole week and never seen your cabin steward since the first night he introduced himself. If that is the case, your steward was doing his job to perfection. Your cabin steward knows your schedule, knows what dining room seating you're at, and knows what your particular preferences are, such as extra towels or a bucket of fresh ice every evening before dinner. Like Santa Claus, he knows when you've been sleeping, he knows when you're awake, he knows when you've been good or bad...and he never makes a comment or passes judgment.

Cabin stewards work long, hard hours. They're up very early in the mornings, sometimes from 5:30 a.m. on, so they can serve cabin-service continental breakfast. They might get a slight break in the afternoon to rest up, but then they're back on the job and working until 10 p.m. or later. Your room will be vacuumed perhaps twice a day, your linen will be changed daily and your bed made each morning and again in the afternoon if you've taken a nap. Your cabin steward might even have a sense of humor, folding your discarded clothes in the shape of a turtle or a frog.

For all of this, you pay a very small amount, usually calculated on a per-day basis. The recommended guideline for tipping your cabin steward is usually $3 per day, or $21 on a seven-day cruise. Of course, you're more than welcome to tip more. If you are sailing on a guaranteed-share basis, your cabin steward has to keep track of *two* schedules and *two* preferences, so a higher tip is appropriate and appreciated. Similarly, you might have the cabin all to yourself and the steward will only be receiving a tip from one person, instead of two people. While it's not necessary to tip for two, a slightly more generous tip again is appropriate and appreciated.

On the last night, perhaps while you're packing, your cabin steward might stop in to say good-bye. This is a perfect time to hand him his envelope and thank him. If you don't see him face-to-face, you can leave the envelope in your cabin with his name printed on the front.

Your Waiter And Busboy

Your dining room waiter and busboy work in partnership to make your meals a delicious and enjoyable experience. While they don't cook the food, they make sure it's cooked the way you like it. If a dish is served to you that is not prepared the way you like it or is not what you anticipated, your waiter will be more than happy to serve you something else. Like your room steward, your waiter wants you to enjoy your experience and it's unfair for you to give him a lower tip if you were unhappy with the food.

In most cases, your waiter is responsible for taking your order, serving the food and making the dining experience flow smoothly. The busboy is responsible for keeping your water glasses and coffee cups full and assisting the waiter, serving the vegetables or salad dressings while your waiter is serving the dishes. The busboy also clears the dishes at the end of a course.

The recommended tip on most cruise lines is $3 a day for your waiter and $1.50 a day to the busboy. Once again, this is a recommended minimum, and you're free to tip more if the service has been exceptional. Many waiters started as busboys and worked their way up as their serving skills and language abilities improved. Waiters try hard to keep a table happy, telling jokes or doing magic tricks in the process. Waiters often have four or more tables to take care of during any one sitting, but when you have a really good waiter, he makes you feel like yours is the only one whose needs he's serving. If you've gotten such a professional, you should thank him monetarily.

At the end of your last dinner, your waiter and busboy should drop by your table to thank you. You'll thank them back by handing them their envelopes. There's no sly "slip-the-money-into-the-palm-during-a-handshake" here. Simply hand over your envelope and express your gratitude.

Even through you're going to be off the ship the next day and never see these people again, it's unfair to stint on the tip. Waiters do know who gave what, and

Courtesy Costa Cruise Lines

Attentive service should always be rewarded.

not only do they rely on the money, they take their tips seriously as an indication of the quality of their service.

Here's an anecdote that will illustrate the point: On the morning of disembarkation, I was the only one who made it to breakfast. My waiter, Roberto, took my order and asked, "Didn't you like my service this week?"

It felt like my heart had stopped when I thought I might have mixed up the envelopes for the waiter and the bus boy, and he thought I had stiffed him on the tip. I replied, "I thought the service was excellent. Did I give you the wrong envelope with my tip?"

He said, "No, your tip was very nice and that lady across from you gave me $35, but that couple on the end only gave me $20 for both of them and the couple over there gave me $32. If they didn't like something, I would have changed it but they never said anything."

Roberto knew the passengers had been informed what a tip should be ("They know it's $21 a week for the tip," he said, "and that's $42 a couple, not $21 a couple!") and he couldn't figure out if those people were just cheap or if they were unhappy with him. Either way, he felt he had worked hard and was dealt with unfairly. I suppose he must have felt that he could confide in me, but out of his sense of professionalism, he would never have said anything to the two couples (nor did he or I have the chance).

Your Head Waiter And Maitre D'

A tip to your head waiter or maitre d' is not necessary, but if there has been some special service performed, a tip is a gracious way to extend your thanks. Perhaps there was a birthday at your table and you took it upon yourself to order a cake. The head waiter rounded up the busboys and they all sang "Happy Birthday." Or you might have been assigned a table or setting that you weren't happy with and the maitre d' changed the arrangements to your satisfaction. In these cases, a tip is not obligatory but a mere $5 or $10 is appreciated. More and more these days, cruise lines are recommending a tip to your head water and maitre d' as standard procedure. If even one out of 10 people on a megacruise ship tipped as suggested, your friendly head waiter or maitre d' would pick up an extra $1,000 a week. If *everyone* tipped $5, these gents could garner up to $13,000 a *week*, in addition to their salaries. Isn't that a lot of money to ensure that the waiters don't drop the Baked Alaska?

Your Wine Steward

When you want to order wine at the table, your wine steward will advise you on a reasonable selection, deliver the bottle to your table, uncork it and serve it. There is already a 15 percent tip added to the bill, so tipping is not necessary. If you order wine every night and your wine steward makes sure the glasses are continually filled, a gratuity of $5 or more is a welcome gift for a hard-working person.

Your Bar Staff

Like the wine steward, the bartenders and bar waiters automatically receive a 15 percent tip on everything you order. Some bar staff personnel are so good that they recollect your name, greet you personally when you sit down, and will even remember that you like a Diet Coke when you're by the pool but a particular cognac when you stop in after dinner. If you want to thank them, you can either add a tip to any bar charge when you sign for it, or you can convey your thanks monetarily near the end of the cruise. There is no standardized amount here; some people add a couple of bucks to their bar tab while others hand over a seemingly exorbitant $20 to their favorite waiter or bartender.

Your Room Service Staff

There's a good chance you may never order room service or any amenities, and so you'll never have to tip anyone. In general, though, you should express your thanks at the time service is delivered. If you order a sandwich to your room, if you have your clothes cleaned and delivered, if a steward drops off your duty-free purchases to your cabin, you should tip at the time service is rendered. The room service staff is not your regular room steward, so a couple of dollars for services rendered is expected and appreciated.

Your Baggage Handlers

If you purchased an all-inclusive package, with air fare and passage, your baggage will be delivered straight from the airport to your room. If you take your own transportation to the dock, you'll drop off your bags with a baggage handler and they will be delivered to your cabin later. When you hand your bags to the handler on the dock, you should also hand over a tip. A gratuity of $1 per bag is sufficient.

Similarly, when you disembark, you may have to claim your luggage on the pier and make sure it gets to the right truck for transportation to the airport. If you don't drag your bags to the truck yourself, a baggage handler will assist you and, again, a tip is expected.

Your Cruise Personnel

There are some personnel on board the ship who are neither officers or crew. This includes the masseuse and the people who work in the salon. Just like back on shore, if you get a massage, manicure or hair styling, you should tip at the time service is rendered.

You may have enjoyed your cruise immensely, and it may have been because of the wonderful personality, service and entertainment of the cruise director and his or her staff. The cruise staff are professional people and should not be tipped. If you really enjoyed your cruise, the best thing you can do is drop a note to the corporate offices of the cruise line and gush about the wonderful people who made your cruise memorable (and do remember to name names!)

Don't embarrass yourself by tipping an officer. He will politely decline—or at least he should.

Turning Lemons Into Lemon Drops

There is no education like adversity.

Benjamin Disraeli

Good-humor makes all things tolerable.

Henry Ward Beecher

It was Eleanor Roosevelt who said, "No one can make you feel inferior without your consent." If she were traveling on a cruise vacation, she might have said, "You can't have a bad cruise trip unless you yourself allow it."

The reality of a cruise trip might not meet up with the fantasy you envisioned, but there's still plenty of room to have a wonderful vacation, if you take minor set-backs in stride. As with anything in life, you might find a few snags that make the situation less than ideal. Taking quick action to right the problem, putting the problem in perspective, or turning a negative into a positive are the solutions that will get you back on an even keel.

Interestingly enough, most complaints and problems you might encounter concerning cruise ships are not the fault of the cruise line but of the passenger or the passenger's perceptions. Flexibility and a sense of humor go a long way in alleviating problems.

Following are some common cruise complaints or glitches and ways to deal with them:

Lost Luggage

Lost luggage aboard a ship is an extremely rare instance, but it has been known to happen. Most likely, your luggage is not lost but merely misplaced. When you consider how many pieces of luggage must be loaded onto a ship and delivered to cabins in such a short period of time, it's a wonder you wind up with the right suitcase at all.

When you receive your documents, you'll also receive baggage tags. You'll be asked to write your cabin number on your baggage tags. If you do not do this, or do not do this legibly, you stand a chance of your luggage not arriving at your cabin at the appropriate time. If you're assigned to ALOHA 33 and think you write A 33, but your writing is so bad it looks more like R 88 (on the RIVIERA deck), you can be pretty sure that your luggage will be outside someone else's door.

It's always possible, of course, that you forgot to affix the baggage tags or that they became detached from your luggage. People who unload and deliver baggage do this every week and are real professionals at what they do. If there's a problem, chances are it's the fault of the passenger, not the cruise line.

If your luggage does not arrive at your cabin within a few hours of the ship's sailing, contact the purser's office and you should have your belongings shortly.

More likely, your luggage will not be lost by the ship but by the airline. When you get off the airplane and are greeted by a ship's representative, you'll probably be escorted to the baggage claim area to identify your luggage. From there, it will be whisked off to the ship and you won't see it again until you're in your cabin.

If you can't locate your luggage in the baggage claim area, you know immediately you've got a problem. Luckily, you have a ship's representative to help you solve this problem.

Wrong Dining Room Seating

You requested second seating in the dining room and when you got your documents, you are confirmed for first seating and wait-listed on second seating. All the way to the ship you envision getting up each morning, bleary-eyed, so you can make it to the 7:30 a.m. breakfast. Frantic calls to the travel agent don't help, and you spend the weeks leading up to your cruise tense and apprehensive.

Would it be an overstatement to tell you to lighten up? In many cases, by the time you get to the ship, your dining room card with the proper seating will be waiting for you in your cabin, and you'll have spent a couple of sleepless nights for nothing.

If, after arriving in your cabin, you still find yourself assigned to an undesirable dining room seating, the maitre d' will be waiting in a lounge or public area to assist you in making new arrangements. When you arrive, you'll see that you're not alone, as the line often snakes around corners. Some of those people in line will be trying to latch onto the seating you're trying to dump.

More than anyone else, the solo traveler might have an advantage in changing dining room seatings. The maitre d' only has to find a table with an odd number of people already seated, and you're set. It's easier to relocate one person than it is to find seating for two. Quite often, I've found myself at a table hosted by an officer, because he made the odd number, and I once again made it even.

If you're looking to change seatings and you're flexible about accepting either a smoking or non-smoking table, your odds at success are much better.

If the maitre d' says he can't help you in changing your table arrangements, don't give up hope. You can try showing up for the appropriate seating and seek out the maitre d'. He will be able to scan the room for any unoccupied seats and may be able to seat you.

Of course, your first request for a seating change is an appropriate time to show your earnestness and appreciation in the form of a gratuity. Keep in mind, though, that a gratuity is not mandatory and you could easily get your desired arrangements without greasing a palm. At the end of the cruise, if you want to remember the maitre d's assistance, it would be appreciated.

Unsatisfactory Table Companions

You come down to dinner on the first night of your trip, and find your table companions are the rudest, crudest, most obnoxious people on the face of the earth. You can't wait until the dinner is over and you can escape.

OR...

You come down to dinner on the first night of your trip, and find your table companions are the quietest, meekest, dullest people on the face of the earth. You can't wait until the dinner is over and you can escape.

What do you do?

Don't do a thing, at least not yet. Consider the fact that everyone at the table, yourself in particular, might be a little over-excited or a little tired this first night. Friendships usually grow stronger as the cruise continues, so don't dismiss the table before you've given it a chance.

There are, however, some circumstances that might warrant an immediate change (and that doesn't mean getting up from the table after five minutes and searching out the maitre d'.).

You might, for example, anticipate a lively table for eight, only to discover it's a husband and wife with their five children (and, of course, you). Surrounded on one side by a tiny waif who needs his meat cut, and a brat on the other who keeps kicking your chair, while all the time trying to have conversation over the baby's crying, might not be your idea of an ideal dinner.

Or, perhaps, you asked for a large table and find yourself seated at a table for four...just a bickering, retired couple, an empty chair, and you. Down the way, you see a seat at a large round table and, while you can't hear what's being said, you see heads close together in conversation and you can sense the laughter among the group. You gaze longingly, feeling like the little match girl staring through the bakery window.

If this is the case, you should discretely see the maitre d' first thing after dinner, or first thing in the morning, whichever is recommended. In almost all cases, a new table assignment will be made available for you.

Bad Food

Since cruises are noted for their variety, quality and quantity of food, it's hard to imagine an entire cruise of bad food. Is it that you were expecting traditional American cuisine and this food is foreign to your palate? Do you like simpler fare and are unhappy with the richness of the food? Are you a plain eater and don't like trying new things?

If your complaint with the food is that you want only simple foods, I'm sure you can work something out with your waiter and maitre d' that will satisfy your appetite. Most cruise lines are even able to accommodate special diets when notified in advance, and many offer low-fat, health-conscious selections.

If you have special meal requirements, it's up to you to have your travel agent notify the cruise line. Even so, there must be something, either room service sandwiches or healthful salads, that you can eat.

It's hard to believe that any ship would serve "bad" food—ships are regularly inspected to ensure that all sanitation and quality standards are met.

And, by the way, if you don't like the food, keep your mouth shut both at the table and around the other passengers. Nobody likes to listen to a complainer, especially when they're enjoying the meal.

Wining At The Table

No, I don't mean whining; I mean the delicate questions of buying and sharing wine at dinner.

As a solo traveler, you'll most often be placed at a large table filled with two, three or four couples. Some people like wine with their dinner, some people do not. Some people like to share wine with the folks next to them, some do not. Some people like to buy wine for the whole table, some like to keep it only for themselves.

The delicacy of wining at the table usually stems from the fact that you're traveling alone and most other people are couples. When you buy a couple of bottles of wine for the table, you're one person paying for two people in marital units.

Surprisingly, many people are aware and sensitive to this fact. Here's the ideal way it has worked out in the past. On Saturday night, the people at the table (three couples and you) meet and greet one other, discovering you all enjoy wine with your meal. The couple from Montreal buys two bottles of the Pouilly-Fuisse to share with everyone. On Sunday, the couple from El Paso selects two bottles of the Burgundy, while the couple from Clearwater chooses a Chardonnay for Monday night's dinner. By Tuesday, it's your turn and you opt for the Gamay Beaujolais. By Wednesday, it's the Montreal folks' turn again, and the cycle is repeated. The reason this works out so well is that each two-person unit has bought wine exactly twice, and you've treated the table to wine once.

Of course, it doesn't always work out so handily. You might end up sharing wine with only one other couple, for example. If they have any sense of fair play, they will make the wine selection twice as often as you.

You may also find out that each couple wants their own wine. You may either ask a bar waiter for an individual glass of wine, or you may order a bottle from the wine steward. Many ships will recork your bottle and return the unfinished portion to you the next night.

Often, people enjoying their wine will ask you if you would like to share some. This is a very kind gesture and you should feel free to accept. If, however, you accept on a regular basis, etiquette demands that you reciprocate by hosting a bottle.

Bad Roommate

When there's a "bad roommate" situation, often the question is which of the two people in the cabin is the "bad roommate." When you agree to a guaranteed-share arrangement, you're doing so because you want to save a single-supplement charge. You pays your money and you takes your chances.

No one said your roommate had to be your best friend, just someone to share a cabin with. If, however, you simply cannot get along with a roommate—he's having parties in the room until four in the morning or she keeps you locked out of the room while she has orgies until all hours—you might have to try and get another cabin.

If you find your situation totally intolerable, you can go to the purser's office and see what your options are, but don't expect the cruise line to be sympathetic to your tale of woe. You paid for half of a cabin and, just because you don't like your roommate, the cruise line is not going to move you into another space. If you want a cabin by yourself at this point, you'll probably have to pay extra. In some cases, there won't be a cabin available if the ship is full.

If you know you're very set in your ways, a light sleeper or very particular about certain habits or with whom you associate, you shouldn't choose a guaranteed share. Continued complaints from dissatisfied roommates will only make the cruise lines reevaluate their policies and ruin things for those who find a guaranteed share the only affordable alternative.

Bad Cabin

You might have thought you were really smart when you booked the very cheapest, bottom-level inside cabin. Then you got on the ship and were unhappy with your accommodations. When you come right down to it, who's fault is that?

When you book a specific cabin, you'll know in advance what the cabin number is. If it's right under the disco, you should decline that cabin and opt for a higher category level, if you know that you'll be bothered.

If, however, you booked for a cabin to be assigned at the discretion of the cruise line and you feel you've been taken advantage of, a discussion with the hotel manager or purser might be in order. If your complaint is valid, and if there is space available, you might be moved.

A malfunction in your cabin is another reason for dissatisfaction. If your air conditioning doesn't work or the telephone is out of order, there's no need for you to suffer in silence (or bore the pants off of any other passenger who'll listen). If you call and report your complaint, the problem should be fixed within a few hours. If the problem is so horrendous that it can't be solved immediately, the cruise personnel will do everything in their power, including upgrading you to a better cabin, to ensure that your stay is enjoyable.

Bumped From The Cruise

I knew airlines bumped passengers but I never heard of a cruise line doing it...until it happened to me.

Two days before I was to leave, my travel agent called and said the cruise line has inquired whether I would agree to be bumped. I was very hesitant at first, but quickly agreed when the travel agent told me what was offered. If I would take the same cruise one week later, the cruise line would upgrade me nine category levels, to an outside deluxe cabin, *and* would refund half my money.

In addition, it was either luck or a planned assignment that had me placed at a dining-room table of people who had all booked suites, a table that was hosted by the very charming hotel manager, a table that was served by one of the most charming and efficient waiters on the ship (as often is the case at tables hosted by officers).

That cruise turned out to be one of the best, most luxurious and, by far, the most inexpensive cruise I've ever taken.

Bad Weather

Let's face it, bad weather is no fun for anyone, least of all the cruise staff. When the weather is nice during a day at sea, people are jovially sitting around the pool, blithely soaking up the rays and amusing each other. When the weather is bad, the cruise staff has to work doubly hard to keep the passengers amused.

When the weather is good during a port day, passengers sign up for shore excursions, beach parties and barbecues, or wander by themselves around the glorious countryside. When the weather is bad, some people don't even bother getting off the ship, choosing instead to mope around and bemoan the fact that *everything* always happens to them.

Bad weather, dear traveler, is not the fault of the cruise line and it shouldn't cloud your judgment of the ship or the vacation experience. Unlike other vacations, like a week in Tahiti, you can still have a very good time despite the weather. When the weather turns sour, the cruise personnel are even *more* responsive to the needs of the passengers. If you have bad weather during a day at sea, there'll be a host of things to do indoors. Sure, you won't be getting any sun but you'll have the opportunity to participate in activities you might otherwise have ignored. Bad weather during a shore day is not always convenient but need not stop you. You can still see the banana plantation in Costa Rica during a rainstorm, and you'll probably be seeing it the way the natives do during most of the year. And when you return from your banana excursion, you'll be returning to a comfortable ship, a hot shower, a fluffy towel and a soothing cup of tea, which is more than can be said for most of those banana farmers.

Missed Port

If your ship has to miss a scheduled port, there's probably a good reason for it. When Hurricane Andrew struck, many ships at sea altered their course to avoid the path of the storm. Weather can affect the docking procedure too; if a captain feels it's unsafe to dock the ship because of turbulent water or other reasons, you can say goodbye to that port. Sometimes, the reason for skipping a port has to do with political turmoil—civil disturbance makes it unsafe to unload passengers in the port city.

Not being able to spend time in a port you've looked forward to can be disappointing, but the cruise line is only looking out for the safety and comfort of its passengers. Take this gesture in the spirit in which it was intended, and enjoy the additional time at sea.

Bad Shore Excursion

Was it really a bad shore excursion, or did you just not have a good time? The ships do a pretty good job of letting you know what's included in a shore excursion and what you should expect. If you sign up for a shore excursion and they deliver what they described, you have little to complain about. If you paid for a barbecue on the beach in Costa Rica and it rained on your parade but you still had a nice lunch, you can't blame the cruise line for the weather. If you went on a city tour but found the sights less than inspiring, is it the fault of the cruise line, or were you just not into the experience on the four hours of sleep you got the night before?

On the other hand, hitches in shore excursions do happen, and the cruise line wants you to be happy. If your bus breaks down in the middle of your trip and you miss half of the tour of the countryside, you have a right to complain. If the air conditioning is malfunctioning and you sweltered for four hours, you should inform the tour director back on the ship. These occurrences are rare but do occasionally happen. The tour director wants to know the level of satisfaction of the various excursions, so informing him or her of any problems in a polite, rational way will help improve the situation in the future. If you experienced a problem that truly interfered with the enjoyment of the excursion, you might be due a partial or total refund of the price you paid.

Seasickness

As ships get bigger and bigger and stabilizing equipment gets more and more sophisticated, seasickness affects fewer people. If you even have an inkling that this might be a cause of concern, there are things you can do to protect yourself *before* this becomes a problem.

Many doctors recommend a patch worn behind the ear which slowly releases the medicine Scopolomine over a three-day period. The patch should be affixed a couple of hours before you get on the ship, and is changed every three days so that the flow of the medicine is never interrupted. This is a prescription drug and the decision as to whether to use the patch is one you and your doctor should make.

Some people swear by cotton wrist bands with built in plastic balls. The wrist bands work on the principle of acupressure—the plastic balls push against the pressure points in the wrist, preventing seasickness. These wrist bands are available through mail-order catalogues or drug stores, and are often sold in the ship's gift stores.

There are a number of over-the-counter motion sickness pills, such as Dramamine and Bonine, that are available in drug stores. You can discuss this choice with your pharmacist.

If you experience choppy waters at sea and really can't control the seasickness, a doctor is on-call 24 hours a day to deal with your illness. In most cases, he will recommend an injection. Keep in mind, that a cabin call from the doctor is not like room service; there is a fee involved in a doctor's visit.

So Long!
Farewell!
Goodbye!

There's a kind of release
And a kind of torment
in every goodbye for every man.

C. Day-Lewis

It was the best of times, it was the worst of time. OOPS, sorry... Charles Dickens already said that, and he wasn't talking about the last day of your cruise, either. But if you feel this way as you get ready to leave the ship, you won't be alone.

You've just spent a week or more relaxing, seeing exciting foreign ports, being pampered in your cabin and served gourmet food in the dining room, all the time meeting new friends throughout the ship. As you enjoy your last day, there's a realization that this is all coming to an end and all that's left is the hard work of packing, saying goodbye, heading off home, and getting back to the reality of your mundane life.

The best of times is what you've experienced for the past week. The worst of times is the whole process of ending the cruise and going through disembarkation.

The last night is also the time to say goodbye to your new circle of friends. Chances are, you'll sit around and moan about the fact that the cruise is over so soon. "Where did the time go?" you'll wonder. "Seems like this was more like a weekend cruise than a whole week," you'll muse. And, because this is the last night, you'll probably stay up later than normal, avail yourself of the last chance

Courtesy Crystal Cruises

Passengers relive the last week and look toward the future in the Avenue Saloon on the *Crystal Harmony*.

to win back your money in the casino, and party harder than normal. And, of course, you'll pay for it the next morning when the real work of disembarkation begins.

Although every cruise line handles disembarkation slightly differently, most cruise passengers agree on one point: Disembarkation is an unpleasant and unwieldy procedure. It starts too early, it takes too long, and there's little to look forward to as you realize your vacation is truly over.

There really isn't a lot to say here, except to walk you through what to expect. Like the last day of your cruise, your journey through this part of the book is almost over. But take a few more minutes and tour through this chapter, and you'll know what you'll encounter at the end of your cruise vacation.

Pack For The Last Time

On the last night of the cruise, you'll have to pack your luggage and leave it outside your door so it can be loaded off the ship the next morning.

As if packing weren't bad enough, you have to keep your wits about you to remember to leave out clothing and toiletries for the next day. It's always amusing to see people wearing the same clothes from the night before because they packed everything, and I do mean everything, so efficiently that all they left out were the clothes on their backs.

Take a few minutes to think through your plans for the day of disembarkation. Lay out the clothes you plan to wear off the ship, keeping in mind what will be comfortable for a long airplane flight. Just like packing to take your cruise, talk yourself through the steps of the day to come. In fact, you can pretty much reverse the process of packing for the trip: Everything you needed in your carry-on luggage, such as travel documents, medicines and the like, should go right back in your carry-on.

Once you're packed, you'll say good-bye to your luggage until you claim it for the trip home. You'll be asked to leave it outside your door before a set time of, say, 10 p.m. Pack carefully—once your luggage is gone, it is inaccessible until the next day.

Complete Your Paperwork

Just when you thought you had the hard part behind you, you'll find there's still a bunch of business to transact. You already know about tipping, but the reality hits you when you find a slew of envelopes left in your cabin, waiting to be filled with solid, American currency. A trip to the purser's office earlier in the day to change large bills will make it easier to fill those envelopes with your green expression of thanks. Make sure you write the appropriate name of the recipient on the envelope—a wad of plain white envelopes is not going to help you reward each person, and few of us are astute enough to remember who gets which tip by merely judging the heft of the envelope.

You'll then look over the forms left for you to complete: a customs declaration, an immigration form, and a cruise-evaluation questionnaire.

If you attended the final lecture, completion of these forms should be a breeze. The cruise director will explain how much merchandise you'll be able to bring into the country without paying additional taxes. You'll learn what information to fill in on the various spaces of the immigration form. And you'll be encouraged to give your honest opinion on the evaluation form.

Cruise lines encourage you to fill in the evaluation form by offering prizes to those passengers whose forms are drawn at random. This form may seem insignificant to you, but they are very important to the crew members who have served you.

I'm spending a little time on the evaluation form because so many crew members have told me how they can make or break their future with a cruise line. After you and your fellow passengers fill out the forms, they go to the central office for computer input and analysis. The cruise lines know what the norm is for each category on the cruise evaluation form, and they know how certain events, such as bad weather or technical problems on the ship, can affect the final numbers. But if there is no major problem on your cruise and the analysis shows the service or product was below the norm, steps will be taken, people will be demoted and careers will be altered.

This should give you a feeling of power, but also a feeling of responsibility. Dining room waiters, for example, strive to give good service so they'll be moved to a larger station with more diners at each table. More tables, more diners equals more tips (while demanding more concentration, energy and work from the the waiter, of course). A poor rating from you because your coffee cup wasn't refilled promptly might cause him to be demoted. While I'm not suggesting that you give blanket approval to every category on the evaluation form, consider the fact that what you are rating is not just the cruise experience but the service and attention of a real person.

With that in mind, fill out your form with a good conscience, and enjoy your last night on board, because morning comes way too early.

Handle Disembarkation

Here's an example of disembarkation that should let you know your vacation is over and you're heading back to reality:

On the morning of disembarkation, you'll be awakened as early as 6:30 a.m. by in-cabin announcements. Either on board the ship or at the pier, you will have to go through customs and immigration. You'll have to vacate your cabin as early as possible and wait in one of the public lounges so the stewards can prepare what was once your room for occupancy by a new group of passengers. You might even start to feel discarded, like a broken-down toy that a child no longer wants.

If the cruise line is on the ball, there might be an urn of coffee available but there's no bar service since your charge account has been cancelled. Breakfast in the dining room is available, but it's no longer the happy, chatty occasion of the days before

Once in the public lounge, you'll have to wait until you're called to leave the ship. This is a perfect opportunity to seek out the people you didn't get a chance to find the night before, although actually making contact with those people seems more like a happy coincidence than a plan, similar to running into your neighbor at a major league baseball game.

Getting 1,000, 2,000 or even 3,000 people off a ship in a short period of time is a major feat and a logistical juggling act. It's a delicate ballet that balances the feats of disembarking the passengers, having them find their luggage, getting the luggage and the passengers to the airport and seeing them safely home. That's why people are called to disembark the ship in small groups, either by cabin number or baggage tag color. Left to their own devices, people would probably queue up to get off the ship starting as soon as the ship docks, creating a line that could rival the Great Wall of China.

Get Thee To An Airport

Unless you live in the port in which you've disembarked, the rest of your journey is spent just getting home. When you're off the ship, you'll probably identify your luggage on the pier and head off the airport. You might see a series of buses and trucks with your airline advertised on the outside. Get your luggage, check it in with the representative there, get your luggage loaded on, and go to the airport.

If your flight is late in the day, you might have some decisions to make. You probably got off the ship in the early morning (between 8 a.m. and 9 a.m.) and now have the rest of the day to wait for your flight. Many cruise lines have a deal with a nearby hotel or resort so passengers can relax by the pool if their flight is in the late afternoon or evening. There might be a shore excursion offering a tour of the port or island that you can enjoy during the hours until your flight.

If your cruise line wants to dump you at the airport at 10 a.m. and your flight doesn't leave until 4:30 p.m., consider taking advantage of your free day by arranging your own entertainment. Your luggage may be taken to the airport at 10 a.m. and your ground transfer certificate may only be valid if you go then, but there's nothing stopping you from a little creative self-amusement. Go to the airport along with your luggage, but grab a cab from the airport and head out to relax on the beach, dine at a restaurant or sightsee around the city. Or let your luggage go on without you (if you've already checked it in and gotten your claim ticket) and simply take a cab from the pier so you can go off and seek adventure. Just make sure you get back to the airport in time for your flight home.

Revel In Your Vacation

Once you're on the plane, it's natural to think about all that awaits you on your return. Take a minute to think about this: the mail that's piled up, the magazines you haven't read, the news you haven't heard, the friends you haven't seen, the bed you you're looking forward to sleeping in, the job you can't wait to get back to. But also take a minute to think about this: the places you've been, the meals you've eaten, the people you've met, the sights you've seen, the growth you've experienced.

And then take a minute to start thinking about your next cruise vacation.

PART TWO

The Cruise Lines

Cruise Ships
&
Solo Traveler Policies

Short of collecting and studying every brochure printed by every cruise line, you have at your fingertips all the information you need to help you decide where you want to cruise and what kind of accommodations you want to book.

Reading a chart, however, doesn't give you the flavor and excitement of the ship you've chosen, so consider this a starting point. After you've narrowed down your choices, you should definitely contact a travel agent, request a brochure and discuss your options. Keep in mind that rates, policies and itineraries change, often only days after a brochure is printed. While this information is up to date at the time of this book's publication, there could be substantial changes by the time you even locate your bathing suit.

The charts below are designed to give you a feeling of each cruise line's options and their policies toward the solo traveler. In no way is any of this information to be perceived as an endorsement of any of the cruise lines. The write-ups are based on details provided by the cruise lines, hopefully conveying their sense of enthusiasm and pride.

When you read about a **single supplement**, it is a comparison to what the double-occupancy rate is. Therefore, if the per-person charge is $1,000 a week, and you're expected to pay $1,500 per week, the single supplement is 50 percent more, or 150 percent the double-occupancy rate. Most cruise lines give their single occupancy rates as 125%, 150%, or 175% the double-occupancy rate, as opposed to noting the rate as 25%, 50% or 75% *above* the double-occupancy rate. These charts follow that format.

Guaranteed share always means two to a cabin, unless otherwise noted. Some ships do not advertise a guaranteed share in their brochure, but will accept it if bookings are light for that cruise or that time of year. As cruise policies change, it is always wise to have your travel agent check with the cruise line, even if they don't advertise a guaranteed share.

Some ships have cabins that are designated **single cabins** because they contain only one berth. Sometimes, these cabins are in more costly price categories. Sometimes, these cabins simply cost more that adjacent cabins which, in effect, means that they've added in a single supplement for facilities that other people paying double-occupancy rates get for less. When a ship has a single cabin, I've tried to relate these rates to those of similarly situated and equipped double cabins so you can compare and see if you would prefer booking a lower-priced cabin and paying the single supplement.

Guaranteed singles rate usually means that the solo traveler pays a flat fee and is assigned a cabin at the discretion of the cruise line. Unlike the single supplement, in which you choose a particular category or cabin, a guaranteed singles rate leaves the mystery of your accommodations to the date of embarkation. On some ships, however, a guaranteed single rate is available on specific double-occupancy cabins, pending confirmation by the cruise line.

Some ships travel the same itinerary all year round. Some split their time between two routes, with repositioning routes in between. Some never make the same route twice in a row. Check with your travel agent about the exact route you're interested in at the time you want to travel. The ports of embarkation and ports of call listed are only representative of the ships' itineraries and do not include every route. Routes listed are meant to give you an idea of the types of itineraries provided by the cruise lines and should not be perceived as future cruise options. Rather, the itineraries should give you an idea of whether a cruise line currently limits itself to one part of the world or chooses a more unstructured approach.

Now, think of the rest of this book as your own personal candy store, and have fun imagining yourself aboard each ship and at each port.

Alaska Marine Highway

P.O. Box R
Juneau, Alaska 99811
(800) 423-0568

The Alaska Marine Highway began in 1960 with a single vessel operating between Haines and Juneau. By 1993, the system included eight ships, six providing ferry service to the Inside Passage, and two ferryliners serving Prince William Sound and southwestern Alaska.

Five of the eight vessels have staterooms, and all carry vehicles, offer food and beverage service, and provide some of the most magnificent scenery available.

The marine system meets the highway at five locations: Bellingham, Washington; Prince Rupert, British Columbia.; and Hyder, Haines and Skagway, Alaska. Travelers can explore Alaska by car, then join up with the marine system. Travelers are allowed—even encouraged—to get off the ferry, plan their own itineraries, see the areas on their own and join up with the ferry later, as long as they've made reservations in advance.

The vessels range in size from the 193-foot *Bartlett* to the 418-foot *Columbia*. Other ships are the *Aurora, Le Conte, Malaspina, Matanuska, Taku* and *Tustumena*. For those traveling without having booked a stateroom, public areas such as solaria, rest areas and observation decks are available. There are also a limited number of recliner chairs and space to roll out sleeping bags, while some vessels make pillows and blankets available.

There are no single cabins aboard the ships, but many trips are merely for transportation and don't require sleeping. For example, the trip from Ketchikan to Wrangell clocks in at under six hours, while Hyder to Ketchikan is less than 10 hours.

American Canadian
Caribbean Line, Inc.

Post Office Box 368
Warren, RI
(800) 556-7450

Innovative vessels and innovative policies are two of the hallmarks of American Canadian Caribbean Line. The line was founded by Captain Luther Blount, a New England shipbuilder. Captain Blount incorporated some of his design concepts, such as a bow ramp and retractable pilot house, so the line's vessels could travel in areas larger ships could only look at.

On ACCL's ships, the dress code is informal. There is a BYOB policy in the bar and an open-seating dinner policy, with tables for 10, allowing passengers to get to know each other in short order.

ACCL caters to a more mature clientele and has a very high percentage of solo travelers, sometimes accounting for as many as 30 per cent of the passengers, according to Yvette Behrendt, vice president of marketing.

Behrendt also said that all of ACCL's programs "are designed so that everyone takes part in them." She added that the small size of ACCL's ships "is conducive to intermingling—passengers often meet other singles and book with them on later trips."

Caribbean Prince

Gross Registered Tonnage: 89.5
Passenger Capacity (double occupancy): 84
Passenger Capacity (all berths): 84
Country of Registry: .... United States
Nationality of Officers: .... American
Length of Cruise: .... 12 to 15 days
Ports of Embarkation: .... Include Belize City, Key West, New Orleans,
Warren, R.I., and Quebec City
Ports of Call: .... Include Livingston, Punta Gorda, Tobacco Cay,
St. Augustine, Charleston, Norfolk, Biloxi,
Montreal and Upper Canada Village
Single Cabins: .... No
Single Supplement: .... "20's" cabins (lower deck cabins): 175%;
all others: 200%
Guaranteed Share: .... Not advertised in brochure, but accepted
in "20's" category at cruise line's discretion

Mayan Prince

Gross Registered Tonnage: 92.3
Passenger Capacity (double occupancy): 92
Passenger Capacity (all berths): 92
Country of Registry: .... United States
Nationality of Officers: ....American
Length of Cruise: .... 12 to 15 days
Ports of Embarkation: ... Include West Palm Beach, St. Thomas, Antigua,
Grenada, Port-of-Spain, Caracas and Quebec City
Ports of Call: .... Include St. John, Tortola, Antigua, Guadeloupe,
Mayreau, Hudson River, Upper Canada Village,
Montreal and Quebec
Single Cabins: .... No
Single Supplement: .... "20's" cabins (lower deck cabins):
175%; all others: 200%
Guaranteed Share: .... Not advertised in brochure, but accepted
in "20's" category at cruise line's discretion

New Shoreham II

Gross Registered Tonnage: 89.7
Passenger Capacity (double occupancy): 72
Passenger Capacity (all berths): 72
Country of Registry: .... United States
Nationality of Officers: ....American
Length of Cruise: .... 7 to 15 days
Ports of Embarkation: .... Include West Palm Beach,
Warren, R.I., and New Orleans
Ports of Call: .... Include Ft. Myers, Sanibel, Sarasota,
Biloxi, Gulfport, New Orleans, Baton Rouge,
New York, Baltimore, Montreal and Quebec City
Single Cabins: .... No
Single Supplement: .... "20's" cabins (lower deck cabins):
175%; all others: 200%
Guaranteed Share: ...... Not advertised in brochure, but accepted in "20's"
and "30's" category at cruise line's discretion

American Hawaii Cruises

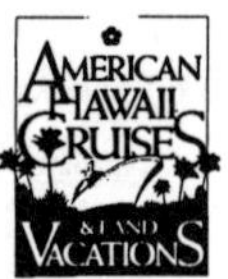

550 Kearny Street
San Francisco, CA 94108
(800) 765-7000

You'll get a true taste of the Hawaiian islands aboard American Hawaii Cruises' two ships, the *Independence* and the *Constitution*. In addition to the regular daily activities offered on other ships, American Hawaii also promises ukelele and hula lessons, lei-making classes and coconut palm weaving demonstrations.

Shore excursions concentrate on the natural beauty and charm of the islands, including helicopter tours of the volcanoes on the Big Island, whale watching and ocean rafting in Maui or kayaking on Kauai.

The cruise line emphasizes its "friendly American crew" and the fact that it is the only cruise line that sails solely among the Hawaiian islands. The ships are also the only "American built, staffed and owned ocean-going cruise ships" currently in operation.

For the solo traveler, the two ships offer a number of cabins for exclusive occupancy at no surcharge, along with a guaranteed-share program.

Constitution

Gross Registered Tonnage: 30,090
Passenger Capacity (double occupancy): 768
Passenger Capacity (all berths): 798
Country of Registry: .... United States
Nationality of Officers: .... American
Length of Cruise: .... 7 days; some 3- and 4-day cruises available
Port of Embarkation: .... Honolulu
Ports of Call: .... Kahului, Maui; Hilo and Kona,
Hawaii; Nawiliwili, Kauai.
Single Cabins: .... 11—2 outside, 9 inside
Single Supplement: .... No supplement on some
cabins in Categories C and G;
Categories B through K, and IO: 160%;
Categories A, AA and Owner's suite: 200%
Guaranteed Share: .... Not advertised in the brochure, but accepted in
Categories C and G at cruise line's discretion

Independence

Gross Registered Tonnage: 30,090
Passenger Capacity (double occupancy): 714
Passenger Capacity (all berths): 798
Country of Registry: .... United States
Nationality of Officers: ....American
Length of Cruise:....................7 days; some 3-and 4-day cruises available
Port of Embarkation: ....Honolulu
Ports of Call: ...... Nawiliwili, Kauai; Kona and Hilo, Hawaii; Kahului, Maui
Single Cabins: .... 18—5 outside, 13 inside
Single Supplement: ....No supplement on some cabins in Categories C,
G and J; Categories B through K and IO: 160%;
Categories A, AA and Owner's Suite: 200%
Guaranteed Share:.......... Not advertised in the brochure, but accepted in
Categories C and G at cruise line's discretion

Bergen Line

505 Fifth Avenue
New York, NY 10017
(800) 666-2374

If you want to see Norway like a native, consider taking a trip on one of the Bergen Line's coastal steamers. The 11 ships travel the coast of Norway 365 days a year, carrying passengers, cargo and mail between Bergen in the south and Kirkenes, near the border with Russia, in the north.

The ships' coastal voyages offer the passengers 6-, 7- or 12-day trips (the 12-day cruise is a round-trip excursion), with an informal atmosphere. According to Chris Lazarus, public relations representative for Bergen, most of the time during the cruise "is spent on deck or in the panorama lounge, watching magnificent scenery. You'll have a chance to meet Norwegians and others Europeans."

In case you want to practice your Norwegian, the names of the ships are: *Finnmarken, Harald Jarl, Kong Olav, Lofoten, Midnatsol, Narvik, Nordnorge, Nordstjernen, Polarlys, Ragnvald Jarl* and *Vesteraalen*.

The vessels offer some single cabins, and a single-supplement rate on the double cabins is available for a fixed amount.

The Bergen Line also offers 4-day cruises from Helsinki to St. Petersburg aboard the *Konstantin Simonov*, as well as 3- and 6-day cruises from Stockholm to St. Petersburg or Stockholm to Riga aboard the *Ilich*.

While there are too many ships in the coastal-voyage itinerary to profile individually, the following will give you an idea of what to expect from the Bergen Line.

Midnatsol

Gross Registered Tonnage:	4,200
Passenger Capacity (double occupancy):	322
Country of Registry:	Norway
Nationality of Officers:	Norwegian
Length of Cruise:	6, 7 or 12 days
Port of Embarkation:	Bergen
Ports of Call:	A total of 35 ports, including Trondheim, Harstad, Hammerfest and others
Single Cabins:	Yes
Comparison to Double Cabins:	Single cabins cost about the same as or slightly higher than double cabins, depending on accommodation and length of cruise
Single Supplement:	Flat rate of $400 to $550, depending on length of cruise
Guaranteed Share:	No

Narvik

Gross Registered Tonnage: 4,073
Passenger Capacity (double occupancy): 310
Country of Registry: .... Norway
Nationality of Officers: .... Norwegian
Length of Cruise: .... 6, 7 or 12 nights
Port of Embarkation: .... Bergen
Ports of Call: .... A total of 35 ports, including Trondheim,
Harstad, Hammerfest and others
Single Cabins: .... Yes
Comparison to Double Cabins: ..... Single cabins cost about the same as
or slightly higher than double cabins,
depending on accommodation and length of cruise
Single Supplement: .... Flat rate of $400 to $550,
depending on length of cruise
Guaranteed Share: .... No

Carlisle Cruises, Ltd.

9110 NE 73rd St.
Vancouver, WA 98662
(800) H$_2$0-WAYS

Imagine floating through the French countryside on your own private hotel barge. (Well, it's almost your own private hotel barge—you'll probably be sharing it with just a few other people.) Carlisle Cruises offers you this opportunity on their two six-passenger barges: *Vios* and *De Hoop*. Even the names are are evocative: Vios means "life" and De Hoop means "hope."

Registered in the United Kingdom, with a crew of three Britains to serve the passengers, the Vios and De Hope start off at Tanlay in the Burgundy region of France and travel down the Nivernais and Burgundy canals.

The barges travel their routes from April through October, and a set price of $2,200 to $2,490 per person, double occupancy, includes accommodations, meals in the French tradition, chauffeured sightseeing with excursion fees paid, special wine tastings, unlimited regional wines at lunch and dinner, use of a specially stocked open bar on the barge, and use of the certain facilities, such as camcorders, VCRs, bicycles and recreational equipment. The barges are also available for charter, if you want to get a small group of friends together.

Because of the very intimate size of the barges, *Vios* and *De Hoop* are a "great place to meet nice people of all ages," according to Alexander Culbertson, managing director. On *De Hoop*, there is one cabin with an upper/lower berth available for solo occupancy at no surcharge, while the surcharge on the other two cabins is 150 percent for solo occupancy. While guaranteed-share requests are uncommon, Carlisle Cruises will attempt to accommodate the solo traveler.

Carnival Cruise Lines

Carnival Place
3655 NW 87 Avenue
Miami, FL 33178-2428
(800) 327-9501

If it's fun you're looking for, Carnival Cruise Lines vows to provide it. Billing itself as "the most popular cruise line in the world," Carnival's fleet of ships includes the newest megaliner *Sensation* debuting in 1993, with the *Fascination* due in 1994 and the *Imagination* scheduled for 1995. Each Carnival ship has so much going on, you'll understand why they call themselves the "Fun Ships."

Whether you're planning a quick three-day getaway or 7-day cruise to the sunny beaches of the popular resort areas, Carnival provides a variety of itineraries, price options and ship sizes. Every Carnival ship offers three different types of live bands and orchestras to fit the dancing and listening tastes of all types of cruisers, along with almost non-stop games, activities and entertainment.

The Carnival ships visit the most popular ports of call in the Bahamas, Caribbean and Mexican Riviera. Solo travelers may choose a single cabin on some ships, a single supplement on all ships, or opt for the guaranteed-share program.

Celebration

```
Gross Registered Tonnage: ............................................... 47,262
Passenger Capacity (double occupancy): ......................... 1,486
Passenger Capacity (all berths): ...................................... 1,896
Country of Registry: ....................................................... Liberia
Nationality of Officers: ...................................................... Italian
Length of Cruise: ............................................................ 7 days
Port of Embarkation: ......................................................... Miami
Ports of Call: ..................................... San Juan, St. Thomas, St. Maarten
Single Cabins: .................................................................... No
Single Supplement: .................................... Categories 1 through 3: 150%;
                                                 Categories 4 through 12: 200%
Guaranteed Share: ...................... Quad-share rate, cruise only, is $650
Note: ... "Superliner" with main lobby featuring moving sculpture-painting
```

Ecstasy

Gross Registered Tonnage: 70,367
Passenger Capacity (double occupancy): 2,040
Passenger Capacity (all berths): 2,594
Country of Registry: .... Liberia
Nationality of Officers: .... Italian
Length of Cruise: .... 3 and 4 days
Port of Embarkation: .... Miami
Ports of Call: .... 3-day cruises stop at Nassau;
4-day cruises stop at Freeport and Nassau
Single Cabins: .... No
Single Supplement: .... Categories 1 through 3: 150%;
Categories 4 through 12: 200%
Guaranteed Share: .... Quad share rate is $275 for three days,
$395 for four days, cruise only
Note: .... "Megaliner" with grand atrium; sister ship to the Fantasy

Fantasy

Gross Registered Tonnage: 70,367
Passenger Capacity (double occupancy): 2,044
Passenger Capacity (all berths): 2,634
Country of Registry: .... Liberia
Nationality of Officers: .... Italian
Length of Cruise: .... 3 and 4 days
Port of Embarkation: .... Port Canaveral
Ports of Call: .... 3-day cruises stop at Nassau;
4-day cruises stop at Freeport and Nassau
Single Cabins: .... No
Single Supplement: .... Categories 1 through 3:150%;
Categories 4 through 12: 200%
Guaranteed Share: .... Quad share rate is $275 for three days,
$395 for four days, cruise only
Note: "Megaliner" with Grand Spectrum atrium; sister ship to the Ecstasy

Festivale

Gross Registered Tonnage: 38,175
Passenger Capacity (double occupancy): 1,146
Passenger Capacity (all berths): 1,400
Country of Registry: .... Bahamas
Nationality of Officers: .... Italian
Length of Cruise: .... 7 days
Port of Embarkation: .... San Juan
Ports of Call: .... St. Thomas, St. Maarten,
Dominica, Barbados and Martinique
Single Cabins: .... 14-12 outside, 2 inside
Comparison to Double Cabins: .... Inside singles are the same price as
outside deluxe cabins; outside singles
are the same price as the deluxe suites.
Single Supplement: .... Categories 1 through 3: 150%;
Categories 4 through 12: 200%
Guaranteed Share: .... Quad-share rate, cruise only, is $650

Holiday

```
Gross Registered Tonnage: .......................................... 46,052
Passenger Capacity (double occupancy): ...................... 1,452
Passenger Capacity (all berths): ................................. 1,800
Country of Registry: ................................................. Bahamas
Nationality of Officers: ................................................. Italian
Length of Cruise: .......................................................... 7 days
Port of Embarkation: ...................................................... Miami
Ports of Call: ............................................. Playa del Carmen/Cozumel,
                                        Grand Cayman and Ocho Rios
Single Cabins: .................................................................... No
Single Supplement: .................................. Categories 1 through 3: 150%;
                                        Categories 4 through 12: 200%
Guaranteed Share: ......................... Quad-share rate, cruise only, is $650
Note: ................................................................... "Superliner"
```

Jubilee

```
Gross Registered Tonnage: .......................................... 47,262
Passenger Capacity (double occupancy): ...................... 1,486
Passenger Capacity (all berths): ................................. 1,896
Country of Registry: ................................................... Liberia
Nationality of Officers: ................................................. Italian
Length of Cruise: .......................................................... 7 days
Port of Embarkation: ........................................... Los Angeles
Ports of Call: ................... Puerto Vallarta, Mazatlan and Cabo San Lucas
Single Cabins: .................................................................... No
Single Supplement: .................................. Categories 1 through 3: 150%:
                                        Categories 4 through 12: 200%
Guaranteed Share: ......................... Quad-share rate, cruise only, is $650
Note: ................................................................... "Superliner"
```

Sensation

```
Gross Registered Tonnage: .......................................... 70,367
Passenger Capacity (double occupancy): ...................... 2,040
Passenger Capacity (all berths): ................................. 2,594
Country of Registry: .................................................. Panama
Nationality of Officers: ................................................. Italian
Length of Cruise: .......................................................... 7 days
Port of Embarkation: ...................................................... Miami
Ports of Call: ......................... Western Caribbean ports include Playa del
                        Carmen/Cozumel, Grand Cayman and Ocho Rios;
                                Eastern Caribbean ports include Nassau,
                                        San Juan and St. Thomas
Single Cabins: .................................................................... No
Single Supplement: .................................. Categories 1 through 3: 150%;
                                        Categories 4 through 12: 200%
Guaranteed Share: ......................... Quad-share rate, cruise only, is $650
Note: ..................................... Newest "megaliner" and sister ship to the
                        Fantasy and Ecstasy; Inaugural sailing Nov. 21, 1993
```

Tropicale

Gross Registered Tonnage: 36,674
Passenger Capacity (double occupancy): 1,022
Passenger Capacity (all berths): 1,400
Country of Registry: .... Liberia
Nationality of Officers: .... Italian
Length of Cruise: .... 7 days
Port of Embarkation: .... San Juan
Ports of Call: .... St. Thomas, Guadeloupe, Grenada,
La Guaira/Caracas and Aruba
Single Cabins: .... No
Single Supplement: .... Categories 1 through 3: 150%;
Categories 4 through 12: 200%
Guaranteed Share: .... Quad-share rate, cruise only, is $650

CAST Freighter Cruises

c/o TravLtips
163-07 Depot Road
Post Office Box 188
Flushing, New York 11358
(800) 872-8584

For the traveler looking for a different experience getting to Europe, CAST offers transatlantic crossings aboard the *Husky*, *Muskox* and *Otter*. Each of the vessels makes journeys that last from 12 to 14 days, and each vessel carries a maximum of 12 passengers. More adventurous passengers can create a round-trip itinerary of 32 days, allowing for a several-day layover in Belgium, using the ship as their hotel.

The staterooms are all air-conditioned, with portholes, lower beds and private facilities, and the vessels feature a dining room and lounge shared with the officers, as well as a passenger lounge. Additional facilities include a library and swimming pool.

During lunch and dinner, complimentary wine is offered, and a pantry is always accessible for a light snack.

Travel aboard CAST's freighters is "ideal for the independent traveler who prefers to entertain self rather than be subjected to typical cruise ship activities," said Steve Wellmeier, director of marketing.

Husky, Muskox and Otter

Dead Weight: .... 70,900 DWT
Passenger Capacity (double occupancy): 12
Passenger Capacity (all berths): 12
Country of Registry: .... Bahamas
Nationality of Officers: .... Croatian
Length of Cruise: .... 12 to 14 days
Port of Embarkation: .... Montreal, Canada or Zeebrugge, Belgium
Single Cabins: .... Yes-4 outside
Comparison to Double Cabins: .... Same as double occupancy rate
Single Supplement: .... None on single cabins
Guaranteed Share: .... No

Celebrity Cruises

500 Blue Lagoon Drive
Miami, FL 33126
(800) 437-3111

Fine cuisine and customized service are the hallmarks emphasized by Celebrity Cruises. The cuisine, designed by Master Chef Michel Roux, includes such culinary specialities as veal "celebrity" with walnuts and marsala sauce, and Caribbean iced rum souffle. As for service, there are butlers provided for the suite accommodations, and 24-hour room service for all passengers.

The three ships in Celebrity's line, the *Horizon*, the *Meridian* and the *Zenith*, all stick fairly close to the United States, sailing in the playgrounds of the Caribbean and Bermuda. While there is no special rate for the solo traveler on the *Horizon* or the *Zenith*, there is a guaranteed single rate aboard the *Meridian*.

Horizon

```
Gross Registered Tonnage: ............................................... 46,811
Passenger Capacity (double occupancy): ......................... 1,354
Country of Registry: ...................................................... Liberia
Nationality of Officers: ................................................... Greek
Length of Cruise: ...................................................... 7 nights
Port of Embarkation: ................................................ San Juan
Ports of Call: .. Martinique, Barbados, St. Lucia, Antigua and St. Thomas
Single Cabins: ................................................................... No
Single Supplement: ................................ Categories 3 through 12: 150%;
                                                  Categories 1 and 2 suites:  200%
Guaranteed Share: ............................................................ No
```

Meridian

```
Gross Registered Tonnage: ............................................... 30,440
Passenger Capacity (double occupancy): ......................... 1,106
Country of Registry: .................................................... Bahamas
Nationality of Officers: ................................................... Greek
Length of Cruise: ................................................ 7 to 11 nights
Ports of Embarkation: ......................... San Juan and New York
Ports of Call: ....... 10-night itinerary includes Aruba, La Guaira, Grenada,
                 Barbados, St. Lucia, Martinique, St. Maarten and St. Thomas;
                 11 nights includes Montego Bay, Aruba, La Guaira, Grenada,
                 Barbados, Martinique, Virgin Gorda/Tortola and St. Thomas;
                 Bermuda itinerary visits King's Wharf
Single Cabins: ................................................................... No
Guaranteed Single rate: ........... Flat rate comparable to lower deck inside
                 cabin; assignment at cruise line's discretion; available
                 on Caribbean itinerary, but not advertised on Bermuda route
Single Supplement: ................................ Categories 3 through 14: 150%;
                                                  Categories 1A through 2 suites: 200%
Guaranteed Share: ............................................................ No
```

Zenith

Gross Registered Tonnage: 47,255
Passenger Capacity (double occupancy): 1,374
Country of Registry: .... Liberia
Nationality of Officers: .... Greek
Length of Cruise: .... 7 nights
Port of Embarkation: .... Fort Lauderdale
Ports of Call: .... Eastern Caribbean includes San Juan, St. Thomas,
St. Maarten and Nassau; Western Caribbean includes
Montego Bay, Grand Cayman, Cozumel,
Playa del Carmen and Key West.
Single Cabins: .... No
Single Supplement: .... Categories 3 through 12: 150%;
Categories 1 and 2 suites: 200%
Guaranteed Share: .... No

Classical Cruises

132 E. 70th St.
New York, NY 10021
(800) 252-7745

Classical doesn't just provide cruises; the company provides "Educational Voyages" in the comfort of the line's *Aurora I* and *II*, sister ships introduced in 1992, and the *Illiria*, refurbished in 1990. After completing its Antarctic itinerary, the *Illiria* will not be open for independent bookings during 1993-1994.

The destinations are exotic, focusing on cultural and natural history. Each ship has an extensive library for exploring through reading, while Zodiac crafts and other launches are provided for access to remote areas. Lectures and cultural themes are an important part of the voyage experience, and journeys include both cruise and land exploration packages.

The line attracts what the cruise company defines as "discriminating, well-traveled consumers who look at travel as a way to expand their minds as well as their horizons."

Classical Cruises President Jamie Rosen said, "Because we attract many older people, there is a high percentage of 'non-couples' on board traveling together. This, combined with the intimate, congenial atmosphere a small ship offers, makes solo travelers feel very comfortable—part of a larger, welcoming family."

Aurora I

Gross Registered Tonnage: 2,928
Passenger Capacity (double occupancy): 74
Passenger Capacity (all berths): 80
Country of Registry: .... Bahamas
Nationality of Officers: .... Greek
Length of Cruise/Tour: .... 13 to 15 nights
Ports of Embarkation: .... Include Luxor, Safaga, Barcelona,
Santorini, Piraeus, Venice and Istanbul
Ports of Call: .... "Egypt & the Red Sea" itinerary includes Aqaba,
Eilat and Masada; "Voyage of Odysseus" includes Malta,
Stromboli and Ithaca; "Art Treasures" include
Bonifacio, Sorrento, Nice and Ravenna
Single Cabins: .... 6—all outside
Comparison to Double Cabins: .... Single cabins cost about 150% of
comparable adjacent double-occupancy cabins
Guaranteed Share: .... Not advertised in the brochure but company
has a "best efforts" policy of locating a
"suitable cabin mate."

Aurora II

Gross Registered Tonnage: 2,928
Passenger Capacity (double occupancy): 74
Passenger Capacity (all berths): 80
Country of Registry: .... Bahamas
Nationality of Officers: .... Greek
Length of Cruise/Tour: .... 9 to 16 nights
Ports of Embarkation: .... Include Caldera, Greenock, Nice,
St. Petersburg, Amsterdam and La Paz
Ports of Call: .... "Sea of Cortez" itinerary includes Isla San Esteban,
Los Islotes and Cabo San Lucas; "Baltic Sea" includes
Helsinki, Riga and Gdansk; "Green & Gentle Lands"
includes Orkney and Shetland Islands
Single Cabins: .... 6—all outside
Comparison to Double Cabins: .... Single cabins cost about 150% of
comparable adjacent double-occupancy cabins
Guaranteed Share: ..... Not advertised in the brochure but company has a
"best efforts" policy of locating a "suitable cabin mate."

Clipper Cruise Line

7711 Bonhomme Ave.
St. Louis, Missouri 63105-1956
(800) 325-0010

When love of the environment and history beckons you, consider taking a vacation aboard Clipper Cruise Lines' ships.

Clipper Cruise Line's three vessels are all geared toward nature appreciation, providing "up-close coastal exploration" of local and exotic destinations. There are naturalist and historians on board each cruise and the cruise line is proud of its commitment to non-intrusive touring with "minimal impact on fragile environments."

Life on board is casual, with single-seating dining featuring healthful, nutritious American cuisine. All staterooms are outside cabins.

According to Clipper representative Karen Kopta, the cruise line welcomes solo travelers and offers the type of "substantive travel experience that doesn't require a spouse to be enjoyable."

Nantucket Clipper

Gross Registered Tonnage: 99.5
Passenger Capacity (double occupancy): 100
Passenger Capacity (all berths): 100
Country of Registry: .... United States
Nationality of Officers: .... American
Length of Cruise: .... 8 to 15 days
Ports of Embarkation: .... Include Charleston, Washington, D.C.,
and St. Thomas
Ports of Call: .... "Antebellum South" itinerary includes Beaufort,
Hilton Head, Savannah; "Colonial Tour" includes Norfolk,
Wilmington and Washington, D.C.; "Art Capitals"
includes Newport, New York and Philadelphia; Caribbean
includes Tortola, Virgin Gorda and Jost Van Dyke;
Single Cabins: .... No
Single Supplement: .... Available on 6 cabins in Category 2
at 150% of the double occupancy rate
Guaranteed Share: .... Not advertised in brochure, but cruise line
will accept a guaranteed share based on availability

World Discoverer

Gross Registered Tonnage: 3,153
Passenger Capacity (double occupancy): 138
Passenger Capacity (all berths): 138
Country of Registry: .... Liberia
Nationality of Officers: .... European
Length of Cruise: .... 11 to 22 days
Ports of Embarkation: .... Include Miami, San Jose,
Prince Rupert, Kodiak and Nome
Ports of Call: .... South American itinerary includes Santiago,
Isla Pan de Azucar, and Paracas; Costa Rica
includes Poerto Escondido and Isla San Jose;
Alaska includes Wrangell, Prince William Sound,
Seward and Katmai Peninsula
Single Supplement: .... Some availability in Categories 1 and 2
at 150% of double occupancy rate
Guaranteed Share: .... Not advertised in brochure, but cruise line
will accept a guaranteed share based on availability

Yorktown Clipper

Gross Registered Tonnage: 99.5
Passenger Capacity (double occupancy): 138
Passenger Capacity (all berths): 138
Country of Registry: .... United States
Nationality of Officers: ....American
Length of Cruise: .... 6 to 15 days
Ports of Embarkation: .... Include Antigua, Port of Spain,
Curacao; Acapulco and Panama City
Ports of Call: .... Caribbean includes Antigua, Anguilla, St. Kitts,
Dominica, Bonaire and Tobago; Sea of Cortez or
Costa Rica itinerary includes Puerto Vallarta, Mazatlan,
Isla Santa Catalina, San Blas Island and Darien Jungle.
Single cabins: .... No
Single Supplement: .... Some availability in Categories 1 and 2 at
140% to 150% of double occupancy rate
Guaranteed Share: .... Not advertised in brochure, but cruise line will
accept a guaranteed share based on availability

Club Med

40 West 57th Street
New York, NY 10019
(800) 258-2633

Club Med ®

If a week of unlimited water sports is your idea of heaven, then a Club Med cruise was made for you.

Each of the five-masted sailing ships has a fold-down platform transforming the vessel into an instant marina. Like the Club Med land villages, use of sports equipment and instruction are included in the tariff. Each ship carries 12 windsurf boards, three sailboats, two water-ski boats, 20 single scuba tanks and four motorized boats.

Also like the Club Med land villages, your all-inclusive vacation includes gourmet meals, wine with lunch and dinner and a strict no-tipping policy. If you have never been a Club Med guest before, you must pay an initiation fee, and all guests must also pay an annual membership fee, in addition to the cruise fare.

Club Med 1

Gross Registered Tonnage: 14,000
Passenger Capacity (all berths): 386
Country of Registry: .... Bahamas
Nationality of Officers: .... French and International
Length of Cruise: .... 7 nights
Port of Embarkation: .... Fort-de-France or Cannes
Ports of Call: .... Caribbean itinerary includes St. Lucia, Bequia,
                                 Barbados, St. Barthelemy, Virgin Gorda or Dominica,
                                 and others; Mediterranean includes Canary Islands,
                                         Cadiz, Malaga, Barcelona and others
Single Cabins: .... No
Single Supplement: 150%
Guaranteed Share: .... Not advertised in the brochure but
                                 cruise line will accept at their discretion

Club Med 2

Gross Registered Tonnage: 14,000
Passenger Capacity (all berths): 392
Country of Registry: .... Wallis and Futuna (French Protectorate)
Nationality of Officers: .... Asian and International
Length of Cruise: .... 3, 4 and 7 nights
Port of Embarkation: .... Noumea or Guam
Ports of Call: .... New Caledonia itinerary includes
                                 Isle of Pines, Ouvea and Vanuatu; Micronesia
                                 itinerary includes Yap, Ulithi, Guam and Saipan
Single Cabins: .... No
Single Supplement: 150%
Guaranteed Share: .... Not advertised in brochure, but
                                 cruise line will accept at their discretion

Color Line

c/o Bergen Line
505 Fifth Avenue
New York, NY 10017
(800) 323-7436

If you're traveling from England to Scandinavia, you can hop aboard a Color Line ship and travel in comfort. Passengers embark at Newcastle and spend a leisurely 21 hours before disembarking in Bergen/Stavanger. Other itineraries on the Color Line include Hirtshals to Oslo, Kiel to Oslo or Hirtshals to Kristiansand.

Prices are based on a flat per-person rate, depending on the amenities of cabin and the number of people it can accommodate. Single supplements are then assessed depending on the number of berths in that cabin that will not be sold.

Ships in the Color Line include the *Kronprins Harald, Prinsesse Ragnhild, Venus, Christian IV, Jupiter* and *Skagen.*

Different ships have different features, but the *Prinsesse Ragnhild*, newest of the Color Line ships, features a shopping center, pub, bistro, cafe, restaurants and entertainment center

Bergen Line is the exclusive booking agent in North America for Color Line.

Prinsesse Ragnhild

Gross Registered Tonnage: 35,500
Passenger Capacity (all berths): 1,875
Country of Registry: .... Norway
Nationality of Officers: .... Norwegian
Length of Cruise: .... 19 hours
Port of Embarkation: .... Oslo or Kiel
Ports of Call: .... None
Single Cabins: .... No
Single Supplement: .... Available in Categories B through D at a flat rate
Guaranteed Share: .... No

Commodore Cruise Line

800 Douglas Road
Suite 700
Coral Gables, FL 33134
(800) 237-5361

Although Commodore offers the same Caribbean ports as other cruise lines, it has scheduled cruises aboard its *Enchanted Seas* from a unique port of embarkation. Trips to the Eastern and Western Caribbean aboard this charming ship leave from the home port of New Orleans.

The *Enchanted Seas* offers a smaller size, a fun atmosphere and competitive, affordable rates. Commodore might be a fine choice for the solo traveler because there are single cabins at some of the lowest rates available. In fact, the single cabins are outside but in the "least expensive Category 12," according to public relations director Nancy Loewenherz, making them "less expensive than inside cabins." Some other cabins are available "with no supplement on select departure dates," she added, making an inquiry into availability worth a phone call from your travel agent.

Enchanted Seas

```
Gross Registered Tonnage: ............................................... 23,500
Passenger Capacity (double occupancy): ........................................ 736
Passenger Capacity (all berths): ........................................ 840
Country of Registry: ................................................... Panama
Nationality of Officers: ................................. European and Scandinavian
Length of Cruise: ..................................................... 7 days
Port of Embarkation: ............................................. New Orleans
Ports of Call: .................................. Different itineraries include Key West,
                                                   Playa del Carmen/Cozumel,
                                                Grand Cayman or Montego Bay
Single Cabins: .......................................................... 2—outside
Comparison to Double Cabins: .................. Priced less than deluxe inside
                                                  cabins or other outside cabins
Single Supplement: ..................................... Category 11:  135%;
                                                 Categories 2 through 10:  150%;
                                                          Category 1:  200%;
Guaranteed Share: ........................................................ No
```

Costa Cruise Lines

World Trade Center
80 S.W. 8th St.
Miami, FL 33130-3097
(800) 462-6782

Costa Cruise Lines' national pride is showing, as they put the emphasis back on the line's Italian spirit of cruising. The waiters are Italian, the cuisine is Italian, and you'll even find pasta stations and pool-side gelato to satisfy your appetite.

The Costa EuroLuxe ships, including the *CostaClassica* and *CostaAllegra*, feature original artwork and unique furnishings to enhance the ships, and the line promises Italian-style hospitality. Public areas and restaurants aboard the two ships sport such atmospheric names as Trevi Piazza Fountain Pool, Alfresco Cafe, Leonardo's Deli, La Trattoria and La Tavernetta Bistro.

Of course, you can enjoy Costa's Italian hospitality while visiting Italian ports during a Mediterranean itinerary. But why not enjoy a bit of Italy while traveling through the Caribbean or Alaska?

CostaAllegra

Gross Registered Tonnage: 30,000
Passenger Capacity (double occupancy): 800
Country of Registry: .... Italy
Nationality of Officers: .... Italian
Length of Cruise: .... 7 days on Caribbean tours;
10 and 11 days on European cruises
Ports of Embarkation: .... San Juan and Venice
Ports of Call: .... Southern Caribbean route includes St. Maarten,
St. Lucia, Barbados, Serena Cay and St. Thomas/St. John;
European tours vary, including ports in Greece,
Turkey, Israel and Egypt and others
Single Cabins: .... No
Single Supplement: .... Categories 1 through 12: 150%;
Categories 13 and 14 suites: 200%.
Guaranteed Share: .... No

CostaClassica

Gross Registered Tonnage: 53,700
Passenger Capacity (double occupancy): 1,300
Country of Registry: .... Italy
Nationality of Officers: .... Italian
Length of Cruise: .... 7 days
Ports of Embarkation: .... Miami and Genoa
Ports of Call: .... Eastern Caribbean stops at San Juan,
St.Thomas/St. John, Serena Cay and Nassau;
Western Caribbean visits Grand Cayman,
Ocho Rios Playa del Carmen/Cancun and Cozumel;
Mediterranean includes Palermo, Tunis,
Ibiza, Palma de Mallorca and Barcelona
Single Cabins: .... No
Single Supplement: .... Categories 1 through 12: 150%;
Category 13 suites: 200%
Guaranteed Share: .... No

CostaRiviera

Gross Registered Tonnage: 31,500
Passenger Capacity (double occupancy): 974
Passenger Capacity (all berths): 1,217
Country of Registry: .... Italy
Nationality of Officers: .... Italian
Length of Cruise: .... 7 days
Ports of Embarkation: .... San Juan and Vancouver
Ports of Call: .... Southern Caribbean route includes
St. Thomas/St. John, Martinique, Caracas,
Aruba and Serena Cay; Alaskan route includes
Inside Passage, Ketchikan, Juneau, Skagway and others
Single Cabins: .... No
Single Supplement: .... 150% to 175%, depending on itinerary
Guaranteed Share: .... No

Crystal Cruises

2121 Avenue of the Stars
Los Angeles, CA 90067
(800) 446-6645

If you have to leave your butler at home, you won't have to worry aboard the *Crystal Harmony*—when you book the Crystal Penthouse, the services of a butler are included. The Penthouse Deck, which includes 32 Penthouses, 26 Penthouse Suites and the four Crystal Penthouses, is looked after by a staff of four specially trained white-gloved butlers and six room stewardesses.

If you're getting the idea that the *Crystal Harmony* is synonymous with luxury, you're on the right track. But if you're traveling in one of the posh cabins on a deck other than those on which the penthouses are located, you'll still be treated with the personal touch. All staterooms feature goose down pillows, terry cloth robes, bathtubs and showers, refrigerators and two hair dryers.

A few other touches make the *Crystal Harmony* unique: a Caesars Palace at Sea casino, two alternative restaurants available for dining at no extra charge (Kyoto for Japanese cuisine and Prego for Italian), and air-conditioned tenders.

Crystal Cruises is "aware and concerned about the solo traveler," according to Eric Graves, director of group sales for the line. The gentleman host program is one area in which this concern is manifested; another is the scaling down of solo-occupancy rates in the future.

Crystal Harmony

```
Gross Registered Tonnage: ........................................................ 49,400
Passenger Capacity (double occupancy): ............................................ 960
Country of Registry: ........................................................... Bahamas
Nationality of Officers: ...................................... Norwegian and Japanese
Length of Cruise: ............................................................. 8 to 88 days
Ports of Embarkation: ........ Include San Juan, Acapulco, Lisbon, London,
                                   Copenhagen, Istanbul, Venice, Piraeus,
                                        Sydney, Yokohama and others
Ports of Call: ................... St. Thomas, St. Maarten, Aruba, Montego Bay,
                            Caldera, Barcelona, Malaga, Dublin, Amsterdam,
                            St. Peterburg, Oslo, Yalta, Odessa, Auckland,
                            Sydney, Brisbane, Singapore and Hong Kong
Single Cabins: ..................................................................... No
Single Supplement: ................... Categories C through K is 140 to 150%;
                                        Categories PS and A are 175%;
                            Categories CP, PS and A suites are 200%
Guaranteed Share: ................................................................. No
Note: ..................... More than half the staterooms have private verandas;
                    paddle tennis court, and Crystal's "Ambassador Host" program,
                            with four gentlemen hosts accompanying each voyage.
```

Cunard Line

555 Fifth Avenue
New York, NY 10017-2453
(800) 221-4770

When most people think of Cunard, they're likely to envision the stately *Queen Elizabeth 2* as it slices across the Atlantic, carrying its precious cargo of passengers in the stylish manner of days gone by. But Cunard is much more than the historic *QE 2*: Its ships also include the yacht-like *Sea Goddess* vessels, the accessible *Princess* and *Countess*, the luxurious *Vistafjord* and *Sagafjord*, and the Crown ships.

Cunard follows the motto: "We're not the best because we're the oldest; we're the oldest because we're the best." Because of the variety of sea-going experiences and availability to the solo traveler, just about any cruiser can assess the truth of this statement.

Another feature of the Cunard sailings is an assortment of "Festivals at Sea" aboard the *QE2, Sagafjord, Vistafjord, Sea Goddess I* and *II* and the *Countess*. Such areas as theatre, bridge, classical music, food and wine, big bands and mystery are given special attention during various cruises on specified weeks.

There are actually three different faces to Cunard: the ships roaming the globe which have sailed in its line for years, the Cunard EuropAmerica River Cruises traveling the Danube, Elbe and Rhone, and the recently formed Cunard Crown Line, which now includes the three ships formerly under the Crown Cruise Line, along with the *Princess* and *Countess*.

Crown Dynasty

```
Division: .................................................................. Cunard Crown Line
Gross Registered Tonnage: ............................................. 20,000
Passenger Capacity (double occupancy): ........................... 800
Passenger Capacity (all berths): ...................................... 840
Country of Registry: .................................................. Panama
Nationality of Officers: ................... Northern European and Scandinavian
Length of Cruise: ..................................................... 7 days
Port of Embarkation: ................................... New York or Montreal
Ports of Call: ..................................... New England/Canada route includes
                          Halifax, Bar Harbor, Portland, Cape Cod Canal,
                          Martha's Vineyard, Montreal,  or Provincetown
Single Cabins: ............................................................ No
Single Supplement: ................................Categories C through F: 150%;
                                     Categories A1, A, B, G and H: 200%
Guaranteed Share: .................................................... Yes
Guaranteed Single Occupancy: .................. Single occupancy guaranteed
                             with no surcharge, subject to confirmation,
                     30 days prior to departure in Categories C through F
```

Crown Jewel

Division: .... Cunard Crown Line
Gross Registered Tonnage: 20,000
Passenger Capacity (double occupancy): 800
Passenger Capacity (all berths): 840
Country of Registry: .... Panama
Nationality of Officers: .... Northern European and Scandinavian
Length of Cruise: .... 7 days
Port of Embarkation: .... Palm Beach
Ports of Call: .... Nassau, Ocho Rios, Grand Cayman and
Cozumel or Bahamas, St. Thomas, San Juan and Nassau
Single Cabins: .... No
Single Supplement: .... Categories C through F: 150%;
Categories A1, A, B, G and H: 200%
Guaranteed Share: .... Yes
Guaranteed Single Occupancy: .... Single occupancy guaranteed with
no surcharge, subject to confirmation,
30 days prior to departure
in Categories C through F

Crown Monarch

Division: .... Cunard Crown Line
Gross Registered Tonnage: 15, 270
Passenger Capacity (double occupancy): 530
Passenger Capacity (all berths): 560
Country of Registry: .... Panama
Nationality of Officers: .... Northern European and Scandinavian
Length of Cruise: .... 7 days
Port of Embarkation: .... Palm Beach
Ports of Call: .... Itineraries vary, including such Caribbean ports
of call as St. Kitts, St. Croix, San Juan, Nassau,
Puerto Plata, Tortola, Grand Cayman,
St. Tomas de Castilla, or Cozumel
Single Cabins: .... Yes
Single Supplement: .... Categories C through F: 150%;
Categories A1, A, B, G and H: 200%
Guaranteed Share: .... No
Guaranteed Single Occupancy: .... Single occupancy guaranteed
with no surcharge, subject to confirmation, 30 days
prior to departure in Categories C through F

Cunard Countess

Division: .... Cunard Crown Line
Gross Registered Tonnage: 17,593
Passenger Capacity (double occupancy): 750
Country of Registry: .... Bahamas
Nationality of Officers: .... European
Length of Cruise: .... 7 days
Port of Embarkation: .... San Juan
Ports of Call: .... "Caribbean Capitals" include Tortola, Antigua,
Martinique, Barbados and St. Thomas.
"7-Plus" route includes St. Maarten, Guadeloupe,
Grenada, St. Lucia, St. Kitts and St. Thomas.
Single Cabins: .... No
Single Supplement: .... Categories C through G: 150%
Guaranteed Share: .... Yes
Guaranteed Single Occupancy: .... Single occupancy guaranteed with
no surcharge, subject to confirmation, 30 days
prior to departure in Categories C through F

Cunard Princess

Division: .... Cunard Crown Line
Gross Registered Tonnage: 17,593
Passenger Capacity (double occupancy): 750
Country of Registry: .... Bahamas
Nationality of Officers: .... European
Length of Cruise: .... 7 to 14 days
Ports of Embarkation: .... Malaga, Athens and Venice
Ports of Call: .... Include Tangier, Lanzarote, Las Palmas,
La Palmas, Tenerife, Funchal, Casablanca,
Gibraltar, Istanbul, Kusadasi, Patmos,
Rhodes, Mykonos, Corfu,
Alexandria, Ashdod, Bodrum and Kos
Single Cabins: .... No
Single Supplement: .... Categories C through G: 150%
Guaranteed Share: .... Yes
Guaranteed Single Occupancy: .... Single occupancy guaranteed with
no surcharge, subject to confirmation,
30 days prior to departure in
Categories C through F

Danube Princess

Division: .... Cunard EuropAmerica River Cruises
Gross Registered Tonnage: 3,400
Passenger Capacity (all berths): 200
Country of Registry: .... Germany
Nationality of Officers: .... German/Austrian
Length of Cruise: .... 7 days
Port of Embarkation: .... Passau, Germany
Ports of Call: .... Durnstein, Budapest, Esztergom,
Bratislava, Slovakia, Vienna, Melk and Grein
Single Cabins: .... 4—all outside
Comparison to Double Cabins: .... About 125% or more of
comparable double-occupancy cabins
Single Supplement: ...... Not listed because of availability of single cabins
Guaranteed Share: .... No
Note: .... Extensive Danube River itinerary

Princesse de Provence

Division: .... Cunard EuropAmerica River Cruises
Gross Registered Tonnage: 2,600
Passenger Capacity (all berths): 144
Country of Registry: .... Germany
Nationality of Officers: .... German, Austrian and French
Length of Cruise: .... 7 days
Port of Embarkation: .... Lyon
Ports of Call: .... Tournus, Chalon Dur Saone, Macon, Trevoux,
Tournon, Arles, Avignon, Vienne
Single Cabins: .... No
Single Supplement: .... Limited number of double cabins
available for single occupancy at about 125%
the double-occupancy rate
Guaranteed Share: .... No
Note: .... Extensive Rhone River itinerary

Prussian Princess

Division: .... Cunard EuropAmerica River Cruises
Gross Registered Tonnage: 2,600
Passenger Capacity (all berths): 144
Country of Registry: .... Germany
Nationality of Officers: .... German
Length of Cruise: .... 7 days
Port of Embarkation: .... Hamburg or Dresden
Ports of Call: .... Include Tangermunde, Wittenberg, Meissen,
Bad Schandau, Decin, Bohemia and Pillnitz
Single Cabins: .... No
Single Supplement: .... Limited number of double cabins
available for single occupancy at about
125% the double-occupancy rate
Guaranteed Share: .... No
Note: .... Extensive Elbe River itinerary

Queen Elizabeth 2

Division: .... Cunard Line
Gross Registered Tonnage: 67,139
Passenger Capacity (double occupancy): 1864
Country of Registry: .... Great Britain
Nationality of Officers: .... British
Length of Cruise: .... 3 days to 128 days
Port of Embarkation: .... Southampton or New York
Ports of Call: .... Tours other than transatlantic include
Barbados, Martinique, St. Thomas, Edinburgh,
Stavanger, Oslo, Copenhagen, Cork,
Brest, Bar Harbor, Halifax, Malaga,
Palma, Gibraltar, or Cherbourg
Single Cabins: 145
Comparison to Double Cabins: ...... Depends on location, class of service
and dining room, but runs about 114% to
154% of similar accommodations in double cabins.
Single Supplement: .... Categories DI through L: 175%;
Categories A1 through C: 200%
Guaranteed Share: .... Not advertised in the brochure, but
accepted at cruise line's discretion
Note: .... Ship features a 40-car garage, kennels,
Epson Computer Center, Spa at Sea,
4 restaurants, Gentlemen Hosts on some sailings;
only ship featuring regularly scheduled transatlantic sailings

Sagafjord

Division: .... Cunard Line
Gross Registered Tonnage: 25,147
Passenger Capacity (double occupancy): 589
Country of Registry: .... Bahamas
Nationality of Officers: .... Norwegian
Length of Cruise: .... 3 days to 96 days
Ports of Embarkation: .... Include Ft. Lauderdale, Vancouver,
Anchorage, Los Angeles and Ft. Lauderdale
Ports of Call: .... Include Grand Cayman, Aruba, Barbados,
St. Lucia, Nawiliwili, Bora Bora, Papeete,
Moorea, Juneau, Skagway, Ketchikan, Valdez,
Seward, Devil's Island, Recife and Belem
Single Cabins: .... 47 outside, 7 inside
Comparison to Double Cabins: .... Similar or slightly higher
in price than double-occupancy
cabins, averaging 3 to 20% higher
than similar accommodations
Single Supplement: 175%
Guaranteed Share: .... No
Note: .... Most cabins are outside, with 90%
providing both shower and tubs; Golden
Door Spa at Sea; some sailings feature
a "Gentleman Host" program

Sea Goddess I

Division: .... Cunard Line
Gross Registered Tonnage: 4,250
Passenger Capacity (double occupancy): 116
Country of Registry: .... Norway
Nationality of Officers: .... Norwegian
Length of Cruise: .... 7 to 11 days
Ports of Embarkation: .... Include St. Thomas, Manaus, Barbados,
Piraeus, Istanbul, Venice and Monte Carlo
Ports of Call: .... Include St. John, St. Barts, Tobago,
Devil's Island, Alter do Chao, Parintins,
Mykonos, Rhodes, Kusadasi, Bodrum,
Patmos, Sorrento, Capri, St. Tropez,
Corfu and Heraklion
Single Cabins: .... No
Single Supplement: .... Not published; available upon inquiry to Cunard
Guaranteed Share: .... No
Note: .... Yacht-like size; Golden Door Spa at Sea,
complimentary wine, liquor and beverages;
tipping discouraged

Sea Goddess II

Division: .... Cunard Line
Gross Registered Tonnage: 4,250
Passenger Capacity (double occupancy): 116
Country of Registry: .... Norway
Nationality of Officers: .... Norwegian
Length of Cruise: .... 5 to 16 days
Ports of Embarkation: .... Include Bali, Singapore, Monte Carlo,
Venice, Piraeus, and Barcelona
Ports of Call: .... Include Komodo, Ujung, Pandang, Phuket,
Kuala Lumpur, Bangkok, Rhodes, Budrum,
Sorrento, Capri, Porto Cervo, Portofino,
Ibiza, Corfu, and Capri
Single Cabins: .... No
Single Supplement: .... Not published; available upon inquiry to Cunard
Guaranteed Share: .... No
Note: .... Yacht-like size; Golden Door Spa at Sea,
complimentary wine, liquor and beverages;
tipping discouraged

Vistafjord

Division: .... Cunard Line
Gross Registered Tonnage: 24,492
Passenger Capacity (double occupancy): 736
Country of Registry: .... Bahamas
Nationality of Officers: .... Norwegian
Length of Cruise: .... 11 to 36 days
Ports of Embarkation: .... Include Ft. Lauderdale, Rio de Janeiro,
Naples, Barcelona, Venice, Hamburg,
Kiel and Piraeus
Ports of Call: .... Include Antigua, Guadeloupe, Barbados,
Buenos Aires, Montevideo, Devil's Island,
Casablanca, Lanzarote, Funchal, Alexandria,
Haifa, Helsinki, Stockholm, Copenhagen and Gibraltar
Single Cabins: .... 36—35 outside, 1 inside
Comparison to Double Cabins: .... Similar or slightly higher in price
than double-occupancy cabins,
averaging 6 to 24% percent higher
than similar outside accommodations,
up to 73% higher on inside accommodations
Single Supplement: 175%
Guaranteed Share: .... No
Note: .... Sister ship of the Sagafjord; Golden Door Spa
at Sea and IBM Computer Center; some
sailings feature a "Gentleman Host" program

Delta Queen Steamboat Company

Robin Street Wharf
New Orleans, Louisiana 70130-1890
(800) 543-1949

The Delta Queen Steamboat Company features two ships that celebrate America and its heritage. Boasting the only two overnight paddle wheel steamboats in America, the *Delta Queen* and the *Mississippi Queen*, the line celebrates America through its itineraries, theme cruises, cuisine and entertainment.

Routes on both ships follow the rivers on one of four itineraries: "The Old South," from New Orleans to Memphis; "Crossroads of America," from Memphis to St. Louis; "America's Heartland," from St. Louis to St. Paul; and "Wilderness Rivers," stopping in such cities as Nashville or Louisville.

Pick up your menu for lunch or dinner and not only will you find such "Traditional River Fare" as Southern Fried Catfish, Shrimp Po' Boy Sandwich or Crab Cakes Louisiane, you'll also be treated to excerpted reading material about Americana, such as Mark Twain's "Life on the Mississippi" or an explanation of the difference between the Creole and Cajun heritage.

Patti Young, vice president of public relations for Delta Queen, noted that the family-like atmosphere is perfect for the solo traveler. She said that "solo travelers are welcomed...the small, intimate on-board atmosphere enables solo travelers to make friends quickly—with fellow passengers and crew members alike." Missy Ellis, director of sales programs, added that she recommends the Delta Queen vessels "to many solo travelers because the cruises are a good way to see the United States and enjoy a variety of activities without being alone."

Delta Queen

Gross Registered Tonnage:	3,280
Passenger Capacity (double occupancy):	176
Passenger Capacity (all berths):	176
Country of Registry:	United States
Nationality of Officers:	American
Length of Cruise:	2 to 12 nights
Ports of Embarkation:	Include New Orleans, Memphis, Cincinnati and St. Louis
Ports of Call:	Include Nachez, Vicksburg, Hannibal, Paducah and Marietta
Single Cabins:	No
Single Supplement:	Categories A through E: 175%
Guaranteed Share:	Certain categories available at cruise line's discretion
Note:	The *Delta Queen* has been designated a national historic landmark

Mississippi Queen

Gross Registered Tonnage: 3,364
Passenger Capacity (double occupancy): 408
Passenger Capacity (all berths): 436
Country of Registry: .... United States
Nationality of Officers: ....American
Length of Cruise: .... 2 to 12 days
Ports of Embarkation: .... Include New Orleans, Memphis,
St. Louis, Pittsburgh and Chattanooga
Ports of Call: .... Include Louisville, Paducah, Marietta,
Portsmouth and Hannibal
Single Cabins: .... No
Single Supplement: ....Categories A through E: 175%
Guaranteed Share:.................................... Certain categories available at
cruise line's discretion
Note: .... Two "Gentlemen Hosts" on all departures,
increased to four on "Big Band" theme cruises

Diamond Cruise

Concorde Centre
2875 North East 191st Street
Suite 304
North Miami Beach, Florida 33180
(800) 333-3333

There is currently only one ship in this fleet, but oh what a ship it is! The *Radisson Diamond's* revolutionary twin-hull design makes the ship look like a fantasy toy in an imaginary bathtub, yet this ship provides luxury and finesse that few other ships can rival.

For water babies, a sports marina can be lowered for jetskiing, windsurfing and aquatic athletics, while the less adventurous can spy on the ocean life through an underwater viewing room. The unique design also provides additional stability for the ship while "noise and vibration levels are a mere 10% of those on conventional ships," according to the company.

Back on board, all warm and dry, you'll enjoy an elegant five-star meal at a single-sitting dinner, while sipping complimentary house wines. Later, you'll retire to your stateroom, where you'll enjoy either your own ocean-view sitting room or private balcony.

Radisson Diamond

Gross Registered Tonnage: 20,000
Passenger Capacity (double occupancy): 354
Passenger Capacity (all berths): 354
Country of Registry: .... Finland
Nationality of Officers: .... Finnish
Length of Cruise: .... Most are 7 nights
Ports of Embarkation: .... San Juan in the Caribbean;
Mediterranean ports of embarkation vary,
including Athens, Rome and Istanbul and others
Ports of Call: .... Caribbean ports include Virgin Gorda,
Antigua, St. Barts, Barbados, Iles des Saintes,
and others; Mediterranean ports include
Rhodes, Portofino, Monaco, Casablanca, St. Tropez,
Kusadasi, Santorini and others
Single Cabins: .... No
Single Supplement: .... Standard single supplement
is 125% the double occupancy rate;
check for special offers lowering the supplement
Guaranteed Share: .... No
Note: .... All cabins are outside staterooms with bath and shower.

Dolphin Cruise Line

901 South America Way
Miami, FL 33132-2073
(800) 222-1003

Dolphin Cruise Line started in the 3- and 4-night Miami cruise and quickly proved so popular that it expanded into the 7-night market.

With only three ships in its line, it's amazing how many itineraries and routes Dolphin has to offer, including the Panama Canal, Southern Caribbean, Eastern Caribbean, Western Caribbean, the Bahamas and Key West.

One of the line's most recent innovations is the tie-in with Hanna-Barbera, creators of the popular cartoon characters of Fred Flintstone, Yogi Bear and other whimsical personalities. Children will be treated to appearances from these come-to-life cartoons during shipboard activities. For the adults, Dolphin has offered a "Laugh Boat" theme, affiliated with National Lampoon, on selected cruises on the *Dolphin IV*.

Dolphin IV

Gross Registered Tonnage: 13,007
Passenger Capacity (double occupancy): 588
Country of Registry: .... Panama
Nationality of Officers: .... Greek
Length of Cruise: .... 3 and 4 nights
Port of Embarkation: .... Miami
Ports of Call: .... 3-night cruises stop at Nassau/Paradise
Island and Blue Lagoon Island;
on 4-night cruises, add Key West
Single Cabins: .... No
Single Supplement: 150%
Guaranteed Share: .... Not advertised in brochure

OceanBreeze

Gross Registered Tonnage: 21,486
Passenger Capacity (double occupancy): 768
Country of Registry: .... Liberia
Nationality of Officers: .... Greek
Length of Cruise: .... 7 Nights
Port of Embarkation: .... Aruba
Ports of Call: .... 7 night Southern Caribbean route stops
at Grenada, Barbados, Martinique and
Curacao, alternating with Cartagena, Panama Canal,
San Blas Islands and Curacao
Single Cabins: .... No
Single Supplement: 150%
Guaranteed Share: .... Not advertised in brochure

SeaBreeze

Gross Registered Tonnage: 21,000
Passenger Capacity (double occupancy): 840
Country of Registry: .... Panama
Nationality of Officers: .... Greek
Length of Cruise: .... 7 nights
Port of Embarkation: .... Miami
Ports of Call: .... Eastern Caribbean visits Blue Lagoon
Island/Nassau, San Juan and St. John/St. Thomas;
Western Caribbean stops at Grand Cayman,
Montego Bay and Playa del Carmen/Cozumel
Single Cabins: .... 2-1 inside, 1 outside
Comparison to Double Cabins: .... Same price as comparable cabins
Single Supplement: 150%
Guaranteed Share: .... Not advertised in the brochure

Epirotiki Cruises

551 Fifth Avenue
New York, NY 10176
(800) 221-2470

Epirotiki is one of the leaders in the Greek cruise market, but over the years has expanded into other areas of the world. Its ships, including the *Pallas Athena, Neptune* and *Hermes*, make one-, four-, and seven-day cruises from such ports as Athens, Rhodes or Crete. Other cruise itineraries include the Red Sea, the Caribbean and a combined Amazon/Caribbean route, known as the Caribazon.

Despite its venture into other locales, Epirotiki has kept its grasp on its Greek origins: Hospitality still abounds in the line's Greek warmth and the cuisine offers many Greek specialties (hardly a meal goes by in which lamb is not on the menu!) While other ships feature a Lido or Caribbean deck, Epirotiki's include the Dionysos, Poseidon or Hera deck.

Apollon

Gross Registered Tonnage:	7,500
Average Passenger Capacity:	800 a day
Country of Registry:	Greece
Nationality of Officers:	Greek
Length of Cruise:	1 day
Port of Embarkation:	Heraklion, Rethymnon or Aghio Nikolaus
Ports of Call:	Santorini

Argonaut

Gross Registered Tonnage:	4,500
Average Passenger Capacity:	160
Country of Registry:	Greece
Nationality of Officers:	Greek
Length of Cruise:	14 days
Ports of Embarkation:	Ravenna and Livorno
Ports of Call:	Include Bari, Syracuse, Valetta, Porto Empedocle, Marsala, Palermo, Lipari, Stromboli, Salerno, Civitacecchia, Milos, Naxos, Samos, Patmos, Hydra, Ithica, Santorini, Andros
Single Cabins:	2
Single Supplement:	150%
Guaranteed Share:	Not advertised in brochure, but accepted at cruise line's discretion
Note:	Originally built as the world's largest yacht

Hermes

Gross Registered Tonnage: 2,100
Average Passenger Capacity: .... 800 a day
Country of Registry: .... Greece
Nationality of Officers: .... Greek
Length of Cruise: .... 1 day
Port of Embarkation: .... Marina Flisvos
Ports of Call: .... Aegina, Poros and Hydra

Jason

Gross Registered Tonnage: 5,500
Average Passenger Capacity: 272
Country of Registry: .... Greece
Nationality of Officers: .... Greek
Length of Cruise: .... 3, 4 and 7 days
Port of Embarkation: .... Piraeus
Ports of Call: .... Include Istanbul, Kusadasi, Rhodes,
Santorini, Heraklion, Patmos and Mykonos
Single Cabins: .... No
Single Supplement: 150%
Guaranteed Share: .... Not advertised in brochure, but accepted
at cruise line's discretion

Mistral II

Gross Registered Tonnage: 2,150
Average Passenger Capacity: .... 643 a day
Country of Registry: .... Greece
Nationality of Officers: .... Greek
Length of Cruise: .... 1 day
Port of Embarkation: .... Rhodes
Ports of Call: .... Tilos and Nisiros; Kos and
Symi; or Kastellorizo and Kas

Neptune

Gross Registered Tonnage: 4,000
Average Passenger Capacity: 184
Country of Registry: .... Greece
Nationality of Officers: .... Greek
Length of Cruise: .... 3 and 4 days
Ports of Embarkation: .... Marina Flisvos and Heraklion
Ports of Call: .... Mykonos, Kusadasi, Patmos, Rhodes,
Heraklion, Santorini, Bodrum and Piraeus
Single Cabins: 5
Single Supplement: 150%
Guaranteed Share: .... Not advertised in brochure, but
accepted at cruise line's discretion

Odysseus

Gross Registered Tonnage: 12,000
Average Passenger Capacity: 452
Country of Registry: .... Greece
Nationality of Officers: .... Greek
Length of Cruise: .... 3, 4 and 7 days
Port of Embarkation: .... Piraeus
Ports of Call: .... Include Istanbul, Kusadasi, Rhodes,
Santorini, Heraklion, Patmos and Mykonos
Single Supplement: 150%
Guaranteed Share: .... Not advertised in brochure, but
accepted at cruise line's discretion

Pallas Athena

Gross Registered Tonnage: 19,940
Average Passenger Capacity: 724
Country of Registry: .... Greece
Nationality of Officers: .... Greek
Length of Cruise: .... 7 days
Port of Embarkation: .... Piraeus
Ports of Call: .... Port Said, Ashdod, Limassol,
Rhodes, Kusadasi, Patmos
Single Cabins: .... No
Single Supplement: 150%
Guaranteed Share: .... Not advertised in brochure, but
accepted at cruise line's discretion

Triton

Gross Registered Tonnage: 14,110
Average Passenger Capacity: 706
Country of Registry: .... Greece
Nationality of Officers: .... Greek
Length of Cruise: .... 3, 4 and 7 days
Port of Embarkation: .... Piraeus
Ports of Call: .... Include Istanbul, Kusadasi, Rhodes,
Santorini, Heraklion, Patmos and Mykonos
Single Cabins: .... No
Single Supplement: 150%
Guaranteed Share: .... Not advertised in brochure, but
accepted at cruise line's discretion

World Renaissance

Gross Registered Tonnage 12,000
Average Passenger Capacity: 536
Country of Registry: .... Greece
Nationality of Officers: .... Greek
Length of Cruise: .... 14 days
Ports of Embarkation: .... Genoa and Venice
Ports of Call: .... Messina, Katakolon, Piraeus, Mykonos,
Istanbul, Odessa, Yalta, Cronith, Sarades,
Corfu, Bari, Valencia, Motril, Malaga, Cadiz,
Lisbon, Casablanca, Tangier, Gibraltar and Ibiza
Single Cabins: .... 5—all outside
Single Supplement: 150%
Guaranteed Share: .... Not advertised in brochure, but
accepted at cruise line's discretion

EuroCruises

303 West 13th Street
New York, NY 10014
(800) 688-EURO

EuroCruises isn't a cruise line but an American-based representative of some of the most intriguing ships sailing around Europe. The organization is also able to combine pre- and post-tour accommodations with the cruises, as well as arranging for car rental and rail passes.

Cruising ground offered by EuroCruises includes the Norwegian Coast, Canary Islands, Baltic Sea, Russian Rivers, the Arctic and other areas that might interest the sophisticated traveler.

In all, EuroCruises represents more than 20 cruise lines with more than 70 vessels. Listed below are just a few options especially geared toward the solo traveler.

Black Prince

```
Cruise Line: ............................................... Fred Olsen
Gross Registered Tonnage: ............................... 11,200
Passenger Capacity (all berths): ........................... 450
Country of Registry: ................................... Norway
Length of Cruise: ............................... 12 to 22 nights
Ports of Embarkation: ...................... Southampton and Tilbury
Ports of Call: .................... Include Lisbon, Agadir, Santa Cruz de
                         Tenerife, Funchal, Tangier, Cadiz, Hardangerfjord,
                              Kristiansund, Bergen, Oslo, Malaga,
                                  Ibiza, Corfu and Heraklion
Single Cabins: ................................ 30—12 outside, 18 inside
Comparison to Double Cabins: ............................ About 118% of similar
                                            double-occupancy cabins
Guaranteed Share: .................................. Not advertised in brochure, but
                                        accepted at cruise line's discretion
```

Funchal

Cruise Line: .... Fritidskryss
Gross Registered Tonnage: 10,000
Passenger Capacity (all berths): 424
Country of Registry: .... Panama
Nationality of Officers: .... Portuguese and Swedish
Length of Cruise: .... 12 to 18 days
Port of Embarkation: .... Gothenburg, Sweden
Ports of Call: .... Geiranger, Honningsvag, Tromso, Molde,
Noordfjord, Bergen, Lysefjord, North Cape,
Pack Ice, Spitzbergen, Iceland, Faroe Islands,
Amsterdam, Rouen, Falmouth, Southampton, Dundee
Single Cabins: .... 14—5 outside, 9 inside
Comparison to Double Cabins: .... About 115 to 120% of similar
double-occupancy cabins
Guaranteed Share: .... 20 of the cabins are specifically designated
as "Single Inside Sharing." Cruise line will also
consider guaranteed shares in other cabins at
their own discretion.
Note: .... Representative Maria Conte said this is
"not a 'couples' ship. Attracts singles and
families, as well as couples."

Sergei Kirov

Cruise Line: .... North West River Shipping Co.
Gross Registered Tonnage: 3,200
Passenger Capacity (all berths): 280
Country of Registry: .... Russia
Nationality of Officers: .... European and Russian
Ports of Embarkation: .... St. Petersburg and Moscow
Ports of Call: .... Include Moscow, Uglich, Goritzy, Kizhy,
Lodenje Pole, Yaroslavi and Zagorsk
Single Cabins: .... Yes
Comparison to Double Cabins: .... About 40% higher
Guaranteed Share: .... Not advertised in the brochure, but
accepted at cruise line's discretion.
Note: .... EuroCruises representative said solo travelers
"never feel left out. Aboard the *Sergei Kirov*,
special seating plans for dinner pair up
solos—but there's flexibility according to
individual tastes and interests."

Fantasy Cruises

5200 Blue Lagoon Drive
Miami, FL 33126
(800) 423-2100

Two nights, five nights, seven nights...choose your time frame and then choose your Fantasy cruise. For those with a limited amount of time, hop aboard the *Britanis* in Miami on Friday and enjoy Saturday in Nassau before returning Sunday to Miami. Take the same ship during the week to the Mexican Caribbean ports, or try the *Amerikanis* and enjoy such ports as Antigua, Barbados or Martinique.

Whichever itinerary you choose, both ships offer the action of the casino, the splash of a swimming pool, the exercise of a gym and the relaxation of a cruise.

Amerikanis

```
Gross Registered Tonnage: ............................................................ 20,000
Passenger Capacity (double occupancy): ........................................... 617
Country of Registry: ................................................................. Panama
Nationality of Officers: ................................................................. Greek
Length of Cruise: ................................................................... 7 nights
Port of Embarkation: ............................................................... San Juan
Ports of Call: ...................... Include St. Thomas, Guadeloupe, Barbados,
                              St. Lucia, Antigua and St. Maarten or St. Thomas,
                                 Martinique, Grenada, La Guaira or Curacao.
Single Cabins: ................................................................... 3—inside
Comparison to Double Cabins: ......................... Comparable in price to a
                                                    mid-deck outside cabin
Single Supplement: ................................. Categories A through H: 150%;
                                                 Categories I and J suites: 200%
Guaranteed Share: .......................................................................... No
```

Britanis

```
Gross Registered Tonnage: ............................................................ 26,000
Passenger Capacity (double occupancy): ........................................... 926
Country of Registry: ................................................................. Panama
Nationality of Officers: ................................................................. Greek
Length of Cruise: ............................................................. 2 and 5 nights
Port of Embarkation: ................................................................... Miami
Ports of Call: ............................................... 2-night cruises visit Nassau;
                                              5-night cruises visit Key West,
                                              Playa del Carmen and Cozumel
Single Cabins: ........................................................................... No
Single Supplement: ................................. Categories B through K:  150%;
                                                 Categories L and M suites:  200%
Guaranteed Share: .......................................................................... No
```

Galapagos

7800 Red Road
Suite 112
South Miami, FL 33143
(800) 327-9854

For those who want to visit the Galapagos Islands in comfort, there's the *Galapagos Explorer*, which bills itself as the "largest, fastest and most comfortable cruise ship operating in the Galapagos." The *Galapagos Explorer* wends its way among the area's 13 major and 5 minor islands on 3- and 4- night excursions, which are often combined into one 7-night voyage.

For those who are looking for an even smaller vessel, the line features Galapagos yacht cruising, with a fleet of eight smaller ships holding 12 to 16 passengers each on the *Dorado, Cruz Del Sur, Estrella, Islas Plazas, Antartida, Moby Dick, Yolita* and *Darwin.*

Galapagos Explorer

Gross Registered Tonnage: 2,204
Passenger Capacity (double occupancy): 90
Country of Registry: .... Ecuador
Length of Cruise: .... 3 and 4 nights; can be combined for 7-night cruise
Port of Embarkation: .... San Cristobal Island
Ports of Call: .... 3-night cruise visits Espanola Island,
Floreana Island and Santa Cruz Island;
4-night cruise stops at Genovesa Island,
Bartolme Island, Isabaela Island,
Fernandina Island and others.
Single Cabins: .... Yes
Comparison to Double Cabins: .... About 125% the cost of standard
double cabin, only slightly higher
than deluxe double
Guaranteed Share: .... Not advertised in brochure
Note: .... Ship features swimming pool, solarium and two bars

Hobo Floating Hotels   **H O B O**

1 Port Hill, Hertford,
Hertfordshire SGI4 1PJ
England
Tel: Hertford (0992) 550616

Hobo Holidays' two floating hotels cruising the Thames are so British, the tariff for passage is listed in pounds. The cruising ground, atmosphere and cuisine are all British, too, featuring kippers along with toast and conserves for breakfast, tea and cakes served mid-afternoon, and perhaps cabinet pudding for your dinner dessert.

The *Swan and Mallard* are a pair of traditional narrowboats that cruise as one unit, weighing in at 50 tons together, and carrying 6 people in the two vessels The *Mallard* has one double bed, while the *Swan* has a double bunk and two single cabins. The *Merganser*, second of the floating hotels and weighing in at a gross registered tonnage of 70, has three twin cabins and two single cabins.

The *Swan and Mallard* cruises the inland waterways of Britain, including the Grand Union Canal, the London Canals, the Oxford Canal, the Stratford Canal and the Rivers Lee and Stort. The *Merganser* cruises from Central London to Windsor and from Windsor to Oxford. All cruises are one week.

Prices per person for a single cabin are actually less than those for a double, at £420 versus £450. Prices on the *Merganser* are £630 per week, and solo occupancy of a twin cabin is an additional £210 .

Because of the high percentage of single cabins, there is also a high percentage of solo travelers. Sheila Purdue, director of Hobo Floating Hotels, estimated that between 30 and 40 percent of their guests are traveling alone. "We welcome them!" Purdue said. "Small capacity means single passengers are always made to feel at home."

Holland America Line

300 Elliott Avenue West
Seattle, WA 98119
(800) 426-0327

Holland America's history dates back as far as 1873, when the company launched its first ocean liner, the original *Rotterdam*, on its itinerary from the Netherlands to New York. Holland America has been providing quality service ever since.

The fleet now includes the *Noordam* and its sister ship, the *Nieuw Amsterdam*, as well as the *Rotterdam* and the *Westerdam*, with the new *Maasdam* debuting in 1993 and the *Ryndam* scheduled for 1994.

While the company provides service to the Caribbean, Panama Canal, South America and the Orient, it also specializes in Alaska tours, providing 73 seven-day sailings during 1992. Choose a cruise for a relaxing week or set off for a cruise of a lifetime on the Grand World Cruise, sailing around the globe for 99 days.

Holland America has a "tipping not required policy," although guests are free to break that rule if they want to reward someone monetarily.

Nieuw Amsterdam

Gross Registered Tonnage 33,930
Passenger Capacity (double occupancy): 1,214
Country of Registry: .... Netherlands Antilles
Nationality of Officers: .... Dutch
Length of Cruise: .... Most are 7 days
Ports of Embarkation: .... Vancouver and Tampa
Ports of Call: .... Caribbean route includes Key West,
Playa del Carmen/Cozumel, Ocho Rios,
Grand Cayman, or Cartagena. Alaskan route
includes Ketchikan, Juneau, Glacier Bay,
Sitka and cruising Inside Passage.
Single Cabins: .... No
Single Supplement: .... Categories B through M: 150%;
Category A: 190%.
Guaranteed Share: .... Available in Categories E and J

Noordam

Gross Registered Tonnage: 33,930
Passenger Capacity (double occupancy): 1,214
Country of Registry: .... Netherlands Antilles
Nationality of Officers: .... Dutch
Length of Cruise: .... Most are 7 days
Ports of Embarkation: .... Vancouver and Ft. Lauderdale
Ports of Call: .... Caribbean Ports include St. Maarten,
Guadeloupe, Barbados, Antigua, St. Thomas,
Curacao, La Guaira, Grenada or Martinique.
Alaska route includes Ketchikan, Juneau,
Glacier Bay, Sitka and cruising Inside Passage
Single Cabins: .... No
Single Supplement: .... Categories B through M: 150%;
Category A: 190%.
Guaranteed Share: .... Available in Categories E and J
Note: .... Gentleman host program included on long cruises

Rotterdam

Gross Registered Tonnage: 38,000
Passenger Capacity (double occupancy): 1,075
Country of Registry: .... Netherlands Antilles
Nationality of Officers: .... Dutch
Length of Cruise: .... Most are 7 days
Ports of Embarkation: .... Vancouver on Alaskan itinerary,
Ft. Lauderdale on Caribbean routes
Ports of Call: .... Caribbean includes St. Thomas, Dominica,
Trinidad, La Guaira, Aruba, Panama
Canal, Grand Cayman. Alaska route includes
Inside Passage, Ketchikan, Sitka, Valdez and Seward
Single Cabins: .... 23—13 outside, 10 inside
Comparison to Double Cabins: .... Inside singles cost about the same
as standard inside cabins; outside
singles cost about the same as deluxe
outside cabins
Single Supplement: .... Categories C through P: 150%;
Categories A and B: 190% on most cruises
Guaranteed Share: .... Available in Categories E and M
Note: .... "Gentleman Hosts" on long cruises

Statendam

Gross Registered Tonnage: 50,000
Passenger Capacity (double occupancy): 1,266
Country of Registry: .... Bahamas
Nationality of Officers: .... Dutch
Length of Cruise: .... 10 to 35 days
Ports of Embarkation: .... Include London, Amsterdam and Rome.
Ports of Call: .... Include Malaga, Monte Carlo, Civitacecchia,
Lisbon, Bordeaux, Copenhagen,
Oslo, St. Petersburg, Helsinki, Naples,
Barcelona, and others
Single Cabins: .... No
Single Supplement: .... On Baltic, Transatlantic and Mediterranean
cruises, Categories C through N: 150%;
Categories S, A & B: 190%
Category PS: 195%; on Grand Europe Cruise,
Categories I-N: 125%; Categories C-H: 150%;
Categories PS, S, A & B: 200% less $300
Guaranteed Share: .... Available in Categories F and K.
Note: .... "Gentleman Hosts" on long cruises

Westerdam

Gross Registered Tonnage: 53,872
Passenger Capacity (double occupancy): 1,494
Country of Registry: .... Bahamas
Nationality of Officers: .... Dutch
Length of Cruise: .... Most are 7 days
Ports of Embarkation: .... Ft. Lauderdale and Vancouver
Ports of Call: .... Caribbean ports include San Juan, Virgin
Gorda and St. Thomas; Alaska route includes
Ketchikan, Juneau, Sitka and cruising Inside Passage
Single Cabins: .... No
Single Supplement: .... In Categories B through N: 150%;
Categories S and A: 190%
Guaranteed Share: .... Available in Categories F and L

Intercruise Ltd.

Olympic Tower
645 Fifth Avenue
New York, NY 10022
(212) 9753-6104

It may seem incongruous to be eating bratwurst and drinking German brew in a Bavarian beer garden, but what else could you expect from a Greek ship that wants to show its international flair?

The *La Palma* travels from Venice through Greece and Turkey and offers all the amenities of a luxury liner: casino, swimming pool, nightly entertainment and shipboard activities.

The seven-day cruise can be extended into a 14-day vacation by adding a one-week stay in Rhodes at a choice of hotels.

Cally Pantelidis, executive vice president of Intercruise Ltd., said, "We welcome solo travelers and know they will enjoy our Greek hospitality."

La Palma

Gross Registered Tonnage: 18,000
Passenger Capacity (double occupancy): 648
Passenger Capacity (all berths): 832
Country of Registry: .... Greece
Nationality of Officers: .... Greek
Length of Cruise: .... 7 days, with shorter segments available
Port of Embarkation: .... Venice
Ports of Call: .... Corfu, Piraeus, Kusadasi, Patmos,
Rhodes and Katakolon
Single Cabins: .... No
Single Supplement: .... Different rates for different cabins,
but runs about 125%
Guaranteed Share: .... Not advertised in the brochure,
but accepted at cruise line's discretion
Note: .... Ship features isolated nudist deck,
swimming pool and Syrtaki dance lessons

Ivaran Lines

111 Pavonia Avenue
Jersey City, NJ 07310-1755
(800) 451-1639

To paraphrase that breath mint ad: It's a freighter! It's a cruise ship! It's two (Click!) two!(Click!) two ships in one!

Yes, Ivaran Lines' *Americana* is a freighter, but promises to deliver the luxury and amenities of many traditional passenger ships. A swimming pool and whirlpool grace the deck, and daily activities include shuffleboard, gambling, bingo and dancing.

And, while the *Americana* is primarily a cargo ship with a capacity of 1,120 containers, it is also the only freighter sailing from the United States with accommodations for more than 12 passengers.

Ivaran claims a 23 per cent repeat business, due in part to the availability of affordable single cabins, according to account executive Louisa Frey-Gaynor. The ship offers inside single cabins costing less than other cabins on board, and outside singles only a few hundred dollars more than doubles.

Americana

Gross Registered Tonnage: 19,500
Passenger Capacity (double occupancy): 88
Passenger Capacity (all berths): 108
Country of Registry: .... Norway
Nationality of Officers: .... Norwegian
Length of Cruise: .... 16 to 45 days
Port of Embarkation: .... Port Elizabeth, New Jersey
Ports of Call: .... Include Rio de Janeiro, Buenos Aires,
Salvador, Montevideo, Norfolk, Savannah,
Miami and others
Single Cabins: .... 20—8 outside, 12 inside
Comparison to Double Cabins: .... Inside singles cost less than
outside singles or outside doubles;
outside single cabins are comparable
in cost to double-occupancy outside cabins
Single Supplement: .... Only single cabins
Guaranteed Share: .... No

KD River Cruises of Europe

170 Hamilton Avenue
White Plains, NY 10601-1788
(800) 346-6525

On KD River cruises, you can travel by the numbers: seven days, six nights, five countries, eight ports, on nine ships cruising four rivers.

The vessels include the *Deutschland, Britannia, France, Austria, Italia, Helvetia* and *Europa*, all passenger ships that wend their way down the Rhine, Moselle and Main Rivers. The two ships cruising the Elbe River are named for pianist and composer Clara Schumann and poet and novelist Theodor Fontane.

Ships' facilities include a glass-walled observation lounge and panoramic windows in the restaurants from which to watch the fascinating river scenery pass by; souvenir and sundry shops on all vessels; and heated outdoor swimming pools on most of the crafts.

Austria, Britannia, Deutschland, Europa, France, Helvetia and Italia

Passenger Capacity (double occupancy): .... 124 to 192
Country of Registry: .... Germany
Nationality of Officers: ....German
Length of Cruise: .... 5 to 7 days
Ports of Embarkation: .... Include Basel, Amsterdam, Strasbourg, Cologne and Frankfurt
Ports of Call: .... Include Basel, Cologne, Dusseldorf, Frankfurt, Heidelberg, Linz, Mainz, Mannheim and Trier
Single Cabins: .... No
Single Supplement: .... Categories B, C and D: 125%; Suites and Category A:150%
Guaranteed Share: .... No
Note: .... Sun decks and souvenir shops on all ships, outdoor pools on most; glass-walled observation lounges

Clara Schumann and Theodore Fontane

Passenger Capacity (double occupancy): .... 124 to 192
Country of Registry: .... Germany
Nationality of Officers: ....German
Length of Cruise: .... 4 to 8 days
Ports of Embarkation: .... Include Wittenberg, Lovosice, Lauenburg, and Schandau
Ports of Call: .... Include Dessau, Hamburg, Havelberg, Prague, Tangermunde and Usti
Single Cabins: .... No
Single Supplement: 150%
Guaranteed Share: .... No
Note: .... Extensive Elbe River itinerary

Le Ponant

c/o Elite Travel International
208 East 58th Street
New York, NY 10022
(212) 752-5440

Le Ponant is a cross between a small cruise ship and a luxury yacht. There are 32 plush double cabins with air-conditioning, mini-bars and safes. There is a decidedly French flair to the ship, with decks named Pont Antigua, Pont Saint Barth and Pont Marie Galante. In the French tradition, unlimited wine is served while dining. A variety of water sports, such as water-skiing, sailboarding and canoeing, along with volleyball and badminton, is offered.

Although not many solo travelers take advantage of Le Ponant's hospitality, "We are happy to have singles," said Robert Hertzka, the line's U.S. representative.

Le Ponant

Passenger Capacity (double occupancy): 64
Passenger Capacity (all berths): 67
Country of Registry: .... France
Nationality of Officers: .... French
Length of Cruise: .... 7 days
Ports of Embarkation: .... Pointe-a-Pitre, Guadeloupe
during winter; Nice during summer
Ports of Call: .... Caribbean route includes The Saintes,
Dominica, St. Martin, Anguilla, St. Bartholomew,
Antigua, Saint Lucia, The Grenadines,
Tobago Cays or Martinique; European route
includes Corsica, Cavallo and Lavezzi,
Poerto Cervo, Ischia and the Aeolian Isles
Single Cabins: .... No
Single Supplement: 150%
Guaranteed Share: .... No

Maine Windjammer Association

Post Office Box 317P
Rockport, Maine 04856
(800) Maine-80

If you want to take a trip back to the country's early beginnings, when tall ships supplied America's east coast with building necessities and fresh seafood, then sail aboard one of Maine Windjammer Association's vessels.

The two- and three-masted schooners depart each Monday from late May to mid-October from Camden, Rockland or Rockport for journeys numbering three and six days.

Meals consist of traditional New England fare: thick chowder, home-baked bread, New England boiled dinner, hot apple pie and hand-cranked ice cream. Each six-day cruise features an authentic lobsterbake, celebrated ashore and featuring those succulent crustaceans, corn on the cob and steamed mussels.

There are thirteen ships in the Maine Windjammer Fleet: At the home port of Rockland are the *American Eagle, Heritage, Isaac H. Evans, Lewis R. French, Nathaniel Bowditch, J. & E. Riggin* and *Timberwind*. At Camden you'll find *Angelique, Grace Bailey, Mary Day, Mercantile* and *Roseway*. Rockport is home to the *Timberwind*.

The vessels range from 64 to 132 feet and carry from 20 to 44 guests. Most of the vessels have some single cabins (at no surcharge), along with some triples and quads, and sharing is quite common and encouraged by the Association.

"Single cabins are available at the same rate, on a first-come, first-served reservation basis. Most singles share a double cabin, unless the vessel is not full, in which case they have a cabin to themselves," said Meg Maiden, public relations director.

Maiden added, "Shipmates develop camaraderie during the cruise, so everyone feels comfortable. Cabins are simple, bathrooms are shared, most time is spent on deck or in common areas."

Majesty Cruise Line

901 South America Way
Miami, FL 33132
(800) 532-7788

Majesty Cruise Line presents a unique itinerary for the passenger looking to enjoy a weekend or mid-week excursion. The *Royal Majesty* claims to be the first major cruise ship offering a four-night cruise from Miami to stop at a port of call in Mexico. During its mid-week tours, the *Royal Majesty* takes passengers to Cozumel/Playa del Carmen, while also allowing its guest to combine the three- and four-day routes into a seven-day vacation.

Taking a unique, healthy approach, the *Royal Majesty* boasts that its dining room is the first to offer a totally smoke-free environment. In addition, 25 percent of the cabins are designated for non-smokers.

In addition, the *Royal Majesty* promotes its meeting and conference facilities, including a meeting room that can accommodate 105 people at one time, as well as smaller executive conference rooms, all with the most modern audio-visual equipment.

Royal Majesty

Gross Registered Tonnage:	32,400
Passenger Capacity (double occupancy):	1,056
Country of Registry:	Panama
Nationality of Officers:	Greek
Length of Cruise:	3 and 4 days
Port of Embarkation:	Miami
Ports of Call:	3-night cruises stop at Nassau/Royal Isle; 4-night cruises visit Playa del Carmen/Cozumel and Key West
Single Cabins:	No
Single Supplement:	Inquire for details
Guaranteed Share:	Not advertised

Marine Atlantic

P.O. Box 250
North Sydney, N.S. B2A 3M3
Canada
(800) 341-7981

Marine Atlantic
Marine Atlantique

The Marine Atlantic system is a network of ferry boats carrying passengers and vehicles from the provinces of Atlantic Canada and the state of Maine. Rates vary depending on the season, the length and distance of the trip, whether a vehicle is to be transported, and whether a cabin is desired.

Following is a brief run-down of just some of the vessels in the Marine Atlantic system, along with cabin availability and amenities.

The *Princess of Acadia* is a 10,050-ton vessel carrying 650 passengers. It operates round trip between St. John, New Brunswick and Digby, Nova Scotia, a distance of 38 nautical miles. The ship has 7 cabins with one berth in each and features a bar lounge, video arcade, cafeteria and news stand. It is registered in Canada and has Canadian officers.

The *Bluenose* carries 1,000 passengers between Yarmouth, Nova Scotia and Bar Harbor, Maine, a distance of 100 nautical miles. It is registered in the Bahamas with Canadian officers and weighs in at 6,524 tons. Passenger capacity in the berths is 105 and ship's amenities include a buffet dining room, movie lounge, duty free shop, video arcade, casino, cafeteria and children's playroom.

The *Northern Ranger* was designed as both a passenger and cargo vessel for "service to the isolated communities of Northern Newfoundland and Labrador." The 2,565-ton vessel carries 131 passengers in deluxe, standard and economy cabins. Single supplement is 150% the double occupancy rate, but Marine Atlantic will consider a guaranteed share upon inquiry.

There are numerous additional vessels in the Marine Atlantic system, including short-distance ferries.

Metropolitan Touring's Galapagos Cruises

c/o Adventure Associates
13150 Coit Road
Suite 110
Dallas, Texas 75240
800-527-2500

The wonders of the Galapagos Islands are waiting to be discovered and Metropolitan Touring wants to help you enjoy them.

You'll travel among the otherwise-isolated islands, possibly retracing the experiences of famed naturalist Charles Darwin. Your day might begin with an exploration of Santa Cruz Island, accompanied by nature guides to point out the sights. Every day is different, as the ship moves among the islands to bring you to each new adventure.

Isabella II

Gross Registered Tonnage: 1,083
Passenger Capacity (all berths): 38
Country of Registry: .... Ecuador
Nationality of Officers: ....Ecuadorian
Length of Cruise:.. 7 nights
Port of Embarkation: .... Baltra
Ports of Call: .... Includes stops at Gardner Bay,
Foreana Island, Tagus Cove and Bartolme.
Single Cabins: .... No
Single Supplement: .... All cabins are double-occupancy and the
same price, but can be booked for single occupancy
at about 120% the double occupancy rate
Guaranteed Share:..................................... Not advertised in brochure, but
accepted at cruise line's discretion

Santa Cruz

Gross Registered Tonnage: 1,500
Passenger Capacity (double occupancy): 90
Passenger Capacity (all berths): 90
Country of Registry: .... Equador
Nationality of Officers: .... Equadorian
Length of Cruise:...... 3 and 4 nights; can be combined for 7-day itinerary
Port of Embarkation: .... Baltra
Ports of Call: .... 3-night itinerary stops at North Islands;
4-night route visits South Islands
Single Cabins: .... 5—all inside
Comparison to Double Cabins: .... About 150%
Single Supplement: .... 200% of other outside cabins
Guaranteed Share:... Not in the brochure, but
accepted at cruise company's discretion

Nabila Nile Cruises

c/o Naggar Tours
605 Market Street
Suite 1310
San Francisco, CA 94105
(800) 443-NILE

Imagine floating down the Nile and watching a blend of ancient and modern-day Egypt floating by. The five Nabila vessels cruising the Nile offer all-suite accommodations and single-seating dining, along with swimming pools and spacious lounge areas. The vessels, with the historic names of *Ramses of Egypt, Queen Nabila I, Ramses King of the Nile, Queen Nabila III* and *Queen of Sheba*, feature interiors inspired by Egyptian and Moorish decor.

There are itineraries available for four and six nights, or you can take the entire tour/cruise package of 15 days and really get to see Egypt.

Although there are no single cabins and no guaranteed share among the Nile ships, single occupancy of a twin cabin is available. Since the rates are figured per cabin instead of per person, solo occupancy of a twin cabin for four- and six-night cruises runs about 165 percent of double occupancy. But on the 15-day cruise tour, solo travelers only pay about 115 percent the double-occupancy rate.

Omar Zaher, senior vice president, commented, "We welcome solo travelers and believe they enjoy interaction with everyone on board."

Queen Nabila I

```
Gross Registered Tonnage: ................................................................ 950
Passenger Capacity (double occupancy): ............................................. 120
Passenger Capacity (all berths): ....................................................... 123
Country of Registry: ....................................................................... Egypt
Nationality of Officers: ............................................................... Egyptian
Length of Cruise/Tour: ........................................................ 4 to 15 days
Port of Embarkation: .................................................... Luxor or Aswan
Ports of Call: .......................................... 4-night tour includes temples at
                        Karnak, Luxor, Esna, Edfu, Kom Ombo and
                        Agha Khan mausoleum; 6-night cruise add
                    temples of Hathor, and Seti First;  15-day tour
                        includes sightseeing in Cairo, Alexandria
                                                   and El Alamein
Single Cabins: ................................................................................ No
Single Supplement: ........................... Single occupancy of twin cabin runs
                        about 165% on shorter cruises but drops
                        to about 115% for 15-day cruise/tour
Guaranteed Share: ......................................................................... No
```

Queen Nabila III

Gross Registered Tonnage: 1,150
Passenger Capacity (double occupancy): 156
Passenger Capacity (all berths): 159
Country of Registry: .... Egypt
Nationality of Officers: .... Egyptian
Length of Cruise/Tour: .... 4 to 15 days
Port of Embarkation: .... Luxor or Aswan
Ports of Call: .... 4-night tour includes temples at Karnak,
Luxor, Esna, Edfu, Kom Ombo and Agha Khan
mausoleum; 6-night cruise add temples of
Hathor, and Seti First; 15-day tour includes
sightseeing in Cairo, Alexandria and El Alamein
Single Cabins: .... No
Single Supplement: .... Single occupancy of twin cabin runs
about 165% on shorter cruises but drops to
about 115% for 15-day cruise/tour
Guaranteed Share: .... No

Queen of Sheba

Gross Registered Tonnage: 1,150
Passenger Capacity (double occupancy): 154
Passenger Capacity (all berths): 157
Country of Registry: .... Egypt
Nationality of Officers: .... Egyptian
Length of Cruise/Tour: .... 4 to 15 days
Port of Embarkation: .... Luxor or Aswan
Ports of Call: .... 4-night tour includes temples at Karnak,
Luxor, Esna, Edfu, Kom Ombo and Agha Khan
mausoleum; 6-night cruise add temples of
Hathor, and Seti First; 15-day tour includes
sightseeing in Cairo, Alexandria and El Alamein
Single Cabins: .... No
Single Supplement: .... Single occupancy of twin cabin runs about
165% on shorter cruises but drops to about
115% for 15-day cruise/tour
Guaranteed Share: .... No

Ramses King of the Nile

Gross Registered Tonnage: 1,150
Passenger Capacity (double occupancy): 152
Passenger Capacity (all berths): 155
Country of Registry: .... Egypt
Nationality of Officers: .... Egyptian
Length of Cruise/Tour: .... 4 to 15 days
Port of Embarkation: .... Luxor or Aswan
Ports of Call: .... 4-night tour includes temples at Karnak,
                          Luxor, Esna, Edfu, Kom Ombo and Agha Khan
                     mausoleum; 6-night cruise add temples of Hathor,
                      and Seti First; 15-day tour includes sightseeing
                                    in Cairo, Alexandria and El Alamein
Single Cabins: .... No
Single Supplement: .... Single occupancy of twin cabin runs
                           about 165% on shorter cruises but drops
                           to about 115% for 15-day cruise/tour
Guaranteed Share: .... No

Ramses of Egypt

Gross Registered Tonnage: 700
Passenger Capacity (double occupancy): 72
Passenger Capacity (all berths): 74
Country of Registry: .... Egypt
Nationality of Officers: .... Egyptian
Length of Cruise/Tour: .... 4 to 15 days
Port of Embarkation: .... Luxor or Aswan
Ports of Call: .... 4-night tour includes temples at Karnak,
                          Luxor, Esna, Edfu, Kom Ombo and Agha Khan
                     mausoleum; 6-night cruise add temples of Hathor,
                      and Seti First; 15-day tour includes sightseeing
                                    in Cairo, Alexandria and El Alamein
Single Cabins: .... No
Single Supplement: .... Single occupancy of twin cabin runs
                           about 165% on shorter cruises but drops
                           to about 115% for 15-day cruise/tour
Guaranteed Share: .... No

Norwegian Cruise Line

95 Merrick Way
Coral Gables, FL 33134
(800) 327-7030

Currently, Norwegian Cruise Line has limited its itineraries to the popular ports of call in the Bahamas, Eastern and Western Caribbean, Mexico, Bermuda and along the California coast. The fleet of ships continues to grow, with the *Dreamward* entering service in 1992 and the *Windward* debuting in 1993.

Noted for their theme cruises, mostly aboard the line's massive *Norway*, NCL promises a schedule featuring such centers of attention as country music, comedy, jazz and big band, with appropriate celebrities entertaining.

The athletically inclined might be interested in NCL's "Sports Afloat" program, which includes lectures, workshops, activities and celebrity appearances centering around golf, tennis, snorkeling, football and other sports.

NCL's ships are popular with solo travelers because of their guaranteed single rates, guaranteed shares and diverse itineraries. The flagship of the fleet, the *Norway*, is currently the largest and longest ship afloat, featuring a variety of accommodations and activities befitting a ship of this stature.

Dreamward

```
Gross Registered Tonnage: ............................................. 41,000
Passenger Capacity (double occupancy): ......................... 1,246
Passenger Capacity (all berths): ..................................... 1,800
Country of Registry: .................................................. Bahamas
Nationality of Officers: ............................................ Norwegian
Length of Cruise: ....................................................... 7 days
Ports of Embarkation: ................................ Ft. Lauderdale for Caribbean;
                                                  New York for Bermuda
Ports of Call: .................................... Eastern Caribbean stops at Nassau,
                              San Juan, St. John/St. Thomas; Western
                              Caribbean visits Grand Cayman, Playa del
                              Carmen/Cozumel, Cancun, Pleasure Island;
                           Bermuda cruise visits St. George's and Hamilton
Single Cabins: ............................................................... No
Single Supplement: ......................................... 150% to 200%
Guaranteed Share: .......................................................... No
Guaranteed Single: ........................................ Comparable to a mid-priced
                                                outside cabin, with assignment at
                                                the discretion of the cruise line
```

Norway

Gross Registered Tonnage: 76,049
Passenger Capacity (double occupancy): 2,022
Passenger Capacity (all berths): 2,548
Country of Registry: .... Bahamas
Nationality of Officers: .... Norwegian
Port of Embarkation: .... Miami
Ports of Call: .... St. John/St. Thomas, NCL's Pleasure Island
and either San Juan or St. Maarten
Length of Cruise: .... 7 days
Single Cabins: .... 20—all inside
Comparison to Double Cabins: .... Comparable to other similar cabins
Single Supplement: .... 150% to 200%
Guaranteed Share: .... Quad share available at cruise line's discretion
Guaranteed Single: .... Comparable to mid-priced cabins,
with assignment at discretion of the cruise line.
Note: .... Ship features 6,000 sq. ft. Roman Spa, a la carte restaurant

Seaward

Gross Registered Tonnage: 42,000
Passenger Capacity (double occupancy): 1,534
Passenger Capacity (all berths): 1,841
Country of Registry: .... Bahamas
Nationality of Officers: .... Norwegian
Length of Cruise: .... 7 days
Port of Embarkation: .... Miami
Ports of Call: .... NCL's Pleasure Island, Ocho Rios,
Grand Cayman, Playa del Carmen/Cozumel
Single Cabins: .... No
Single Supplement: .... 150% to 200%
Guaranteed Share: .... No
Guaranteed Single: .... Comparable to mid-priced cabin with
assignment at discretion of the cruise line

Southward

Gross Registered Tonnage: 16,607
Passenger Capacity (double occupancy): 752
Passenger Capacity (all berths): 1,005
Country of Registry: .... Bahamas
Nationality of Officers: .... Norwegian
Length of Cruise: .... 3 and 4 days
Port of Embarkation: .... Los Angeles
Ports of Call: .... Catalina Island and Ensenada on 3-day
cruises; add San Diego on 4-day cruises
Single Cabins: .... 9—all outside
Comparison to Double Cabins: .... Same as double occupancy, but
discount programs do not apply
Single Supplement: .... 150% to 200%
Guaranteed Share: .... Quad share available at
cruise line's discretion
Guaranteed Single: .... Comparable to mid-priced or
upper-priced cabins with assignment
at the discretion of the cruise line

Starward

Gross Registered Tonnage: 16,107
Passenger Capacity (double occupancy): 758
Passenger Capacity (all berths): 1,003
Country of Registry: .... Bahamas
Nationality of Officers: .... Norwegian
Length of Cruise: .... 7 days
Port of Embarkation: .... Los Angeles
Ports of Call: .... Cabo San Lucas, Mazatlan, Puerto Vallarta
Single Cabins: .... No
Single Supplement: .... 150% to 200%
Guaranteed Share: .... Quad share available at cruise line's discretion
Guaranteed Single: .... Comparable to mid-priced outside
cabin with assignment at discretion
of the cruise line

Westward

Gross Registered Tonnage: 28,000
Passenger Capacity (double occupancy): 829
Passenger Capacity (all berths): 831
Country of Registry: .... Bahamas
Nationality of Officers: .... Norwegian
Length of Cruise: .... 3 and 4 days
Port of Embarkation: .... Ft. Lauderdale
Ports of Call: .... Key West and NCL's Pleasure Island on 3-day cruises;
Nassau, Pleasure Island and Freeport on 4 -day cruises
Single Cabins: .... No
Single Supplement: .... 150% to 200%
Guaranteed Share: .... No
Guaranteed Single: .... Comparable to a mid-priced outside
cabin, with assignment at the
discretion of the cruise line

Windward

Gross Registered Tonnage: 41,000
Passenger Capacity (double occupancy): 1,246
Passenger Capacity (all berths): 1,806
Country of Registry: .... Bahamas
Nationality of Officers: .... Norwegian
Length of Cruise: .... 7 days
Port of Embarkation: .... San Juan
Ports of Call: .... Aruba, Curacao, Tortola/Virgin Gorda and
St. John/St. Thomas alternate with Barbados,
Martinique, St. Maarten, Antigua and St. Thomas
Single Cabins: .... No
Single Supplement: .... 150% to 200%
Guaranteed Share: .... No
Guaranteed Single: .... Comparable to a mid-priced outside
cabin, with assignment at the discretion
of the cruise line
Note: .... NCL's newest ship

Oceanic Cruise Lines

5757 W. Century Blvd.
Suite 390
Los Angeles, CA 90045
(800) 545-5778

Its unique itinerary, including visits to ports in Japan, China and South Korea, make the *Oceanic Grace* an ideal choice for the traveler yearning for the charm of the Orient.

In addition, the cuisine on the *Oceanic Grace* is prepared by chefs trained at Tokyo's Palace Hotel, and incorporates fresh ingredients bought at ports along the way. All menus are printed in both Japanese and English.

According to Bill Balfour of the sales office, "The *Oceanic Grace* is a very friendly ship. We will always try our best to assist a solo passenger and will attempt to find another customer who is willing to share."

Oceanic Grace

```
Gross Registered Tonnage: .............................................. 5,050
Passenger Capacity (double occupancy): ............................. 120
Passenger Capacity (all berths): ......................................... 120
Country of Registry: ...................................................... Japan
Nationality of Officers: ........................... Japanese, American and British
Length of Cruise: ................................................. 3 to 12 days
Ports of Embarkation: ...................... Various cities throughout the Orient,
                                             including Yokohama, Kobe and Tokyo
Ports of Call: ................................... Include Osaka, Hiroshima, Shanghai,
                                                 Tiensin, Shimizu and Akita
Single Cabins: ................................................................. No
Single Supplement: ........................................................ 150%
Guaranteed Share: ................... Not advertised in the brochure, but cruise
                                        line will attempt to make a match
```

OdessAmerica Cruise Company

170 Old Country Road
Suite 608
Mineola, NY 11505
(800) 221-3254

Cruises through the Russian and Ukrainian waterways, trips down the Dnieper River, expeditions to Antarctica and Mayan country are all included in the unusual itineraries offered by OdessAmerica Cruise Company.

Adventurous passengers can tour Russia aboard the *Andropov* from May through September, or take passage on the *Gruziya* October through May on a Mayan adventure, affording passenger the opportunity to experience a real Russian-style ship.

OdessAmerica calls itself the "Cruise Line of the Czars," and each of its ships provides traditional Russian food, entertainment and hospitality.

Most of OdessAmerica's ships have either single cabins, a slew of cabins with no supplement, or a guaranteed-share policy, allowing for a great deal of flexibility for the solo traveler. OdessAmerica Vice President Claudia Casson said that on the *Columbus Caravelle*, the percentage of solo travelers often comprises 60 percent of the ship, noting: "The fact that single travelers are not forced to pay a supplement or surcharge for occupying a cabin alone is a real selling point."

Andropov

Gross Registered Tonnage:	4,800
Passenger Capacity (double occupancy):	250
Passenger Capacity (all berths):	287
Country of Registry:	Russia
Nationality of Officers:	Russian, with American cruise staff
Length of Cruise/Tour:	16 days
Port of Embarkation:	Moscow or St. Petersburg
Ports of Call:	Uglich, Kostroma, Yaroslavl, Irma, Gortitzy, Kizhi, Valaam and St. Petersburg
Single Cabins:	12—all outside
Comparison to Double Cabins:	Only $100 more over the 16 day cruise than comparable double cabins
Guaranteed Share:	Accepted at the cruise line's discretion
Note:	Some meals feature Blini de Czar with red and black caviar, Russian vodka and other traditional Russian fare; included in the price are sightseeing tours in each city. Itinerary is a river cruise along the Neva, Svir and Volga Rivers

Azerbaydzhan

Gross Registered Tonnage: 15,000
Passenger Capacity (double occupancy): 500
Passenger Capacity (all berths): 650
Country of Registry: .... Ukraine
Nationality of Officers: .... Ukranian/Russian with British cruise staff
Length of Cruise: .... 15 days
Ports of Embarkation: .... Include Tilbury, Liverpool,
Perth and Southampton
Ports of Call: .... Include Lisbon, Nice, Livorno, Gibraltar,
Casablanca, Liverpool, Dublin, Malaga and Tangier
Single Cabins: .... No
Single Supplement: .... Single occupancy of a 3rd Deck outside
cabin runs 150% the double occupancy rate
Guaranteed Share: .... Inquire about availability

Columbus Caravel

Gross Registered Tonnage: 7,560
Passenger Capacity (double occupancy): 250
Passenger Capacity (all berths): 270
Country of Registry: .... Ukraine
Nationality of Officers: .... Ukrainian and Russian
Length of Cruise: .... Most are 14 days
Ports of Embarkation: .... Include Punta Arenas, Chile; Belem,
Brazil; and Bremerhaven, Germany
Ports of Call: .... Various ports in Russian Arctic, Antarctic,
Greenland, Iceland, South America and the Amazon
Single Cabins: 70
Comparison to Double Cabins: .... No additional supplement
Single Supplement: .... Single cabins only
Guaranteed Share: .... No
Note: .... Ship is rated "Ice Class IA," certifying
maximum safety for polar regions.

Glushkov

Gross Registered Tonnage: 4,910
Passenger Capacity (double occupancy): 288
Passenger Capacity (all berths): 300
Country of Registry: .... Ukraine
Nationality of Officers: .... Ukrainian with American staff
Length of Cruise: .... 7 nights
Port of Embarkation: .... Odessa or Kiev
Ports of Call: .... Include Khanev, Kremenchug, Dnepropetrovsk,
Zaprorozhye, New Kakhovka and Kherson
Single Cabins: .... No
Single Supplement: .... Single occupancy rate of a double cabin
is same as the price for an outside deluxe suite
Guaranteed Share: .... Accepted at cruise line's discretion
Note: .... Itinerary cruises Dnepr River; price includes
Russian-style entertainment and sightseeing

Gruziya

Gross Registered Tonnage: 15,500
Passenger Capacity (double occupancy): 400
Passenger Capacity (all berths): 650
Country of Registry: .... Ukraine
Nationality of Officers: .... Ukrainian and Russian with
North American cruise staff
Length of Cruise:.. 6 to 16 days
Ports of Embarkation: .... Include St. Petersburg, Florida
and Montreal, Canada
Ports of Call: .... Mayan route includes Puerto Cortes,
Belize City, Cancun; Canadian route includes
Montreal, Prince Edward Island, Gaspe and Quebec City
Single Cabins: .... No
Single Supplement: .... Single occupancy in Categories 8 and 9,
(outside upper and lower) is available
at about 150% the double occupancy rate
Guaranteed Share:......................... Accepted at the cruise line's discretion
Note: .... Single-seating dining with Russian cuisine;
Russian/Ukrainian gift shop

Kareliya

Gross Registered Tonnage: 15,000
Passenger Capacity (double occupancy): 500
Passenger Capacity (all berths): 650
Country of Registry: .... Ukraine
Nationality of Officers: .... Ukrainian/Russian with British cruise staff
Length of Cruise:... 15 days
Port of Embarkation: .... Tilbury, England
Ports of Call: ...... Include ports in Africa, western Europe, Canary Island,
Mediterranean, Scandinavia and other areas
Single Cabins: .... No
Single Supplement: .... Single occupancy of 3rd Deck outside
cabin runs about 150% the double-occupancy rate
Guaranteed Share:............................. Accepted at cruise line's discretion

Pacific Cruises Inc.

#620-1090 West Georgia Street
Vancouver, British Columbia
Canada V6E 3V7
(800) 661-4646

The 44-passenger *Malecite* has a video entertainment area, stand-up bar, 360-degree panoramic viewing area and a galley with dining area—but no cabins.

The reason there are no cabins is that the *Malecite* cruises from port to port during the day, dropping off guests to settle in for dinner and the evening's stay at various waterfront inns and lodges each night. Pacific Cruises features calm-water cruising along British Columbia's magnificent coastline, emphasizing the history, nature and heritage of the area.

A typical day features a morning of island hopping from South Pender Island to Plumper Sound to Saturna Island and others, after which the Malecite arrives at Cowichan Bay. After touring the Duncan Forestry Museum and Native Heritage Centre, guests will be transported to Inn at the Water for dinner and a relaxing night before once again embarking on the *Malecite* and other adventures.

There is always a naturalist on board, featuring lectures on heritage and culture of the areas to be visited.

"Solo travelers have the company of other passengers during cruising and private time once we dock, if they choose," said Christine Murphy, director of marketing and sales.

Malecite

```
Gross Registered Tonnage: ..................................................... 97
Passenger Capacity (double occupancy): ............................... 44
Country of Registry: ................................................... Canada
Nationality of Officers: ............................................ Canadian
Length of Cruise: .................................................... 6 days
Port of Embarkation: .............. Sidney or Quadra Island, British Columbia
Ports of Call: ......................... Roche Harbor, Cowichan Bay, Chemainus,
                                Nanoose Bay, Marina Island, Cortes Island,
                                             along with island hopping.
Single Cabins: ........................................................... No
Single Supplement: ............................................ About 120%
Guaranteed Share: ..................... Not advertised in brochure but
                                   accepted at cruise line's discretion
```

Premier Cruise Lines, Ltd.

400 Challenger Road
Cape Canaveral, FL 32920
(800) 327-7113

If you're looking out over the ocean and see a big, red boat sailing by, chances are it's one in the Premier fleet. In fact, each of the three ships in the line, the *Atlantic*, *Majestic* and *Oceanic*, is probably better known as the "Big Red Boat" than by its official name.

Premier is also the "Official Cruise Line of Walt Disney World," so the three- and four-night cruises are most often combined with packages to the Magic Kingdom. In addition, children will be treated to roaming Disney characters aboard ship, when they're not busy making their own ice cream sundaes or playing in the arcade or teen center

Although the vast majority of passengers on Premier are families, there is also a special single-parent rate for a parent traveling alone with a child or children. As for the solo traveler, Premier's public relations coordinator Paula Meyer commented: "Singles are always welcome on Premier. It's a great place for singles to meet new friends and share all the excitement of a Premier cruise."

Atlantic

Gross Registered Tonnage: 36,500
Passenger Capacity (double occupancy): 1,070
Passenger Capacity (all berths): 1,500
Country of Registry: .... Liberia
Nationality of Officers: .... International
Length of Cruise: .... 3 and 4 days
Port of Embarkation: .... Port Canaveral
Ports of Call: .... Nassau and Port Lucaya
Single Cabins: .... No
Single Supplement: .... Categories 3 through 8: 175%
Guaranteed Share: .... No
Single Parent Plan: .... Parent pays 125% double-occupancy rate
plus lower third- or fourth-person rate for each child

Majestic

Gross Registered Tonnage: 17,750
Passenger Capacity (double occupancy): 760
Passenger Capacity (all berths): 1,006
Country of Registry: .... Bahamas
Nationality of Officers: .... International
Length of Cruise: .... 3 and 4 days
Port of Embarkation: .... Port Everglades
Ports of Call: .... Nassau and Port Lucaya
Single Cabins: .... No
Single Supplement: .... Categories 3 through 7: 175%
Guaranteed Share: .... No
Single Parent Plan: .... Parent pays 125% double-occupancy rate plus
lower third- or fourth-person rate for each child

Oceanic

Gross Registered Tonnage: 40,000
Passenger Capacity (double occupancy): 1,132
Passenger Capacity (all berths): 1,609
Country of Registry: .... Bahamas
Nationality of Officers: .... International
Length of Cruise: .... 3 and 4 days
Port of Embarkation: .... Port Canaveral
Ports of Call: .... Nassau and Port Lucaya
Single Cabins: .... No
Single Supplement: .... Categories 3 through 8: 175%
Guaranteed Share: .... No
Single Parent Plan: .... Parent pays 125% double-occupancy rate plus
                           lower third- or fourth-person rate for each child

Princess Cruises

10100 Santa Monica Boulevard
Los Angeles, CA 90067
(800) 568-3262

You won't find Doc, Gopher and Julie running around this "Love Boat," but you will find friendly, helpful people making you feel like one of television's pampered guests. And, while the Princess line was the setting for the popular TV show which is no longer in production, Gavin McLeod (Captain Stubing) still remains the company spokesperson.

The ships in the fleet, all with Princess in their name, roam the world covering more ports and more itineraries than any other cruise line, according to "Princess Cruises News."

The cuisine aboard is definitely Continental and Italian: Six of the ships have their own pizzerias and, on a typical 10-day cruise, more than 25 different types of pasta are served.

Princess is so beloved by their passengers that at least one-third of the passengers on any cruise are repeat sailors, and the number goes as high as 80 per cent on certain exotic destinations, according to recent figures.

"Solo travelers are welcome," said Kathey Truschel of Princess' P.R. department, and the line will continue to develop special booking discounts and incentives for those traveling alone.

Crown Princess

Gross Registered Tonnage: 70,000
Passenger Capacity (double occupancy): 1,590
Country of Registry: .... Liberia
Nationality of Officers: .... Italian
Length of Cruise: .... Most are 7 days
Ports of Embarkation: .... Ft. Lauderdale and Vancouver
Ports of Call: .... Caribbean routes include Princess Cays,
Montego Bay, Grand Cayman, Playa del
Carmen/Cozumel, San Juan, St. Maarten
or St. Thomas ; Alaska route includes
Juneau, Skagway, Glacier Bay, Ketchikan
and Inside Passage
Single Cabins: .... No
Single Supplement: .... Categories CC through M on Mexico
Caribbean routes: 150%; Categories CC
through M on Alaskan route: 160%;
Categories AA through B on all routes: 200%
Guaranteed Share: .... Not advertised in the brochure, but cruise line
will accept in certain categories at their discretion

Fair Princess

Gross Registered Tonnage: 25,000
Passenger Capacity (double occupancy): 890
Country of Registry: .... Liberia
Nationality of Officers: .... Italian
Length of Cruise: .... Most are 7 to 11 days
Ports of Embarkation: .... Include Anchorage/Seward or Vancouver;
Papeete, Honolulu and Los Angeles
Ports of Call: .... Alaskan ports include cruising Sitka or
Glacier Bay, Skagway, Juneau and Ketchikan;
Mexican ports include Cabo San Lucas,
Mazatlan and Puerto Vallarta; South Pacific
ports include Moorea, Bora Bora, Christmas
Island, Hilo and Lahaina
Single Cabins: .... No
Single Supplement: .... For Categories CC through P on
Mexico cruises: 150%; Categories
CC through P on Alaska and Hawaii/Tahiti
cruises: 160%; Categories A and B on
all routes: 200%
Guaranteed Share: .... Not advertised in the brochure, but cruise line
will accept in certain categories at their discretion

Golden Princess

Gross Registered Tonnage: 28,000
Passenger Capacity (double occupancy): 830
Country of Registry: .... Bahamas
Nationality of Officers: .... Finnish, British and Italian
Length of Cruise: .... Most are 7 and 10 days
Ports of Embarkation: .... San Francisco and Los Angeles
Ports of Call: .... Alaska itinerary includes Victoria, Vancouver,
Juneau, Sitka, and Ketchikan; Mexico route
includes Puerto Vallarta, Ixtapa/Zijuatenejo,
Acapulco, Mazatlan and Cabo San Lucas
Single Cabins: .... No
Single Supplement: .... Categories FF through K on Mexican
routes: 150%; Categories FF through K
on Alaska and Hawaii routes: 160%;
All other categories: 200%
Guaranteed Share: .... Not advertised in the brochure, but cruise line
will accept in certain categories at their discretion

Island Princess

Gross Registered Tonnage: 20,000
Passenger Capacity (double occupancy): 610
Country of Registry: .... Great Britain
Nationality of Officers: .... British
Length of Cruise:... Most are 12 to 14 days
Ports of Embarkation: .... Include Venice, Barcelona, Athens,
Syndey, Auckland and Papeete
Ports of Call: .... Mediterranean/Black Sea routes include
Olympia, Mykonos/Delos, Messina, Rome, Livorno,
Cannes, Yalta, Odessa, Constanta, Istanbul,
Izmir or Santorini; South Pacific includes
Wellington, Moorea, Pago Pago or Melbourne
Single Cabins: .... Two—outside deluxe singles
Comparison to Double Cabins: .... Slightly higher than outside deluxe
mini-suites and about 125% the cost
of comparable outside deluxe cabins
Single Supplement: .... Categories FF through K: 160%;
Categories A, B, DD, D and E: 200%.
Guaranteed Share: .... Not advertised in the brochure, but cruise line
will accept in certain categories at their discretion

Pacific Princess

Gross Registered Tonnage: 20,000
Passenger Capacity (double occupancy): 610
Country of Registry: .... Great Britain
Nationality of Officers: .... British
Length of Cruise:... Most are 12 to 16 days
Ports of Embarkation: .... Include London, Barcelona, Venice,
Bangkok, Hong Kong and Kobe
Ports of Call: .... Mediterranean/Atlantic routes include Lisbon,
Tangier, Cannes, Gibraltar, Athens or Livorno;
Asian routes include Singapore, Bali and Canton
Single Cabins: .... Two—outside deluxe singles
Comparison to Double Cabins: .... Slightly higher than outside deluxe
mini-suites and about 125% the cost of
comparable deluxe cabins
Single Supplement: .... Categories FF through K: 160%;
Categories A, B, DD, D and E: 200%.
Guaranteed Share: .... Not advertised in the brochure, but cruise line
will accept in certain categories at their discretion

Regal Princess

Gross Registered Tonnage: 70,000
Passenger Capacity (double occupancy): 1,590
Country of Registry: .... Liberia
Nationality of Officers: .... Italian
Length of Cruise: .... Most are 7 to 11 days
Ports of Embarkation: .... Ft. Lauderdale and Vancouver
Ports of Call: .... Caribbean routes include Princess Cays,
Montego Bay, Grand Cayman,Playa del
Carmen/Cozumel, San Juan, St. Maarten,
St. Thomas, Ocho Rios, Cartagena, or
Puerto Caldero; Alaskan route includes
Juneau, Skagway, Glacier Bay and Ketchikan
Single Cabins: .... No
Single Supplement: .... Categories CC through M on Caribbean
and Mexico routes: 150%;
Categories CC through M on Alaskan and
Transcanal routes: 160%;
Categories AA through B on all routes: 200%
Guaranteed Share: .... Not advertised in the brochure, but cruise line
will accept in certain categories at their discretion
Note: .... Ship features pizzeria, wine & caviar bar,
patisserie, in-pool bar and domed observation
lounge with casino; some cabins with
verandas and balconies

Royal Princess

Gross Registered Tonnage: 45,000
Passenger Capacity (double occupancy): 1,200
Country of Registry: .... Great Britain
Nationality of Officers: .... British
Length of Cruise: .... Most are 10 to 14 days
Ports of Embarkation: .... Include Acapulco, San Juan,
London, New York and Montreal
Ports of Call: .... Transcanal route includes Puerto Caldera,
Cartagena, St. Maarten, St. Thomas, Curacao or
Grenada; European routes include Stockholm,
Helsinki, St. Petersburg, Copenhagen and
Amsterdam; New England Route includes
Newport, Boston, Halifax and Quebec City
Single Cabins: .... No
Single Supplement: .... Categories EE through K : 160%;
Categories AA through D: 200%
Guaranteed Share: .... Not advertised in the brochure, but cruise line
will accept in certain categories at their discretion
Note: .... All outside staterooms

Sky Princess

Gross Registered Tonnage: 46,000
Passenger Capacity (double occupancy): 1,200
Country of Registry: .... Great Britain
Nationality of Officers: .... British
Length of Cruise: .... 7 to 15 days
Ports of Embarkation: .... Include Acapulco, Los Angeles,
Vancouver and Anchorage/Seward
Ports of Call: .... Transcanal routes include Puerto Caldera,
Cartagena, Ocho Rios, Cabo San Lucas
or Princess Cays; Alaskan route includes Sitka,
Skagway, Juneau and Ketchikan
Single Cabins: .... No
Single Supplement: .... Categories C through M on Caribbean
routes: 150%; Categories C through M on
Alaska and Transcanal routes: 160%;
Categories AA and B: 200%
Guaranteed Share: .... Not advertised in the brochure, but cruise line
will accept in certain categories at their discretion

Star Princess

Gross Registered Tonnage: 63,500
Passenger Capacity (double occupancy): 1,490
Country of Registry: .... Liberia
Nationality of Officers: .... Italian
Length of Cruise: .... Most are 7 days
Ports of Embarkation: .... Include San Juan, Anchorage/Seward
and Vancouver
Ports of Call: .... Caribbean route includes Barbados, Mayreau,
Martinique, St. Maarten and St. Thomas;
Alaskan route includes Sitka, Skagway,
Juneau and Ketchikan
Single Cabins: .... No
Single Supplement: .... Categories CC through M on Caribbean
and Mexico routes: 150%; Categories CC
through M for Alaska and Transcanal routes: 160%;
Categories AA and A: 200%
Guaranteed Share: .... Not advertised in the brochure, but cruise
line will accept in certain categories at their discretion
Note: .... Ship features pizzeria, wine and caviar bar,
patisserie, three-story atrium lobby

Renaissance Cruises

1800 Eller Drive
Suite 300
P.O. Box 350307
Fort Lauderdale, FL 33335-0307
(800) 525-5350

From the small, intimate islands of the Caribbean to the popular destinations of the Mediterranean to the exotic ports of the Asia and Africa, there is a yacht-like Renaissance ship waiting to transport you. The eight ships in the Renaissance fleet are "designed for adventure, not just for luxury," as the brochures advertises, but luxury is hard to ignore, nonetheless.

Each of the eight ships (with *Renaissance I* in dry dock) features either four or five different types of outside suites, and the vessels house a maximum of 114 pampered guests. Take advantage of the line's "Blue Water Adventures" program and use their equipment for scuba, snorkeling, sailing and jet skiing, while getting instruction on how to master these water sports. Then mingle easily with the other passengers during the single-seating gourmet dinner.

Although there are no guaranteed shares offered and a single supplement is added, the solo traveler is advised to check for special offers on selected sailings. According to marketing assistant Nancy Pierce, the single supplement is waived on selected sailing dates.

"Renaissance caters to the discerning traveler interested in quaint, pristine ports of call which attracts the traveler in all of us, whether traveling alone or with a companion," she added.

Renaissance II

Gross Registered Tonnage:	4,000
Passenger Capacity (double occupancy):	100
Passenger Capacity (all berths):	100
Country of Registry:	Italy
Nationality of Officers:	European
Length of Cruise:	7 to 14 nights
Ports of Embarkation:	Include Barcelona, Rome, Istanbul and Athens
Ports of Call:	Include Port-Vendres, Monte Carlo, Portofino, Ibiza, Paros, Kos, Lesbos or Canakkale
Single Cabins:	No
Single Supplement:	200% on top-level suites but flat-rate supplement added to other cabins, running between 125% and 150% of double-occupancy rate, depending on accommodations selected.
Guaranteed Share:	No

Renaissance III

Gross Registered Tonnage: 4,000
Passenger Capacity (double occupancy): 100
Passenger Capacity (all berths): 100
Country of Registry: .... Italy
Nationality of Officers: .... European
Length of Cruise: .... 7 to 14 nights
Ports of Embarkation: .... Include Antigua in the Caribbean;
Rome, Istanbul, Athens and Athens in
the Mediterranean and Aegean
Ports of Call: .... Caribbean routes include Dominica,
St. Lucia, St. Vincent and Bequia; Mediterranean
and Aegean include Sorrento, Lipari, Zante,
Pylos, Ithira, Paros, Kos, Bodrum, Chios,
Lesbos, Monte Carlo and Portofino.
Single Cabins: .... No
Single Supplement: .... 200% on top-level suites but flat-rate
supplement added to other cabins, running
between 125% and 150% of double-occupancy
rate, depending on accommodations selected.
Guaranteed Share: .... No

Renaissance IV

Gross Registered Tonnage: 4,000
Passenger Capacity (double occupancy): 100
Passenger Capacity (all berths): 100
Country of Registry: .... Italy
Nationality of Officers: .... European
Length of Cruise: .... 7 to 14 nights
Ports of Embarkation: .... Include Rome, Barcelona, Istanbul,
Athens, Stockholm, Copenhagen and Antigua
Ports of Call: ....Mediterranean and Aegean routes include
Portofino, Monte Carlo, Paros, Mykonos, Rhodes,
Patmos, Kusadasi; Scandinavian route includes
Tallinn, St. Petersburg, Helsinki and Amsterdam;
Caribbean includes St. Kitts, St. Croix, Virgin Gorda,
St. Maarten and St. Barts
Single Cabins: .... No
Single Supplement: .... 200% on top-level suites but flat-rate
supplement added to other cabins, running
between 125% and 150% of double-occupancy
rate, depending on accommodations selected.
Guaranteed Share: .... No

Renaissance V

Gross Registered Tonnage: 4,300
Passenger Capacity (double occupancy): 114
Country of Registry: .... Italy
Nationality of Officers: .... European
Length of Cruise: .... 7 to 14 nights
Ports of Embarkation: .... Include Barcelona, Rome, Istanbul,
Copenhagen, Athens, and Antigua
Ports of Call: .... Include Ibiza, Mahon, Port-Vendres, Port
St. Louis, Monte Carlo, Corfu, Santorini, Athens,
Lesbos, Zeebrugge, Amsterdam, Copenhagen,
Helsinki, St. Petersburg, Dominica, St. Lucia,
St. Vincent and Bequia.
Single Cabins: .... No
Single Supplement: .... 200% on top-level suites but flat-rate
supplement added to other cabins, running
between 125% and 150% of double-occupancy
rate, depending on accommodations selected.
Guaranteed Share: .... No

Renaissance VI

Gross Registered Tonnage: 4,300
Passenger Capacity (double occupancy): 114
Passenger Capacity (all berths): 114
Country of Registry: .... Italy
Nationality of Officers: .... European
Length of Cruise: .... 7 to 14 nights
Ports of Embarkation: .... Include Barcelona, Rome, Istanbul,
Copenhagen, Athens, Antigua; Bombay,
Singapore and Monaco
Ports of Call: .... Include Ibiza, Mahon, Port-Vendres, Port St. Louis,
Monte Carlo, Sorrento, Lipari, Corfu, Santorini,
Athens, Zeebrugge, Amsterdam, Copenhagen, Helsinki,
St. Petersburg, Dominica, St. Lucia, St. Vincent,
Bequia, Goa, Phuket, Kuala Lumpur, Singapore,
Krakatau, Jakarta, Bali
Single Cabins: .... No
Single Supplement: .... 200% on top-level suites but flat-rate
supplement added to other cabins, running
between 125% and 150% of double-occupancy
rate, depending on accommodations selected.
Guaranteed Share: .... No

Renaissance VII

Gross Registered Tonnage: 4,300
Passenger Capacity (double occupancy): 114
Passenger Capacity (all berths): 114
Country of Registry: .... Italy
Nationality of Officers: .... European
Length of Cruise: .... 14 days
Ports of Embarkation: .... Include Athens, Istanbul, Bombay and Singapore
Ports of Call: .... Include Santorini, Mykonos, Rhodes, Patmos, Kusadasi, and Istanbul
Single Cabins: .... No
Single Supplement: .... 200% on top-level suites but flat-rate supplement added to other cabins, running between 125% and 150% of double-occupancy rate, depending on accommodations selected.
Guaranteed Share: .... No

Renaissance VIII

Gross Registered Tonnage: 4,300
Passenger Capacity (double occupancy): 114
Passenger Capacity (all berths): 114
Country of Registry: .... Italy
Nationality of Officers: .... European
Length of Cruise/Tour: .... 10 to 18 days
Port of Embarkation: .... Mahe
Ports of Call: .... Curieuse, La Digue, Descroche, Poivre, Praslin
Single Cabins: .... No
Single Supplement: .... Available on request
Guaranteed Share: .... No
Note: .... Passengers can combine a 10- or 11-day cruise with a 4-day African safari.

Royal Caribbean Cruise Line

⚓ Royal Caribbean Cruise Line

1050 Caribbean Way
Miami, Florida 33132
(800) 327-6700

Look! Up in the sky! It's a bird! It's a plane! It's....Royal Caribbean's Viking Crown Lounge! Recognized as a trademark of the Royal Caribbean ships, the Viking Crown Lounge is situated high in the sky, affording a 360 degree view of the sea and making it the perfect place to watch the sun sizzle as it sinks into the sea. The lounge, cantilevered from the ship's smokestack, was first introduced on the *Song of Norway* and is now a focal point of every RCCL ship.

The Viking Crown Lounge isn't all RCCL has going for it, however. Long recognized as a leader in passenger service, the line claims its vessels have been named ships of the year by the World Ocean & Cruise Liner Society more than any other cruise line. The ships have also been consistently named "#1 in Passenger Satisfaction," according to the cruise line.

RCCL has a variety of programs geared toward solo travelers, including some single cabins, guaranteed-share programs and a flat rate for solo occupancy. Sandra Richards, public relations coordinator, said, "Royal Caribbean attracts many single cruisers. Due to the variety of activities, singles can either easily meet others or spend time relaxing alone—whatever they choose."

Majesty of the Seas

```
Gross Registered Tonnage: ............................................... 73,941
Passenger Capacity (double occupancy): ........................... 2,354
Passenger Capacity (all berths): ....................................... 2,744
Country of Registry: ......................................................... Norway
Nationality of Officers: ............................................. International
Length of Cruise: ............................................................. 7 days
Port of Embarkation: ........................................................ Miami
Ports of Call: ..................... Playa del Carmen/Cozumel, Grand Cayman,
                                   Ocho Rios and RCCL's private island
Single Cabins: ...................................................................... No
Single Supplement: ............... 150% plus air supplement,when applicable
Guaranteed Single: ............... Flat rate comparable to mid-priced outside
                           stateroom plus air supplement when applicable,
                       with cabin assignment at the discretion of the company
Guaranteed Share: ................... Flat rate comparable to mid-priced inside
                               cabin, plus air supplement when applicable,
                       with cabin assignment at the discretion of the company
Trivia Fact: ...................... Christened in 1992 by Queen Sonja of Norway
```

Monarch of the Seas

Gross Registered Tonnage: 73,941
Passenger Capacity (double occupancy): 2,354
Passenger Capacity (all berths): 2,744
Country of Registry: .... Norway
Nationality of Officers: .... International
Length of Cruise: .... 7 days
Port of Embarkation: .... San Juan
Ports of Call: .... Martinique, Barbados, Antigua,
St. Maarten and St. Thomas
Single Cabins: .... No
Single Supplement: .... 150% plus air supplement, when applicable
Guaranteed Single: .... Flat rate comparable to mid-priced outside
stateroom plus air supplement when applicable,
with cabin assignment at the discretion of the company
Guaranteed Share: .... Flat rate comparable to mid-priced
inside cabin, plus air supplement when
applicable, with cabin assignment at
the discretion of the company
Trivia Fact: .... Christened in 1991 by actress Lauren Bacall

Nordic Empress

Gross Registered Tonnage: 48,563
Passenger Capacity (double occupancy): 1,600
Passenger Capacity (all berths): 2,020
Country of Registry: .... Liberia
Nationality of Officers: .... International
Length of Cruise: .... 3 and 4 days
Port of Embarkation: .... Miami
Ports of Call: .... 3-day cruises stop at Nassau and RCCL's
private island, Coco Cay; 4-day cruises add Freeport
Single Cabins: .... No
Single Supplement: .... 150% plus air supplement, when applicable
Guaranteed Single rate: .... Available at a flat rate comparable to
a medium-priced outside stateroom plus air
supplement when applicable, with cabin
assignment at the discretion of the cruise line.
Guaranteed Share: .... Available for a flat rate comparable to
a middle-lower-priced stateroom plus
air supplement when applicable, with cabin
assignment at the discretion of the cruise line
Trivia Fact: .... Christened in 1990 by singer Gloria Estefan

Nordic Prince

Gross Registered Tonnage: 23,200
Passenger Capacity (double occupancy): 1,012
Passenger Capacity (all berths): 1,127
Country of Registry: .... Norway
Nationality of Officers: .... International
Length of Cruise: .... 7 to 11 nights
Ports of Embarkation: .... Include Miami, San Juan,
Vancouver and Los Angeles
Ports of Call: .... Caribbean routes includes St. Kitts, Grenada,
Trinidad, and one of RCCL's private islands; Alaskan
route includes Skagway, Juneau, Ketchikan and Inside
Passage; Mexico route stops at Cabo San Lucas,
Mazatlan and Puerto Vallarta
Single Cabins: .... No
Single Supplement: .... 150% plus air supplement, when applicable
Guaranteed Single rate: .... Available at a flat rate comparable to a
lower-priced stateroom, plus air supplement when
applicable, with cabin assignment at the
discretion of the cruise line.
Guaranteed Share: .... Available for a flat rate comparable to a
lower-priced inside stateroom, plus air supplement
when applicable, with cabin assignment at the
discretion of the cruise line
Trivia fact: .... Christened in 1971 by film star Ingrid Bergman

Song of America

Gross Registered Tonnage: 37,584
Passenger Capacity (double occupancy): 1,402
Passenger Capacity (all berths): 1,552
Country of Registry: .... Norway
Nationality of Officers: .... International
Length of Cruise: .... 7 to 11 nights
Ports of Embarkation: .... Include Los Angeles, New York,
Miami and San Juan
Ports of Call: .... Mexican Riviera stops at Cabo San Lucas,
Mazatlan and Puerto Vallarta; Bermuda route
stops at St. George's and Hamilton; Caribbean
route includes Dominica, St. Kitts, Trinidad and
RCCL's private island
Single Cabins: .... No
Single Supplement: .... 150% plus air supplement, when applicable
Guaranteed Single: .... Flat rate comparable to mid-priced
stateroom, plus air supplement when
applicable, with cabin assignment at
the discretion of the company
Guaranteed Share: .... Flat rate comparable to lower-priced
inside stateroom plus air supplement
when applicable, with cabin assignment
at the discretion of the company
Trivia Fact: .... Christened in 1982 by opera singer Beverly Sills

Song of Norway

Gross Registered Tonnage: 23,005
Passenger Capacity (double occupancy): 1,016
Passenger Capacity (all berths): 1,138
Country of Registry: .... Norway
Nationality of Officers: .... International
Length of Cruise: .... 10 to 14 nights
Ports of Embarkation: .... Include Amsterdam, Venice, Harwich, England and Barcelona
Ports of Call: ....Mediterranean route includes Barcelona, Naples and Corfu; Scandinavian routes include Stockholm, Helsinki and Copenhagen
Single Cabins: .... No
Single Supplement: .... 150% plus air supplement, when applicable
Guaranteed Single: .... Flat rate comparable to medium-priced stateroom, plus air supplement when applicable, with cabin assignment at the discretion of the cruise line
Guaranteed Share: .... Flat rate comparable to lower-priced stateroom, plus air supplement when applicable, with cabin assignment a the discretion of the cruise line
Trivia Fact: .... Christened in 1970 by Mrs. Per Borten, wife of the Norwegian Prime Minister

Sovereign of the Seas

Gross Registered Tonnage: 73,192
Passenger Capacity (double occupancy): 2,276
Passenger Capacity (all berths): 2,524
Country of Registry: .... Norway
Nationality of Officers: .... International
Length of Cruise: .... 7 nights
Port of Embarkation: .... Miami
Ports of Call: .... San Juan, St. Thomas and RCCL's private island
Single Cabins: .... No
Single Supplement: .... 150% plus air supplement when applicable
Guaranteed Single: .... Flat rate comparable to mid-priced outside stateroom, plus air supplement when applicable, with cabin assignment at the discretion of the company
Guaranteed Share: .... Flat rate comparable to mid-priced inside cabin, plus air supplement when applicable, with cabin assignment at the discretion of the company
Trivia Fact: .... Christened in 1988 by former first lady, Rosalynn Carter

Sun Viking

Gross Registered Tonnage: 18,556
Passenger Capacity (double occupancy): 714
Passenger Capacity (all berths): 818
Country of Registry: .... Norway
Nationality of Officers: .... International
Length of Cruise: .... 7 to 12 nights
Ports of Embarkation: .... Include San Juan, Genoa, Athens
and Harwich, England
Ports of Call: .... Caribbean route includes St. Croix, St. Barts, Aruba,
Curacao or St. Thomas; Italy/Greek route includes
Athens, Naples, and Mykonos; other European routes
include Kristiansand, Oslo, Amsterdam and Le Havre
Single Cabins: .... No
Single Supplement: .... 150% plus air supplement, when applicable
Guaranteed Single: .... Flat rate comparable to mid-priced stateroom,
plus air supplement when applicable, with cabin
assignment at the discretion of the company
Guaranteed Share: .... Flat rate comparable to lower-priced
stateroom plus air supplement when applicable,
with cabin assignment at the discretion of the company
Trivia Fact: .... Christened in 1972 by Mrs. Sigurd Skaugen,
wife of one of RCCL's owners

Viking Serenade

Gross Registered Tonnage: 40,132
Passenger Capacity (double occupancy): 1,512
Passenger Capacity (all berths): 1,863
Country of Registry: .... Bahamas
Nationality of Officers: .... International
Length of Cruise: .... 3 and 4 nights
Port of Embarkation: .... Los Angeles
Ports of Call: .... 3-night cruises stop at Catalina Island and
Ensenada; 4-night cruises add San Diego
Single Cabins: .... No
Single Supplement: .... 150% plus air supplement when applicable
Guaranteed Single: .... Flat rate comparable to mid-priced stateroom,
plus air supplement when applicable, with cabin
assignment at the discretion of the company
Guaranteed Share: .... Flat rate comparable to mid-priced inside
stateroom, plus air supplement when applicable, with
cabin assignment at the discretion of the company
Trivia Fact: .... Christened in 1982 by Liv Ullman;
Christened in 1991 by Whoopi Goldberg

Royal Cruise Line

One Maritime Plaza
Suite 1400
San Francisco, CA 94111
(800) 662-0538

The three ships in the Royal Cruise Line fleet all take you on an odyssey. In fact, odyssey is in each of their names: *Crown Odyssey, Golden Odyssey* and *Royal Odyssey*. Each ship promises the same spacious cabins and top-of-the-line service that has won the cruise line its Number One ranking from *Conde Nast Traveler* readers, while each ship also maintains its own unique character.

All of the ships also offer alternative health-conscious cuisine, called "Dine to Your Heart's Content." However, for those who want to splurge a bit, the *Royal Odyssey* features Yanni's Hearth, with its fresh hot cinnamon buns and cookies.

One of the more popular features of Royal Cruise Line is its extensive Gentleman Host program. Started in 1982, the program now incorporates Gentlemen Hosts into all itineraries on all ships. "Our host program is extremely popular with mature single women—many cruise with us specifically because of the program," said Valerie Gadway, public relations representative.

Whether you're looking for a companion or not, Royal Cruise Line would be glad to have you aboard. Gadway added, "We recognize the growing market of single travelers and offer programs designed to accommodate them, and, in fact, encourage them to travel with us."

"Cruises are ideal for singles—they offer a relaxed, non-threatening social atmosphere," she said.

Crown Odyssey

Gross Registered Tonnage: 34,250
Passenger Capacity (double occupancy): 1,052
Country of Registry: .... Bahamas
Nationality of Officers: .... Greek
Length of Cruise: .... 8 to 21 days
Ports of Embarkation: .... Include Los Angeles, San Juan, Lisbon, London, Copenhagen, Venice and Athens
Ports of Call: .... Include Panama Canal, Aruba, Acapulco, Puerto Vallarta, Hawaii, Rome, Monte Carlo, Dublin, Paris, Amsterdam and Helsinki.
Single Cabins: .... No
Single Supplement: .... Categories CA through FC: 160%; Categories AA through BC: 200%; on selected departures, single supplements are only $75 a day more.
Guaranteed Share: .... Not advertised in the brochure, but the cruise line will accept shares in Categories CA through FC at their discretion
Comment: .... Eight Gentlemen Hosts on every sailing

Golden Odyssey

Gross Registered Tonnage: 10,500
Passenger Capacity (double occupancy): 450
Country of Registry: .... Bahamas
Nationality of Officers: .... Greek
Length of Cruise: .... 7 to 14 days
Ports of Embarkation: .... Include Singapore, Bombay, Hong Kong,
Anchorage, Vancouver and New York
Ports of Call: .... Include Panama Canal, Curacao, Singapore,
Bali, Saigon, Phuket, Colombo, Zanzibar,
Mombasa, Pusan, Juneau, Skagway and Quebec
Single Cabins: .... No
Single Supplement: .... Categories 7 through 14: 160%;
Categories 1 through 6: 200%; on selected
departures, single supplements are only
$75 a day more.
Guaranteed Share: .... Not advertised, but accepted at the
cruise line's discretion in Categories 7 through 14
Note: .... Four Gentlemen Hosts on every cruise

Royal Odyssey

Gross Registered Tonnage: 28,000
Passenger Capacity (double occupancy): 765
Country of Registry: .... Bahamas
Nationality of Officers: .... Greek
Length of Cruise: .... 11 to 28 days
Ports of Embarkation: .... Include Los Angeles, Barbados, Malaga,
Athens, Rome, Venice, Genoa and Lisbon
Ports of Call: .... Include Panama Canal, Gibraltar, Tangier,
Casablanca, Rhodes, Cairo, Yalta, Istanbul,
Naples, Genoa, Devil's Island and Santarem
Single Cabins: .... 56—29 outside, 27 inside (About 15% of all cabins)
Comparison to Double Cabins: .... Deluxe Outside Single comparable
in price to Superior Outside Deluxe Double;
Deluxe Inside Single comparable to Deluxe
Outside double.
Single Supplement: .... 200% on all cabins except singles
Guaranteed Share: .... No
Note: .... Single-seating dining; eight hosts on every cruise; extra
discount for early booking of single cabins

Royal Viking Line

95 Merrick Way
Coral Gables, FL 33134
(800) 422-8000

Royal Viking Line invites you to join their world and become a member of their "Community At Sea." At Royal Viking, the whole world is a community, and their two ships, the *Royal Viking Sun* and the *Royal Viking Queen*, travel the world, visiting 165 ports in more than 60 countries on six continents.

The line's "World Affairs Program" is affiliated with Georgetown University's School of Foreign Service and offers lectures, seminars and field trips to consuls and embassies around the world, eventually netting a "Certificate of Merit" for the participant. Another affiliation is with the Cousteau Society, to provide passengers insight into the mysteries of the deep.

In addition to the emphasis on learning and knowledge, Royal Viking also promises spectacular entertainment from around the world, including internationally known performers, and fine wine and connoisseur dining, ranging from French cuisine to "spa fare."

Royal Viking Queen

Gross Registered Tonnage: 10,000
Passenger Capacity (double occupancy): 200
Passenger Capacity (all berths): 212
Country of Registry: .... Bahamas
Nationality of Officers: .... Norwegian
Length of Cruise: .... 10 to 21 days
Ports of Embarkation: .... Include London, Copenhagen, Amsterdam, Athens, Monte Carlo, Istanbul, Venice, Cairns, Hong Kong, Singapore, Nairobi and Beijing
Ports of Call: .... Include Bali, Bangkok, Oslo,Bergen, Rhodes, Solomon Islands, Dublin, Kuala Lumpur, Colombo, Alexandria, Shanghai, Ho Chi Minh City, Mombasa and Djibouti
Single Cabins: .... No
Single Supplement: .... Category A suites—125% to 200%
All other categories: 200%
Guaranteed Share: .... No

Royal Viking Sun

Gross Registered Tonnage: 38,000
Passenger Capacity (double occupancy): 740
Passenger Capacity (all berths): 758
Country of Registry: .... Bahamas
Nationality of Officers: .... Norwegian
Length of Cruise: .... 10 to 102 days
Ports of Embarkation: .... Include San Francisco, Hong Kong, Athens,
                              Lisbon, Copenhagen, Rome and Ft. Lauderdale
Ports of Call: .... Include Aruba, Barbados, Trondheim, Bergen,
                         Riga, St. Petersburg, Odessa, Alexandria, Waterford,
                              Bordeaux, Naples, Amsterdam, and Malaga
Single Cabins: ....2—Outside
Comparison to Double Cabins: .... Outside singles run about the same
                                      price as outside doubles with verandas
Single Supplement: .... Categories B through JI: 125% to 175%;
                                            200% on all other categories
Guaranteed Share: ..... Accepted in Category E1 at cruise line's discretion
Note: .... Berlitz Ship of the Year 1992; only ship with a golf
                                  simulator; up to six Gentleman Hosts

St. Lawrence Cruise Lines, Inc.

253 Ontario Street
Kingston, Ontario
K7L 2Z4 Canada
(800) 267-7868

Retrace the routes of early Canadian explorers aboard the *Canadian Empress*, a replica steamship reminiscent of the early days of splendor.

The *Canadian Empress* provides calm-water cruising from May through October, offering such itineraries as the "Upper St. Lawrence Excursions," "St. Lawrence River Passage," and the "St. Lawrence and Ottawa River Journey." Unlike most vessels, the *Canadian Empress'* all-outside staterooms are equipped with windows that open, so passengers can actually smell the river breeze.

Traveling aboard the *Canadian Empress* provides an opportunity to explore the wonders of our neighbor to the north. Experience the Canadian Tulip Festival in Ottawa or glory in the turning fall foliage. The price of passage also includes all tours, admission costs and transportation required during the tours.

James Clark, vice president of the St. Lawrence Cruise Line, noted, "Since our per diems are low in comparison to most small inland water passenger vessels, we find that our product is very affordable for the single traveler."

Canadian Empress

Gross Registered Tonnage: 467
Passenger Capacity (double occupancy): 64
Passenger Capacity (all berths): 66
Country of Registry: .... Canada
Nationality of Officers: .... Canadian
Length of Cruise: .... 4 and 5 nights
Ports of Embarkation: .... Include Kingston, Montreal,
Quebec City and Ottawa
Ports of Call: .... Various itineraries include Brockville, Prescott,
Rockport, Montreal, Cote St. Catherines, Montebello,
Upper Canada Village, Coteau Landing, Montreal,
Trois Rivieres, Upper Canada Village and 1000 Islands Retreat
Single Cabins: .... No
Single Supplement: .... 150% on limited number of staterooms;
175% on the rest
Guaranteed Share: .... Not advertised in the brochure, but the cruise
line will arrange a share upon request

Seabourn Cruise Line

55 Francisco Street
San Francisco, CA 94133
(800) 351-9595

Travel & Leisure Magazine once called Seabourn "the one to beat." The two sister ships, the *Seabourn Pride* and the *Seabourn Spirit*, are intimate, all-suite ultra-luxury vessels that accommodate about 200 passengers in the same space others house 400, according to the cruise line's literature.

Both ships feature a "fold-out" water sports marina with sailboard, paddleboats and sailboats, although the itineraries are not limited to warm-water cruising. In fact, Seabourn features individualized itineraries throughout the world, or, as Seabourn puts it, throughout "The Americas, Europe, Scandinavia, The Mediterranean and The Far East." Added to that is single-seating dining (with cuisine individually prepared when ordered) and a no-tipping policy.

For the 1993-1994 season, Seabourn instituted an innovative "Single Traveler's Savings" policy. While the single supplement is normally 150 percent the double-occupancy rate, selected sailings offer the solo traveler a rate of only 110 or 125 percent. The brochure notes: "We see to it that singles are always included in the social mainstream. (Unless they prefer to be left alone.) Our officers and staff personally invite and accompany single guests to parties, dinners, dances and other events."

Seabourn Pride

Gross Registered Tonnage: 10,000
Passenger Capacity (double occupancy): 204
Passenger Capacity (all berths): 204
Country of Registry: .... Norway
Nationality of Officers: .... Norwegian
Length of Cruise: .... From 7 to 23 days
Ports of Embarkation: .... Include Bridgetown, Ft. Lauderdale,
Acapulco, Oranjestad, New York,
San Juan, Manaus and Lisbon
Ports of Call: .... Include Bonaire, Curacao, Aruba, Panama Canal,
Baltimore, Savannah, Devil's Island, Madeira, Tangier,
Gibraltar, Ibiza, St. Tropez and Monte Carlo
Single Cabins: .... No
Single Supplement: .... Standard single occupancy rate is
150% but on many itineraries, solo occupancy
of Type A suites is offered at 110% or 125%
Guaranteed Share: .... No
Note: .... Seabourn was voted the Best Cruise Line in the
Fifth Annual Reader's Choice poll of
Conde Nast Traveler Magazine.

Seabourn Spirit

Gross Registered Tonnage: 10,000
Passenger Capacity (double occupancy): 204
Passenger Capacity (all berths): 204
Country of Registry: .... Norway
Nationality of Officers: .... Norwegian
Length of Cruise: .... 7 to 23 days
Ports of Embarkation: .... Include Singapore, Ashod, Haifa,
Piraeus, Nice, Venice, Istanbul
Ports of Call: .... Include Kuala Lumpur, Bangkok, Bali, Colombo,
Aden, Bombay, Phuket, Port Said, Alexandria,
Rhodes, Taormina, Rome, Malta, Barcelona, Odessa,
Single Cabins: .... No
Single Supplement: .... Standard single occupancy rate is
150% but on many itineraries, solo occupancy
of Type A suites is offered at 110% or 125%
Guaranteed Share: .... No

Sea Spirit Cruise Line, Inc.   ≦ *SeaSpirit*

RSVP Travel Productions, Inc.
2800 University Avenue SE
Minneapolis, MN 55414
(800) 533-1482

RSVP Travel discovered they were so successful packaging cruises for their gay clientele that the organization took the plunge and bought their own ship. The *Sea Spirit* features seven-day cruises around the Caribbean during the winter and along the eastern United States during summer.

The *Sea Spirit* is the first gay-owned and operated cruise ship, according to Andy Schmiedel, director of advertising and sales, and features a predominantly gay staff and crew. The *Sea Spirit* offers amenities and programs for the enjoyment of their clientele—special-interest cruises include Singles' Week and Leather Week. There are assigned tables in the ship's totally non-smoking single-seating dining room, but a unique "Dine Around" program allows passengers to enjoy different table companions at each meal if they request it in advance.

Sea Spirit

Gross Registered Tonnage:	100
Passenger Capacity (double occupancy):	100
Passenger Capacity (all berths):	109
Country of Registry:	United States
Nationality of Officers:	American
Length of Cruise:	7 days
Port of Embarkation:	St. Thomas for the Caribbean itinerary; New York or Boston for the Eastern U.S. route
Ports of Call:	Caribbean route includes U.S. and British Virgin Islands; Eastern U.S. route includes Newport, New Bedford, Martha's Vineyard, Nantucket and Provincetown.
Single Cabins:	No
Single Supplement:	200% in all categories
Guaranteed Share:	Available in Category B

Seawind Cruise Line

1750 Coral Way
Miami, FL 33145
(800) 258-8006

The only ship in the Seawind Cruise Line fleet is the *Seawind Crown*, sailing year-round out of Oranjestad, Aruba and calling at ports in Curacao, Grenada, Barbados and St. Lucia, with two days at sea. Billing itself as the "Classic Cruise For Connoisseurs," the line makes note of its generous space-per-passenger ratio. The ship's gross registered tonnage is 24,000, but maximum passenger capacity is only 624.

According to Seawind officials, the *Seawind Crown* sets itself apart from other cruise lines by combining a "unique itinerary to the unspoiled Southern Caribbean...with a very sanely sized ship, a European on-board atmosphere and competitive pricing."

For the solo traveler looking for a bargain, the line adds no surcharge for single occupancy of Category M cabins, which consists of inside cabins with upper and lower berths. While these staterooms might not be ideal for a couple on a romantic honeymoon, they serve quite well for the solo cruiser, and are the lowest priced cabins on the ship.

Seawind Crown

Gross Registered Tonnage: 24,000
Passenger Capacity (double occupancy): 624
Passenger Capacity (all berths): 624
Country of Registry: .... Panama
Nationality of Officers: .... Portuguese and Greek
Length of Cruise: .... 7 nights
Port of Embarkation: .... Oranjestad, Aruba
Ports of Call: .... Curacao, Grenada, Barbados and St. Lucia
Single Cabins: .... No
Single Supplement: .... Category M: No surcharge;
                                             Categories E through L: 150%:
                                             Categories A through D: 200%
Guaranteed Share: .... No

Seven Seas Cruise Line

333 Market Street
San Francisco, CA 94105
(800) 285-1835

When *Agents Cruise Monthly* newsletter created a "Best Cruise Value" award in 1992, the top prize for "Ultra-Deluxe 5-Star +" went to Seven Seas Cruise Line's *Song of Flower.*

The ship features all outside staterooms, some with sliding glass doors that open up to private balconies. Single, open-seating dining is standard, there is an "Open Bridge Policy" to encourage passengers to observe the ship's navigation, and gratuities are "neither expected nor accepted." Enjoy 24-hour room service, along with complimentary wines and liquors available in the staterooms and public rooms

Itineraries are highly individualized, with such poetic names as "Tropical Splendour,""Jewels of the East" or "Voyage through Byzantium."

Song of Flower

Gross Registered Tonnage: 8,282
Passenger Capacity (double occupancy): 172
Passenger Capacity (all berths): 172
Country of Registry: .... Norway
Nationality of Officers: .... Norwegian
Length of Cruise: .... 8 to 15 days
Ports of Embarkation: .... Include Athens, Venice, Monte Carlo,
                    Barcelona, Bangkok, Bombay, London and Stockholm
Ports of Call: .... Include Aden, Bali, Komodo, Jakarta,
                    Phuket, Lisbon, Trondheim, Riga, Helsinki,
                    Copenhagen, Zeebrugge, Gibraltar, Suez, Santorini,
                    Mykonos, Sorrento, and Istanbul
Single Cabins: .... No
Single Supplement: .... Categories C through F: 125%;
                    Categories A and B: 200%.
Guaranteed Share: .... No

Silja Line

c/o Bergen Line
505 Fifth Avenue
New York, NY 10017
(800) 323-7436

The Silja Line provides transportation for travelers heading to Scandinavia from Finland, Sweden, or Germany. While these are not cruise ships in the traditional sense, it's a great way to get from Point A to Point B in comfort.

The ships include the *Silja Serenade, Silja Karneval, Silja Festival,* and *Silja Symphony,* The vessels travel routes between Helsinki and Stockholm, Turku and Stockholm, Helsinki and Travemunde, as well as featuring two-day Baltic Sea cruises.

The ships travel overnight and will get you to your destination between 7 a.m. and 8:30 a.m., in time to enjoy the new sights.

Bergen Line is the exclusive booking agent in North America for Silja Line.

Silja Symphony

Gross Registered Tonnage: 56,000
Passenger Capacity (all berths): 2,670
Country of Registry: .... Sweden/Finland
Nationality of Officers: .... Swedish and Finnish
Length of Cruise: .... Overnight
Port of Embarkation: ....Helsinki or Stockholm
Ports of Call: .... None
Single Cabins: .... No
Single Supplement: .... Around 150%, depending on class of cabin
Guaranteed Share: .... No

Special Expeditions   **SPECIAL EXPEDITIONS** 👁

720 Fifth Avenue
New York, NY 10019
(800) 762-0003

A recent expedition staff included a zoologist, a tropical plant ecologist, two divemasters and two expedition staff members—all this on a ship that holds a maximum of 80 passengers. On Special Expeditions, it's hard for a passenger to tell if the emphasis is on the word *special* or *expedition.*

Some of the itineraries aboard the *Polaris*, *Sea Bird* and *Sea Lion* focus on nature, such as the Costa Rican coast. Some emphasize history, providing the opportunity to retrace the route of the Spanish Armada.

Special Expedition packages include meals on shore, as well as aboard ship, services and lectures by the staff. They also feature shore excursions and sightseeing, including transportation to and from the sites, entrance fees, and services of local guides.

The company does "recognize that solo travelers are extremely valuable to the cruise industry," according to Gina Cerami, sales manager, and the line is currently seeking more vessels that have facilities to better serve this "ever-growing community."

Polaris

Gross Registered Tonnage: 2,214
Passenger Capacity (double occupancy): 80
Passenger Capacity (all berths): 80
Country of Registry: .... Bahamas
Length of Cruise: .... 9 to 18 days
Ports of Embarkation: .... Include Limon, Belize, Balboa, Antigua, Lisbon, London, Bergen, Belem, Iquitos and Caldera
Ports of Call: .... Include Honduras, Mosquito Coast, San Blas Island, Trinidad, St. Lucia, Cote Basque, Iona and Staffa Islands, Amsterdam, St. Emilion, Gdansk, Riga, Oslo, Madeira, Manaus and Iles du Salut
Single Cabins: .... No
Single Supplement: .... Categories 1 and 2: 150%
Guaranteed Share: .... Available in Categories 1 and 2

Sea Bird

Gross Registered Tonnage: 99.7
Passenger Capacity (double occupancy): 70
Passenger Capacity (all berths): 70
Country of Registry: .... United States
Length of Cruise: .... 4 to 14 days
Ports of Embarkation: ... Include Guaymas, La Paz, Portland, Vancouver, Sitka, San Francisco and Cabo San Lucas
Ports of Call: .... Include Bahia Magdalena, Isla Santa Catalina, San Ignacio, Islas San Jose, Hells Canyon, Columbia River Gorge, Bonneville Dam, Glacier Bay National Park, Misty Fiords, Portland and Astoria.
Single Cabins: .... No
Single Supplement: .... Categories 1 and 2: 150%
Guaranteed Share: .... Available in Categories 1 and 2

Sea Lion

Gross Registered Tonnage: 99.7
Passenger Capacity (double occupancy): 70
Passenger Capacity (all berths): 70
Country of Registry: .... United States
Length of Cruise: .... 4 to 14 days
Ports of Embarkation: ... Include Guaymas, La Paz, Portland, Vancouver, Sitka, San Francisco and Cabo San Lucas
Ports of Call: .... Include Bahia Magdalena, Isla Santa Catalina, San Ignacio, Islas San Jose, Hells Canyon, Columbia River, Gorge, Bonneville Dam, Glacier Bay National Park, Misty Fiords, Portland and Astoria.
Single Cabins: .... No
Single Supplement: .... Categories 1 and 2: 150%
Guaranteed Share: .... Available in Categories 1 and 2

Star Clippers

4101 Salzedo Avenue
Coral Gables, FL 33146
(800) 442-0551

Gaze up at the masts and you'll see a cloud of sails unfurl, with 36,000 square feet of material blowing in the breeze. You can learn how to handle the sails, discover the art of navigation, or practice tying a sailor's knot. But if you consider that to be "work," then simply spend your time relaxing and enjoying the impromtu activities offered aboard these "Tallest of the Tall Ships."

Once aboard one of the Star Clippers' ships, you'll visit a variety of ports in the Leeward or Windward Islands year round on the *Star Clipper*, or experience a unique Mediterranean itinerary on the *Star Flyer* during the summer.

For those who love water sports, these two tall ships come equipped with windsurfers, waterskis, scuba and snorkeling gear, along with an experienced sports staff to help you use it. The atmosphere is open and spontaneous, with no set daily program, although there is a "Captain's Story Time" after breakfast, at which the day's events are described, according to Alan Bell, a Star Clippers representative.

Bell added that he often travels solo and is "made very welcome." The solo traveler "can join in any activity and sit anywhere (there is open, single-session dining.) Nothing is rigidly planned on this informal luxury sail 'yacht,'" he said.

Star Clipper

Gross Registered Tonnage: 3,050
Passenger Capacity (double occupancy): 180
Passenger Capacity (all berths): 180
Country of Registry: .... Luxembourg
Nationality of Officers: .... International
Length of Cruise: .... 7 Days
Port of Embarkation: .... St. Maarten or Antigua
Ports of Call: .... Leeward Island itinerary includes Saba/Statia,
St. Kitts, Antigua, Iles Des Saintes, Nevis and
St. Barthelemy. Windward Islands itinerary
includes Iles des Saintes, Martinique, St. Vincent,
St. Lucia and Dominica.
Single Cabins: .... No
Single Supplement: 150%
Guaranteed Single: .... Comparable to a mid-priced outside cabin,
with assignment at the discretion of the cruise line
Guaranteed Share: .... Available in Categories 2 through 6

Star Flyer

Gross Registered Tonnage: 3,050
Passenger Capacity (double occupancy): 180
Passenger Capacity (all berths): 180
Country of Registry: .... Luxembourg
Nationality of Officers: .... International
Length of Cruise: .... 7 days
Ports of Embarkation: .... St. Maarten and Antigua in Caribbean;
Nice in the Mediterranean
Ports of Call: .... Treasure Islands itinerary includes Anguilla,
St. Thomas/St. Croix, Tortola, Norman Island,
Virgin Gorda and St. Barthelemy; Leeward Islands
itinerary includes St. Kitts, Anguilla, St. Maarten,
St. Barthelemy, Saba/Statia and Nevis; Mediterranean
includes Cannes, St. Tropez, Port-Vendres,
Barcelona, Corsica, Elba or Portofino
Single Cabins: .... No
Single Supplement: 150%
Guaranteed Single: .... Comparable to a mid-priced outside cabin,
with assignment at the discretion of the cruise line
Guaranteed Share: .... Available in Categories 2 through 6

Starlite Cruises

1520 State Street
Suite 100
San Diego, CA 92101-2930

Starlite Cruises offers the neophyte traveler the opportunity to board a passenger vessel and spend the day at sea. The *Pacific Star* offers one-day cruises leaving out of San Diego and stopping in Ensenada, Mexico, all for one flat fee. Included in the tariff is three buffet meals, a full casino, a children's playroom, hot tubs, gift shop and an assortment of bars and lounges.

While meals are included in the price, discriminating passengers may choose to pay an additional $20 fee for a sit-down lunch and dinner, selecting from sirloin steak or angel hair pasta at lunch and ordering escargot, Caesar salad and Chateaubriand for dinner.

Since all pricing is individual, there is no single supplement. "We are a great way for inexperienced cruisers to try a first voyage with a minimum investment of time and money," said Kevin Weisner, director of sales and marketing.

Pacific Star

```
Gross Registered Tonnage: ............................................. 10,500
Passenger Capacity : ....................................................... 1,050
Country of Registry: ..................................................... Bahamas
Nationality of Officers: .................................................... Greek
Length of Cruise: ........................................................ One day
Port of Embarkation: ................................................. San Diego
Ports of Call: ................................................ Ensenada, Mexico
Single Cabins: ...................................... 150 passenger cabins, rented by
                                                   the cabin, not per person
Comparison to Double Cabins: ............................... Charged at a flat rate
```

Sun Line Cruises, Inc.

One Rockefeller Plaza
New York, NY 10020
(800) 872-6400

Enjoy the authentic Greek atmosphere as the officers and crew of the Sun Line ships extend their hospitality and share their culture while you cruise the playgrounds of the Caribbean, Greek islands and the Mediterranean.

Sun Line Cruises currently operates three ships: The *Stella Solaris,* with a passenger capacity of 620; the *Stella Oceanis*, carrying 300 guests, and the *Stella Maris*, with an intimate 180.

The cruise line strives to make the solo passenger comfortable, noting it "welcomes single passengers, couples and families with the same legendary Greek hospitality for which their crew is known," according to Meg Duncan, public relations manager for Sun Line. She said that Sun Line's intimate size on the smaller ships encourages "passenger interaction and serves as a catalyst for sociability and friendship on board."

Stella Maris

```
Gross Registered Tonnage: ............................................... 3,500
Passenger Capacity (double occupancy): ............................. 180
Passenger Capacity (all berths): ....................................... 230
Country of Registry: ...................................................... Greece
Nationality of Officers: ..................................................... Greek
Length of Cruise: ........................................................... 7 days
Ports of Embarkation: ..................................... Piraeus for Greek Islands;
                                     Venice and Nice for Mediterranean
Ports of Call: ................. Greek Islands/Turkey itinerary includes Istanbul,
                            Kusadasi, Rhodes, Heraklion and Mykonos; Italy
                            and Mediterranean route includes Tremiti Islands,
                                  Corfu, Messina, Capri and Elba;
Single Cabins: ................................................................... No
Single Supplement: .................................... Categories 2 through 6: 150%;
                                     Category 1 Deluxe cabins: 200%
Guaranteed Share: .................... Not advertised in brochure, but accepted
                                           at cruise line's discretion
```

Stella Oceanis

Gross Registered Tonnage: 5,500
Passenger Capacity (double occupancy): 300
Passenger Capacity (all berths): 360
Country of Registry: .... Greece
Nationality of Officers: .... Greek
Length of Cruise: .... 3 and 4 days
Port of Embarkation: .... Piraeus
Ports of Call: .... 3-day cruises visit Mykonos, Rhodes, Kusadasi
and Patmos; 4-day cruises include Hydra, Heraklion,
Rhodes, Kusadasi and Mykonos
Single Cabins: .... No
Single Supplement: .... Categories 4 through 8: 150%;
Categories 1 through 3 Deluxe Cabins
and Suites: 200%
Guaranteed Share: .... Not advertised in brochure, but accepted
at cruise line's discretion

Stella Solaris

Gross Registered Tonnage: 18,000
Passenger Capacity (double occupancy): 620
Passenger Capacity (all berths): 700
Country of Registry: .... Greece
Nationality of Officers: .... Greek
Length of Cruise: .... 7 to 14 days
Ports of Embarkation: .... Galveston and Piraeus
Ports of Call: .... Caribbean/Mexican cruises include Grand Cayman,
Cozumel and Montego Bay or Key West; Panama
Canal route includes Ocho Rios, Colon, Gatun Locks,
San Blas Islands, Port Limon, and Cozumel;
Greek Islands/ Turkey route includes Istanbul,
Kusadasi, Rhodes, Santorini and Mykonos;
Single Cabins: .... No
Single Supplement: .... Categories 4 through 11: 150%;
Categories 1 through 3 Suites: 200%
Guaranteed Share: .... Not advertised in brochure, but accepted
at cruise line's discretion
Note: .... Gentleman Host program on winter cruises

Swan Hellenic Cruises

Esplanade Tours
581 Boylston Street
Boston, MA 02116
(800) 426-5492

Swan Hellenic combines in-depth sightseeing, knowledgeable guides and numerous guest lecturers to provide an experience of travel and learning while cruising the Mediterranean, Aegean and other exotic areas.

The line promotes its "all-inclusive cruising" policy, which takes care of excursion costs, entrance fees to museums and landmarks, as well as all gratuities on land and at sea.

The cruise line is aware of the needs of the solo traveler (estimating that as many as 30 percent travel solo) and promotes a single-seating policy at all meals. As noted in the brochure, the dining policy "is particularly satisfying if you are traveling alone; friendships soon flourish and with so many experiences to share day by day, an opening to any conversation is never hard to find."

Marketing manager Jill Walker added, "Swan Hellenic has earned a reputation for taking exceptional care of its travelers—whether traveling alone or with a companion. They attend to every possible detail, especially appealing to someone traveling alone."

Nile Monarch

Gross Registered Tonnage: 2,000
Passenger Capacity (double occupancy): 76
Country of Registry: .... Egypt
Nationality of Officers: .... Egyptian
Length of Cruise: .... 12 to 20 days
Port of Embarkation: .... Cairo
Ports of Call: .... Include Aswan, Edfu, Luxor, Dendera, Esna, Kom-Ombo, El-Kab and Nag-Hamadi
Single Cabins: .... 6—all outside
Comparison to Double Cabins: ... About the same price as double cabins
Single Supplement: .... Deluxe cabins and suites—190%; other cabins are charged a flat rate, ranging from 105% to 130%, depending on the time of year
Guaranteed Share: .... Yes

Orpheus

Gross Registered Tonnage: 5,100
Passenger Capacity (double occupancy): 275
Country of Registry: .... Greece
Nationality of Officers: .... Greek
Length of Cruise: .... 14 to 17 days
Ports of Embarkation: .... Include Piraeus, Thessaloniki, Nice,
Venice, Corfu and Aqaba
Ports of Call: .... Include Kusadasi, Elos, Mykonos, Rhodes,
Malta, Istanbul, Dikili, Tripoli, Casablanca,
Tunis, Algiers, Tangier, Cadiz, Malaga,
Naples, Ithaca, Varna, Odessa, Yalta,
Trieste, Syracuse and Livorno
Single Cabins: .... 12—6 outside, 6 inside
Comparison to Double Cabins: .... About the same price
Single Supplement: .... Categories G, H, I and J: 140%
Guaranteed Share: .... Yes, in both double and triple cabins

Rembrandt Van Rijn

Gross Registered Tonnage: 1,700
Passenger Capacity (double occupancy): 90
Country of Registry: .... Netherlands
Nationality of Officers: .... Dutch
Length of Cruise: .... 5 to 12 days
Ports of Embarkation: .... Include Amsterdam, Arnhem, Basel,
Bamberg, and Wuerzberg
Ports of Call: .... Include Rotterdam, Delft, Gouda, Cologne,
Strasbourg, Dusseldorf, Wertheim,
Ruedesheim and Cochem
Single Cabins: .... No
Single Supplement: .... Flat rate is added, varying by itinerary,
making single supplement about 120%
Guaranteed Share: .... Yes
Note: .... Itineraries features cruises on the Rhine,
Main and Mosel Rivers

Tall Ship Adventures, Inc.

1010 South Joliet Street
Suite 200
Aurora, Co 80012
(800) 662-0090

Tall Ship Adventures' *Sir Francis Drake* is a three-masted tall ship that was originally built in 1917, but has been extensively refurbished through the years.

The vessel provides a relaxed, natural atmosphere, featuring beach parties and barbecues, along with sailboats, windsurfing and snorkeling equipment provided for the enjoyment of the passengers.

The *Sir Francis Drake* travels in the Caribbean to the smaller islands where the megaships can't go, allowing maximum time and exposure for those who enjoy water exploration.

The line does welcome passengers traveling alone, according to public relations representative Oscar Kolb, and offers guaranteed shares. There is also a flat per-day rate for an additional third adult sharing a cabin with two others, "which appeals to three singles traveling together," Kolb said.

Sir Francis Drake

Tonnage:	450 DWT
Passenger Capacity (double occupancy):	28
Passenger Capacity (all berths):	34
Country of Registry:	Panama
Length of Cruise:	3, 4 and 7 days
Port of Embarkation:	St. Thomas, St. John or St. Maarten
Ports of Call:	3-day cruises visit Caneel Bay, St. James Island and Trunk or Francis Bay; 4-day cruises stop at Tortola, Jost Van Dyke, Sandy Cay and Norman or Peter Island; 7-day cruises stop at at a variety of Caribbean islands
Single Cabins:	No
Single Supplement:	Call for rates
Guaranteed Share:	Yes

Windjammer
Barefoot Cruises

Post Office Box 120
Miami Beach, FL 33119-0120
(800) 327-2600

If you want to feel free as the wind, look into a cruise on one of Windjammer Barefoot Cruises' tall ships. The captains of the vessels pick the routes best suited for the currents and weather conditions, so the ships are "very much at the call of the winds," according to Mike Vegis of Windjammer. There is also considerably less structure than on other cruise lines, with shore excursions up to the passengers and daily programs non-existent.

Windjammer provides a unique opportunity for the solo traveler: throughout the year, Windjammer offers a number of "Singles Sailings." There is a "balanced booking" policy to ensure an even number of passengers of both sexes. For those willing to share "Bachelor/ette Quarters," (a six-bunk cabin), prices are as low as $600 per person for the week, not including air fare. And don't let the single supplement scare you; guaranteed share is available on all vessels.

"Since our inception in 1947, Windjammer has courted the solo traveler," Vegis said. "We've always had a guaranteed-share program because of the smaller, intimate nature of our ships. For the last 3 years, we also hosted special Singles-Only sailings with a concerted effort to insure a 50/50 male/female ratio."

Vegis said the singles-only sailing has proved so successful, the line has added an additional date for 1993 and will be expanding the program for 1994.

Amazing Grace

Gross Registered Tonnage: 1,585
Passenger Capacity (double occupancy): 96
Passenger Capacity (all berths): 96
Country of Registry: .... Honduras
Nationality of Officers: .... British
Length of Cruise: .... 13 days
Ports of Embarkation: .... Freeport and Grenada
Ports of Call: .... Include Martinique, Tortola, Grand Turk,
St. Lucia, Bequia, St. Kitts, St. Barts or Jost Van Dyke
Single Cabins: .... No
Single Supplement: 175%
Guaranteed Share: .... Yes
Note: .... *Amazing Grace* is a supply vessel for the Windjammer fleet

Fantome

```
Gross Registered Tonnage: ............................................. 2,400
Passenger Capacity (double occupancy): ............................ 120
Passenger Capacity (all berths): ....................................... 132
Country of Registry: .................................................. Honduras
Nationality of Officers: ................................................. British
Length of Cruise: ...................................................... 6 days
Ports of Embarkation: ............................... Antigua and Nassau/Freeport
Ports of Call: ............................ From Antigua, ports includes a selection
                                  of St. Barts, Sint Maarten, St. Kitts,
                                  Monserrat, Dominica and others.
                          From Nassau or Freeport, ports may include
                          Gun Cay, Bimini, Rose Island and others.
Single Cabins: ............................................................. No
Single Supplement: ..................................................... 175%
Guaranteed Share: ...................................................... Yes
```

Flying Cloud

```
Gross Registered Tonnage: ............................................. 399
Passenger Capacity (double occupancy): ............................. 70
Passenger Capacity (all berths): ......................................... 76
Country of Registry: .................................................. Honduras
Nationality of Officers: ................................................. British
Length of Cruise: ...................................................... 6 days
Port of Embarkation: .................................................... Tortola
Ports of Call: .............................. Include a selection of Salt Island Virgin
                              Gorda, Beef Island, Green Cay. Sandy Cay,
                                             Deadman's Bay and others.
Single Cabins: ............................................................. No
Single Supplement: ..................................................... 175%
Guaranteed Share: ...................................................... Yes
```

Mandalay

```
Gross Registered Tonnage: ............................................. 500
Passenger Capacity (double occupancy): ............................. 72
Passenger Capacity (all berths): ......................................... 72
Country of Registry: .................................................. Honduras
Nationality of Officers: ................................................. British
Length of Cruise: .................................................... 13 days
Ports of Embarkation: ..................................... Antigua and Grenada
Ports of Call: .................................... Includes a selection of Palm Island,
                           Mayreau, Tobago Cays, Bequia, St. Vincent,
                                                Dominica and others
Single Cabins: ............................................................. No
Single Supplement: ..................................................... 175%
Guaranteed Share: ...................................................... Yes
```

Polynesia

Gross Registered Tonnage: 600
Passenger Capacity (double occupancy): 108
Passenger Capacity (all berths): 126
Country of Registry: .... Honduras
Nationality of Officers: .... British
Length of Cruise: .... 6 days
Port of Embarkation: .... Sint Maarten
Ports of Call: .... Includes a selection of Columbier Beach,
                   St. Barts, St. Kitts, Saba, Statia, Anguilla and others
Single Cabins: .... No
Single Supplement: 175%
Guaranteed Share: .... Yes

Yankee Clipper

Gross Registered Tonnage: 300
Passenger Capacity (double occupancy): 64
Passenger Capacity (all berths) 65
Country of Registry: .... Honduras
Nationality of Officers: .... British
Length of Cruise: .... 6 days
Port of Embarkation: .... Grenada
Ports of Call: .... Includes a selection of Petit St. Vincent,
                   Bequia, Mayreau, Carriacou, Palm Island and others.
Single Cabins: .... Yes—One
Comparison to Double Cabins: 175%
Single Supplement: 175%
Guaranteed Share: .... Yes

Windstar Cruises

300 Elliott Avenue West
Seattle, WA 98119
(800) 258-7245

Read the brochure, and you'll find Windstar describing itself as "unregimented...unstructured...flexible...approachable...imaginative.... unassuming" But don't let this fool you: Windstar Cruises offers three ships complete with sails furling in the breeze and elegant service meant to pamper and please.

With a passenger capacity of only 148, there are 91 members of the crew on board to serve your every need. From fluffy bathrobes in the cabins to unique shore excursions and unique itineraries, Windstar entices.

Dining structure is open seating and a "no-tipping required" policy prevails. Each ship features six computer-directed sails with 21,500 square feet of surface area that unfurl in two minutes, as well as a water sports platform and sporting equipment, such as waterskis, windsurfing boards and small sailboats.

While the vast majority of passengers on Windstar travel as couples, the company notes that "Windstar is excellent for the solo traveler who is not cruising to make a match. Singles who are open, friendly, enjoy privacy and don't require an escort or hand-holding to enjoy their travel love their cruises on Windstar," said Kathlene Dunlop, public relations manager for the company.

Wind Song

```
Gross Registered Tonnage: ............................................................... 5,350
Passenger Capacity (double occupancy): .......................................... 148
Passenger Capacity (all berths): ....................................................... 148
Country of Registry: ................................................................. Bahamas
Nationality of Officers: ................................................................. British
Length of Cruise: ............................................................. Most are 7 days
Port of Embarkation: ...................................................... Papeete, Tahiti
Ports of Call: ............................. Huahine, Bora Bora, Raiatia and Moorea
Single Cabins: ................................................................................. No
Single Supplement: ................... 150% on all cabins except owner's suite,
                                          which is 200%; single occupancy
                                                  subject to availability
Guaranteed Share: .......................................................................... No
Note: ..................... Ship features six computer-directed sails with 21,500
                        square feet of surface area that unfurl in 2 minutes
```

Wind Spirit

Gross Registered Tonnage: 5,350
Passenger Capacity (double occupancy): 148
Passenger Capacity (all berths): 148
Country of Registry: .... Bahamas
Nationality of Officers: .... British
Length of Cruise: .... Most are 7 days
Ports of Embarkation: .... Include St. Thomas, Piraeus,
Istanbul and Singapore
Ports of Call: .... Include St. Barthelmy, Nevis, St. Kitts,
Virgin Gorda, Tortola, Mykonos, Santorini, Rhodes,
Kusadasi, Penang, Phuket and Langkawi
Single Cabins: .... No
Single Supplement: .... 150% on all cabins except owner's
suite,which is 200%; single occupancy
subject to availability
Guaranteed Share: .... No

Wind Star

Gross Registered Tonnage: 5,350
Passenger Capacity (double occupancy): 148
Passenger Capacity (all berths): 148
Country of Registry: .... Bahamas
Nationality of Officers: .... British
Length of Cruise: .... Most are 7 days
Ports of Embarkation: ..... Include Monte Carlo. Bridgetown andBarbados
Ports of Call: .... Include Corsica, Sardinia, Elba, Portofino,
Barcelona, St. Tropez, St. Lucia, St. Martin,
St. Barthelemy, St. Kitts, Grenada and Bequia
Single Cabins: .... No
Single Supplement: .... 150% on most cabins, 200% for owner's
suite, subject to availability
Guaranteed Share: .... No

World Explorer Cruises

555 Montgomery Street
San Francisco, CA 94111-2544
(800) 854-3835

For the true aficionado of the Alaskan scenery, World Explorer is a top option. The *Universe* sails the Inside Passage during the summer months, and stops at nine ports during its 14-day tour. In fact, the line claims to offer more ports of call and longer time in each port (averaging 9 hours) than most other Alaskan cruises.

The ship's clientele tends to be older and more educated, according to the cruise line's literature, and emphasis is placed on lectures and exploring. There is a fresh herbarium on board, and passengers are encouraged to contribute unique specimens. Shore excursions focus on the distinctive qualities of Alaska, including helicopter rides and panning for gold.

It's obvious that the cruise line welcomes the solo traveler: There is an abundance of single cabins, with a goal of increasing the number of single-occupancy cabins by 1994 or 1995, according to Dennis Myrick, vice president. The line also sponsors one or two Gentlemen Hosts on each voyage.

Myrick added, "We feature a destination and on board product that has wide appeal to single travelers with ample opportunity to socialize with other travelers in a relaxed, informal, educational environment."

Universe

Gross Registered Tonnage: 18,100
Passenger Capacity (double occupancy): 532
Passenger Capacity (all berths): 602
Country of Registry: .... Liberia
Nationality of Officers: .... Chinese
Length of Cruise: .... 14 days
Port of Embarkation: .... Vancouver, British Columbia
Ports of Call: .... Include Wrangell, Juneau, Skagway, Glacier Bay,
                            Valdez, Seward, Sitka, Ketchikan and Victoria
Single Cabins: .... 25—13 outside, 12 inside
Comparison to Double Cabins: .... About same price as comparable
                                            double-occupancy cabins
Single Supplement: .... Not available; only single cabins
Guaranteed Share: .... No
Note: .... Gentleman Host program, 12,000-volume library

Zeus Tours & Yacht Cruises

566 Seventh Avenue
New York, NY 10018
(800) 447-5667

Zeus Cruises takes you to a different island every day and then offers bouzouki music and ouzo at night. You'll sail on one of Zeus' ten intimate yachts and motorsailers, holding an average of 40 people each, while traveling one of three unique itineraries.

The size and facilities on Zeus' vessels vary, but all offer windsurfing, waterskiing and fishing equipment for the enjoyment of the passengers.

Included in the line is the *Zeus I, II, III,* and *V*, accommodating between 40 and 49 passengers. The smaller vessels, including the *Nicholas A.* and *Viking Star*, accommodate 26 to 32 passengers.

More important, the Zeus fleet offers three itineraries on the seven-day cruises. Choose the "Cycladic Jewels" tour and embark at Piraeus for stops at Paros, Santorini/Ios, Naxos, Delos/Mykonos and Tinos/Sounioun. On the "Greco-Turkish Mystique" cruise, you'll embark at Rhodes and visit Kos, Lipsi, Samos, Kusadasi, Patmos/Kalymnos and Chalki. The "Ionian Odyssey" leaves Corfu for Paxi/ Antipaxi, Lefkas, Kefalonia, Zakynthos, Ithaki and Parga.

There is no guaranteed share-program on these cozy yachts, but cabins used as a single are charged only a $300 supplement for solo use.

Index of Cruise Lines & Ships

Entries in **bold** indicate cruise lines. Entries in *italics* are cruise ships